Image of the New World

Image of
the New World

*The American continent
portrayed in native texts*

GORDON BROTHERSTON

Translations prepared in collaboration with
ED DORN

with 118 documentary texts and illustrations

THAMES AND HUDSON

For Jenny, Lucy, Katie and Isabel

Library of Congress Catalog Card Number: 78-55194

Printed in Great Britain by BAS Printers Ltd, Over Wallop, Hampshire

Contents

List of maps, tables and figures

Preface

THIS book has grown out of an idea for a volume on native American literatures planned and worked on since 1969; it has benefited from my experience of teaching that subject at graduate and undergraduate levels at Essex University from about the same date, and owes much to my colleagues there. Of these, by far the most important has been Ed Dorn, poet and mentor, whose name appears on the title page; and Dawn Ades has contributed a great deal from her knowledge of Mexican and Maya art, and in choosing and editing pictorial texts. I should like to make clear my indebtedness to Ric Luxton's work. His unpublished manuscript 'The Hidden Continent of the Maya and the Quechua' which was prepared in close collaboration with the Mayan Indian Don Pablo Canche, has established connections which I had not perceived independently in my own work. Most significant amongst these are that the *Nueva corónica* of Guaman Poma de Ayala, the sixteenth-century Quechua author, is best considered as a transcription of *quipu* (knotted cord) records, or '*quipu*-literacy'; and that this insight, in Luxton's words, 'demonstrates the existence of a common epistemology between the north and south parts of the continent, of notable formal complexity'. Also Luxton and Canche have shown how this epistemology is relevant to the Yucatec Maya and Quechua 'walk' of today. I have also learned much from conversations with American Indians, especially the Maya friends of William Brito in Teabo, Yucatan; the Paez Indian Francisco in Tierradentro, Colombia; and Cuthbert Simon, an Arawak at the settlement on the upper Mahaica River, Guyana, who told the story found in item *VI.8*.

Others to whom I am grateful for their conversation and correspondence, as well as for help of other kinds, are: the late Eric Thompson; Munro Edmonson; Alfredo Barrera Vásquez and his colleagues in Merida, Yucatan; the late Günter Zimmermann; Gerdt Kutscher and the staff of the Ibero-Amerikanisches Institut, Berlin; Elizabeth Carmichael, Jonathan King and the staff of the

Museum of Mankind, London; Clemency Coggins; Joseph Rykwert; George Dekker; Michael Podro; Val Fraser; Kurt Egger; Margaret Iversen; John Stratton; Michael Lane; John Bierhorst; Tony Khater; Joel Benjamin; and my wife Gisela. I am also extremely grateful to Barry Woodcock for his expert camera work, and to the staff of Thames and Hudson for their encouragement and patience.

I have received financial help in the preparation of the American Indian texts from the American Philosophical Society (1972), the Humboldt Stiftung (1970–1 and 1976), the Nuffield Foundation (1975–6), and from the University of Essex Research Endowment Fund.

ACKNOWLEDGMENTS
Acknowledgment is due to the following institutions for supplying photographs (numbers in parentheses refer to illustrations in this book):

Arts Council of Great Britain, for the birchbark scroll (*IX.2a*).

Bodleian Library Oxford, for the Laud screenfold, pp. 1 (*III.8*), 2 (*III.6*) and 25–6 (*III.11*); the Selden screenfold, p. 7 (*IV.4*); and the Mendoza Codex, p. 39 (*VII.10*).

British Library and Museum of Mankind, London, for the Nuttall screenfold, pp. 15 (*III.13*) and 75 (*VII.3*); the Osuna Codex, p. 38 (*VIII.7*); the facsimile (1892) of the Lienzo of Tlaxcala, scene 42 (*I.2*); the facsimile (1899) of the Borbonicus screenfold, pp. 21–2 (*IV.2*); the Cheyenne robe, item 917 (*VII.1*); the Midewiwin scroll, cat. no. 2252 (*III.2*); and the uncatalogued song-board (*IX.2b*).

Horniman Museum, London, for the 'Whirling Logs' sand-painting (*III.4*).

Merseyside County Museums, for the Fejérváry screenfold, pp. 34–33 (*VI.12*).

Bibliothèque Nationale, Paris, for the Annals of Texcoco, p. 3 (*IV.3*); the Aubin manuscript, no. 20 (*VII.2*); the Contrat de Commanderie (*I.4*); the Manuscrito del Aperramiento (*I.5*); and the Annals of Cuauhtinchan, pp. 24–5 (*VII.5*).

Vatican Library, for pages from the Codex Ríos (*VIII.6* and *I.1*); the Borgia screenfold, pp. 17 (*III.9*), 27 (*VI.13*), 30 (*III.5*) and 59 (*III.10*); and the *Libellus de Medicinalibus Indorum Herbis*, p. 53v. (*VIII.4*).

Museum für Völkerkunde, Staatliche Museen (Preussischer Kulturbesitz), Berlin, for the Sioux robe, cat. no. IV b205 (*VI.2*).

Ibero-Amerikanisches Institut, Berlin, for the Chilam Balam Book of Kaua, p. 4 (*VIII.2*).

American Philosophical Society, Philadelphia, Pa., for pages from the Cherokee Notebooks of K. Thomson and W. W. Long (*VIII.9*).

Acknowledgment is due to the following for permission to quote: Oklahoma University Press (*I.9; IV.7; VIII.3*); Munro Edmonson and Tulane University Press (*V.6; IX.10*); John Bierhorst and Farrar, Straus & Giroux, Inc. (*VIII.8*); University of Nebraska Press (*III.3*).

I have published parts, and drafts of parts, of this study in various places, in the form of essays and articles in: *Estudios de cultura náhuatl*; *Ibero-Amerikanisches Archiv*; *Indiana*; *Mesoamerican Archeology: New Approaches* (ed. N. Hammond, 1974); *The New Scholar*; the *Times Literary Supplement*; and *Maya Archeology and Ethnohistory* (ed. Hammond and Willey, 1978). Also translations, mostly in collaboration with Ed Dorn, have appeared in: *Stand*; *Poetry Review*; *Sixpack*; *Alcheringa*; *New World Journal*; and *Seneca Review*.

Wivenhoe, 1978   GORDON BROTHERSTON

Author's note

THE alphabetic spelling of native American names and words usually depends on the phonetics of the European language into which they were first transcribed, hence: Quechua (Spanish; 'Kechwa'), Sioux (French; 'Soo') and Cherokee (English). These renderings are at best approximate; in the Roman alphabet there are not ready-made ways of expressing, say, Quechua gutturals, Maya 'fortis' consonants (c̆h. p′), or the Nahua 'tl' palatal. Where choice is possible I have preferred the Romance to the English vowel values, e.g. tipi not tepee; and Mide ('Meeday'). In the case of the Spanish spelling I have retained established forms: hua (wa), hui (wee), que (kay), qui (kee), x (sh), ll (l), though 'qua' becomes 'cua' (kwa). For consistency I have not marked accents on Indian words. In some cases, accents which these words have acquired are actually incorrect in Indian terms; for example, as Nahua words Cuauhtítlan and Teotihuácan characteristically have the stress on

11

the penult, despite the fact that the accent is placed on the final syllable in Mexican Spanish. The following standardized terms have been used: Algonkin (Algonquin, Algonkian), Nahua (Nahuatl), Navajo (Navaho), Ojibwa (Ojebway, Chippewa), Texcoco (Tezcoco).

In referring to native manuscripts known under several different titles I have chosen and used only one of them; and my preference has been not to italicize except where there is a clear bibliographical obligation to do so. Appropriate details are given in the Notes and Bibliography. In the case of traditional Mesoamerican books, these are always specified as 'screenfolds' when they have that format; the term 'codex' is reserved for non-screenfold manuscripts. Toltec and Maya calendar dates are given according to the correlations proposed, respectively, by Alfonso Caso and J. E. S. Thompson.

Introduction:
The idea of the New World,
and American Indian texts

AMERICA, the Americas, the Western Hemisphere, the New World: geographically these are all the same. As a name, the 'New World' is the most dramatic. It recalls the astonishment caused by the discovery of the continent which separates the Atlantic from the Pacific. For the maps of Columbus and his successors quite changed the Old World's ideas about itself, more subtly perhaps than the demonstration that we live on a globe. In the maps of Graeco-Roman antiquity, as in the mappamundi of the Middle Ages, there is no room even for the *notion* of America. The three 'worlds' of Asia, Europe and Africa fully occupy the earth's disk (the first as its eastern top half, the other two below), an arrangement radically upset by the addition of the new 'fourth world', as America came to be called. Once discovered, its terrain, climates, flora and fauna had to be reconciled with the known world. And above all, the people who lived there – the 'Indians', so named because of Columbus's famous misapprehension that he had reached Asia from the other side – had to be fitted into the scheme of things.

In the first European debates on the subject of native Americans – whether they were human or not, for example, or whether they were mentioned in the Bible – the 'Indians' were taken to be a single race. Their newness on the historical stage of the Old World outweighed the many regional and other differences between them. As Europeans strove to appropriate American territory, they imposed new differences of their own. Variously christened – as Nueva España, Nouvelle France, New England, Nieuw Nederland, Nova Scotia – the New World acquired frontiers it had not known before. With the struggles for political independence in what became Latin America and the United States, this process was only reinforced. Today, the fragmentation has gone so far that in English popular usage the term 'American Indian' most often refers just to Indians happening to have survived within the modern frontiers of the United States. In this, we may detect a linguistic imperialism, destructive in its way of larger coherences in New World cultures, represented today by the millions of 'first Americans' who hold out still, largely in and near the mountain chains which form the backbone of the continent, from Chile to Canada.

The Old World's first view of American Indians was doubtless too simple. Among the 45 or so million people living in the continent in AD 1492, great differences, and enmities, certainly existed. The life-style of the metropolitan Aztecs or Incas had little in common with the habits of fishermen around the Great Lakes, or down in Tierra del Fuego. And the tightly knit confederacies of the Iroquois and Cherokee in the Appalachians hardly resembled the loosely organized and very widespread language family of the Guarani and Tupi in Brazil and Paraguay. Yet that initial notion of a continental homogeneity has always haunted 'Americanist' scholars; and contrary to certain expectations, it has gained rather than lost strength with the recent growth of knowledge held by us to be scientific.[1]

Genetically, all native Americans living south of the intercontinental Eskimo are now recognized to have characteristic blood-groups. They lack blood-group B, a highly eloquent testimony to their millennial isolation from the rest of the world after their migrations from Asia. For their part, linguisticians have shown that Indian languages are closer to each other than they are to languages elsewhere; and what in the nineteenth century was thought to be a plethora of hundreds of quite distinct languages has now been reduced to five or six main groups. Further, the kind of evidence used in support of these claims also underlies the arguments of anthropologists who detect an unbroken chain of mythic thought from South to North America. In the four volumes of his *Mythologiques*, Lévi-Strauss has suggested that this ancient 'syncretism' will one day shape the true history of early America, when it comes to be written. As for archaeology, explorations made from about the turn of this century have much enhanced our knowledge of the main foci of American civilization: in Mesoamerica, the cities of the Toltecs and Aztecs in central Mexico, and of the Maya, now divided by the national boundaries of Mexico, Guatemala, Belize, Honduras and El Salvador; in South America, the empires of the Inca and their predecessors; and in northern

America,[2] the towns and so-called 'Mound Builder' monuments along the Ohio and the Mississippi rivers and in the ancient territory of the Cherokee. More important, archaeologists point to the thoroughness of the contact between these foci. We learn of trade from the Inca empire in Peru up to Mesoamerica, and then on up to the urban centres of the Mississippi. It has become clear that, whether they knew it or not, conquistadors like Coronado, who travelled from the Aztec capital Tenochtitlan through Pueblo towns in present-day New Mexico and Arizona on up to Kansas, were following well-established routes.

It is with Americanist history[3] of this order in mind that we attempt here to approach the literatures of the New World, texts in which the Indians, the people concerned, speak for themselves. As in most other literatures, many older traditional texts were originally oral compositions, eventually – after the arrival of Europeans – written down in the Roman alphabet. Other American Indian literature cannot be accounted oral in this sense, however. Before the appearance of Europeans, a number of recording systems were in use in America, which have a literary legacy of their own. Until recently, these New World signs and scripts have been neglected, even as unparalleled evidence of how man began to write. The neglect stemmed in part, perhaps, from the blank disbelief that American Indians were ever capable of writing anything down themselves. Even those wanting to champion the Indians have also wanted them free of the 'corrupting' effects of literacy. In his much-quoted paragraphs on the discovery of the New World, Montaigne spoke of the Indian as 'so new and infantine, that he is yet to learn his A.B.C.'. Applied to the Tupi-Guarani of Brazil, whom Montaigne knew most about, the description is possibly accurate; but elsewhere it is quite wrong. And when Europeans did encounter undeniable evidence of writing, of literacy equivalent to their own, they did their best to eradicate it, because it posed a threat to the Scripture (the Bible) they brought with them. In Mesoamerica, great bonfires were made of parchment and paper books, in Toltec and in Maya writing, palpable volumes paginated in screenfold or 'accordion' fashion. The books the missionaries did not burn were remitted to secret archives at headquarters in Rome, as classified information, keys to the pagan systems that the Church sought to undo. The Anglican Church in northern America dealt in much the same way, though some time later and on a smaller scale, with the birchbark scrolls of the Algonkin, examples of which were remitted to Canterbury for

Table I MAIN WORKS QUOTED, ROUGHLY CLASSIFIED BY AREA

NORTHERN AMERICA

Culture	Native writing	Language	Roman alphabet	
North-west	totem poles			
	Midewiwin scrolls	Ojibwa-Algonkin	Midewiwin chants	Pontiac's speech, 1763
	Walam Olum	Lenape-Algonkin	Walam Olum gloss, 1820	
	Wampum belt	Iroquois	Condolence Ritual	Grangula's speech, 1684
	Cherokee syllabary			Cusick's Cosmogony, 1825
	Winter Counts	Sioux	Winnebago narrative, 1910	
	records of hunting and conquest			Memoirs of Black Elk, 1932
	Red Horse, *The Battle of Little Big Horn*			
South-west	sandpaintings	Navajo	chants	

MESOAMERICA

Culture	Native writing		Language	Roman alphabet	
Toltec	1350–1650				
	Aztec:	Borbonicus and Boturini screenfolds and Annals of Texcoco; Ríos and Mendoza codices; de la Cruz Herbal	Nahua	Twenty Sacred Hymns; Aztec Priests' Speech, 1524; *Annals of Tlatelolco, c.* 1551; Legend of the Suns, 1558;	*Annals of Cuauhtitlan*, 1570; Florentine Codex, 1575–80; Histories by: Castillo, *c.* 1600; Chimalpahin, 1606–3
		Sun stone		*Cantares mexicanos,* 1550–60	Curing formulas
	Tlaxcalan:	legal documents Borgia screenfold; Lienzo of Tlaxcala			
	Cholulan:	*Annals of Cuauhtinchan*		*Annals of Cuauhtinchan,* 1550	
	Mixtec:	Fejérváry and Laud screenfolds Vienna, Nuttall, Selden screenfolds			
			Otomi	songs	
	[Oaxcaca:	carving, 300 BC]			
Maya	[Olmec: carving, 31 BC] Classic inscriptions, AD 200–900				
	Yucatec paper screenfolds, 1200–1500: Dresden, Paris, Madrid		Yucatec-Maya	Chilam Balam Books (of Chumayel, Kaua etc.), 1550 and later;	Ritual of the Bacabs; Chronicle of Nakuk Pech, 1562
	hieroglyphs in Chilam Balam books				
			Chontal-Maya	Paxbolon Papers, 1612	
			Quiche-Maya	*Popol vuh,* 1550–5	
			Cakchiquel-Maya	Book of the Cakchiquel, 1604	

Culture	Native writing	Language	Roman alphabet	
North	*timehri*, ideographs	Arawak	Carib snake story, 1978	
		Chibcha	Tundama's speech, 1541	
	Serkan Ikala	Cuna-Chibcha	Serkan Ikala	
Tahuan-tinsuyu	*quipu*, knotted cords	Quechua	Zithuwa ritual	*New Chronicle* of Guaman Poma, 1613
			hymns to Viracocha	
			Huarochiri Narrative, 1597–1608	Tarmap Pacha Huaray, 1905
	Chimu: scenic designs, on pottery			
Amazon and South		Witoto	Genesis	
		Tupi	chants	
		Guarani	Ayvu Rapyta	

examination. The literature of the Inca, recorded in *quipus* (knotted cords), was deemed no less significant, though the few examples which survived the burning of the *quipu* libraries resisted Spanish attempts at decipherment at the Council of Lima (1582–3). A tiny residue of the Mesoamerican screenfold books (Maya and Toltec) is today kept in libraries of the old Holy Roman Empire (Italy, Germany, Austria) and of the pirate nations England and France. Through transcription and adaptation to the Roman alphabet, the native literary traditions of Mesoamerica weathered the European invasion and to some extent persist even today.

Of the two kinds of American texts, those in native script and those in the Roman alphabet, this book concentrates on the former. It endeavours to show what these New World signs and symbols look like, how they are put together and may be read, what purposes they were and are used for, and how they are related to each other. For recording conventions still in use in northern America, like Mide writing and Southwestern sandpainting, have a close affinity with the pre-Columbian scripts of Mesoamerica – Toltec and Maya – the latter being connected in turn with the *quipu* of northern South America. Besides this mainstream tradition, we also touch on such marginal or special phenomena as Eskimo pictography, the totem carving of the Northwest, the signs used by the Chibcha and by their neighbours, the scenic designs of the Chimu, and the Cherokee syllabary invented by Sequoyah in 1819. Further, in Mesoamerica, the centre of native book production, definite genres of writing emerge, and major works representative of those genres: ritual practice (Borgia and Dresden screenfolds), ritual exegesis (Vienna screenfold), and calendrical history (Selden screenfold), for example.

It is classic native texts of this kind which give shape to this 'image' of the New World and provide the criterion of selection for the alphabetic texts with which they are complemented. The range of American Indian literature in the Roman alphabet is large, extremely so when it includes fragments gathered by travellers, anthropologists, philologists and others over the centuries.[4] Here we focus on writing which has some direct precedent in native script, either as direct transcription, like the versions of Maya hieroglyphic texts found in the community books of Yucatan, or as matching commentary, like the Nahua versions of Toltec writing or the Lenape-Algonkin gloss on the Walam Olum. A number of purely oral texts, chiefly from South America, provide a term for specific comparison with these more literate traditions.

Though sometimes inscrutable, as much by design as accident, these two kinds of American texts may be seen converging on certain fundamental topics, which may also be distinguished in the early literature of the Old World like Hesiod's *Theogony* and *Works and Days*, the Bible and Gilgamesh: the past and present ages of the world; man's need to eat; and the authority of such professionals as the warrior, the healer, and the poet or scribe himself. While the chapters which it devotes to these topics are thematic, this book as a whole nonetheless attempts to take account of chronology. In the first instance this is achieved by tracing the (unfinished) story of encounter between the Old and New World throughout the continent, relying on native sources only. By this means we gain an idea of the longer-lived civilizations, with their foci in Meso-america, with the Inca Tahuantinsuyu to the south and the Ohio valley to the north. In the case of the Maya, unrivalled in their calendrical expertise, we are not just given a clear description of the three main periods of their own history (the Classic to *c.* AD 900, the post-Classic to *c.* 1550, and the post-Columbian) but are shown an understanding of time decidedly less arbitrary than that enjoyed by Columbus and his companions. This temporal dimension is also important for the appreciation of texts which diverge in some way from the dominant social ideology of one period or another.

The readings, translations and interpretations which follow rely heavily on the work of scholars in particular cultures and literacies, notably the Algonkin and Sioux (Brinton; Mallery; Radin; Landes), Navajo (Reichard), Toltec (Caso; Nowotny; Handbook of Middle American Indians, vols 14–15), Maya (Morley; Roys; Thompson; Kelley; Edmonson), Chibcha (Holmer and Wassen), and Quechua (Nordenskjöld; Means; Trimborn; Arguedas). At the same time they incorporate some original work. Close comparison of the alphabetic texts with each other and with their pre-Columbian precedents has suggested new readings of the Walam Olum, for example, and has generally affected the structuring of sentences, paragraphs and chapters.[5] Perhaps the most important single innovation has been formally to separate the ritual iconography from the calendrics of Mesoamerica. For instance, the ritual signs set out as the 'Twenty Signs' in Table 2 have been customarily referred to by the misleadingly explicit term the 'Day Signs'. This separation has made it possible, on the one hand, to find analogies over the whole continent, in iconography and numbers, design and format, reading order and sequence; and, on the other, to make a cleaner distinction between the two main calendars of Meso-america, Toltec and Maya, which use the same sets of symbols in radically different ways. Consistent with this is the argument that the shaman's trance journey follows a paradigm found in northern and Mesoamerican texts alike, especially as regards the west-east transit and its correlation with the inferior conjunction of the planet Venus, measured at nine nights and eight days. Further, this circuit of cosmic movement, proper to the hunter, in which zenith and nadir take precedence over north and south as moments between east and west, proves antithetical to the 'rooted' time and space of the planter, the two modes of existence being intricately opposed in economies from which the pastoral is absent.[6] Also, new readings are made of texts concerned with such major matters as world ages, parthenogenesis and power; the importance of song as tribute; and the idea of the text as an artificial (specifically textile) object.

The literatures of the American Indians have long affected Western thinking in such subjects as government, anthropology and psychology. And from Montaigne and Rabelais to the Surrealists, from Herder and Chamisso to the novelists and poets of Latin America and the U.S.A., Western literature proper has again and again been indebted to that of the original New World. While we cannot trace these connections in detail, we do present, as far as possible, their common source, with its own energy and reason.

I Invasion from the Old World

THE first thrust of the European invasion of America was into the Caribbean. Quickly so devastated as to require slaves from Africa, the islands of Cuba and Hispaniola became the base for military operations on the mainland, to west, south and north. This stage of the Conquest has no Indian chronicler, itself an apt comment on the bestiality which drove the loyal and Christian Las Casas to become the Indians' anguished spokesman. The three decades spent by the Spaniards in the West Indies (1492–1519), impeccably described in Carl Sauer's *The Early Spanish Main*, provide a grim prologue to the tales of derring-do told of the subsequent conquests on the mainland, in Meso-, South and northern America.

Mesoamerica

From Cuba, the Spaniards made several expeditions westward to the mainland in the early sixteenth century. The most spectacular was the one led by Hernán Cortés who, at Veracruz, made a bridgehead from which to attack the Aztec empire, at that time the dominant military power in Mesoamerica, or New Spain as the Spaniards christened it. Between the years 1519 and 1521, helped by local armies resentful of Aztec power, Cortés besieged and took the Aztec capital Tenochtitlan, now Mexico City, up in the highland Valley of Mexico. One of the wonders of the New World, this metropolis received tribute from city states all over Mesoamerica. Having disposed of the Emperor Moctezuma II and his successor, Cuauhtemoc, Cortés found himself well supplied with all kinds of food and goods, including the metals and jewels he was so greedy

Opposite. Map 1: The American continent, *c.* 1550.
Overleaf. Map 2: The Valley of Mexico and its surroundings, with (inset) the metropolitan area.

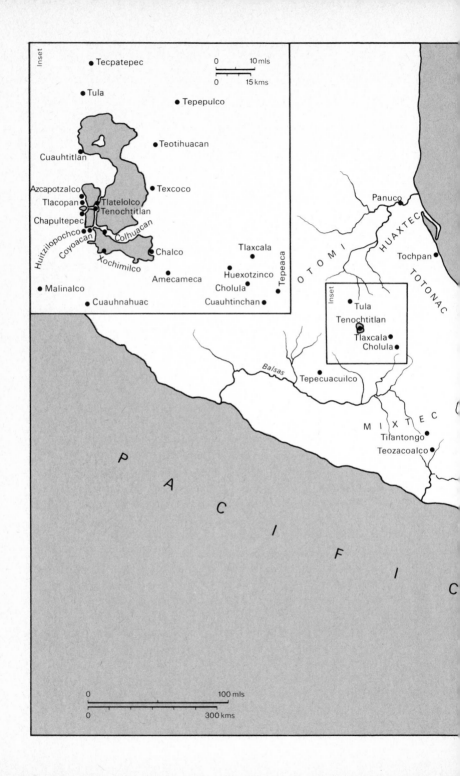

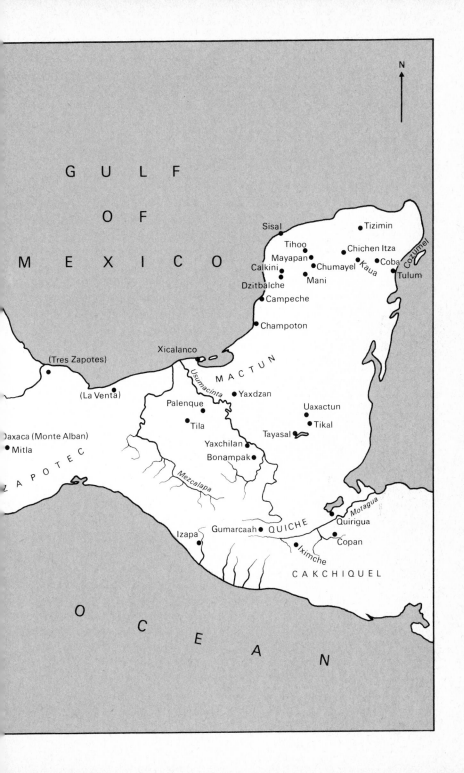

for. In their turn the Aztecs had inherited this vast economic empire from the Toltecs, who were named after their city – Tula – which was and is not far north of Tenochtitlan. Like the Toltecs before them, the Aztecs had come from the north, being closely related to the Tarahumara who still live in the mountains of northern Mexico, and to the Hopi in New Mexico and Arizona, the area known in English as the 'Southwest'. Like the Toltecs, the Aztecs spoke Nahua and used the same calendar and writing conventions.

Within Mesoamerica, the Aztecs had several rivals, among them fellow Nahua-speakers like the Tlaxcalans to the east; the old-established Otomanguan peoples (Otomi, Mixtec and Zapotec, centred to the west and north of Tenochtitlan, and on the Valley of Oaxaca to the south, though these had been largely subdued and are known to us by Nahua names); and, above all, the Maya. From AD 1000 the Maya had suffered invasion by Nahua-speakers from the north and west, who had pressed through their territory right to the southern limits of Mesoamerica in Nicaragua (itself a Nahua name). To this extent they were ready for the Spaniards when they set off on the same routes. The part of Mesoamerica to withstand the Spanish invaders most resolutely was the Yucatan peninsula, called Peten, or the Land, by the Maya. Attacked several times after 1517, and on a large scale by Francisco de Montejo from the east coast in 1542, the Maya there were never fully 'pacified'. They held close to the traditions of the Classic Maya who early in the first millennium had built the famous cities of the Maya territory, at Tikal, Palenque, Copan and elsewhere. The hieroglyphic writing and the calendar of the Classic Maya still flourished in Yucatan when the Spaniards arrived.

South America

Besides the Aztec, the other flourishing empire of sixteenth-century America was the Inca. While Cortés took over the one in the north, Francisco Pizarro and his companions appropriated the other, no less grand, to the south. Inca influence was felt in Colombia, through Ecuador, Bolivia and Peru, down to northern Chile and Argentina. Like Cortés, Pizarro spent much of his early career in the Caribbean and took part in attacks on Darien and other native towns in Panama in 1510. There, the Chibcha population, whose language extended over the area between Mesoamerica and the

Opposite. Map 3: The Tahuantinsuyu.

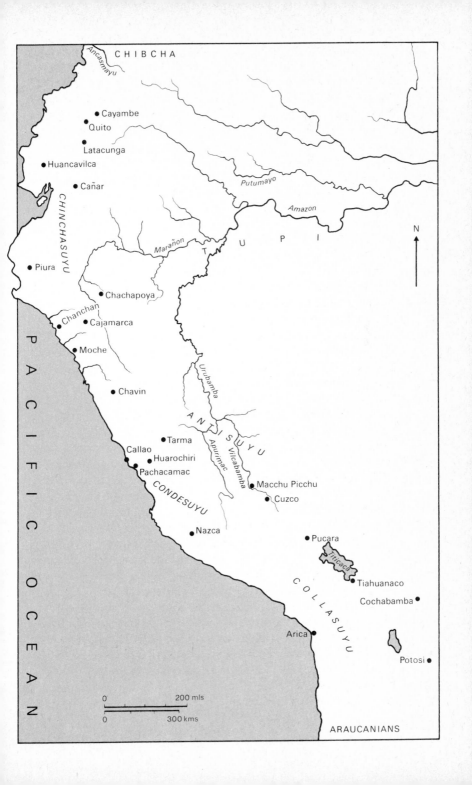

Inca empire, gave reports of maritime trade with the Inca in Peru along the Pacific coast. When he arrived in Peru, Pizarro was fortunate enough to find the Inca in a state of civil war. On the death of the royal or 'Sapa' Inca, Huayna Capac, in 1525, two of his sons – half-brothers – disputed the imperial title. From Quito (the capital of modern Ecuador) in the north, Atahuallpa came to do battle with Huascar, who was residing in the traditional Inca capital Cuzco, both cities being high in the Andes. Atahuallpa had the upper hand over Huascar when Pizarro attacked with his band of Spaniards and troops of Indian allies recruited from the fringes of the empire and from recently conquered peoples within it. Pizarro soon managed to dispose of both Huascar and Atahuallpa and to claim the Inca for Spain. He made this dramatic gesture against a groundswell of popular resistance which is still in evidence today. Military resistance continued for several decades but was left leaderless at a national level with the execution of the last heir to the imperial title, Tupac Amaru ('Shining Snake'), in 1572.

Like the Aztecs, the Inca had only recently risen to prominence when the Spaniards arrived. And both within and beneath the official religion and language of the Inca state lay traces of civilizations at least as old as those of Mesoamerica. The main language, Quechua, was adopted by the Spanish missionaries and today is the second official language of Peru. The boundaries of the empire were clearly drawn and have in part determined political divisions in modern South America. To the north and still part of the Andean culture, lay the fabulous Chibcha kingdoms of El Dorado, whose history was deeply enmeshed with that of the wide ranging Arawak and Caribs. To the south, the Spaniards were no more successful than the Inca had been in dislodging the Araucanians of Chile from the towns which guarded their northern frontier. As for the eastern frontier of the empire, the Spaniards soon learned to regard it with Inca eyes, as the home of hostile jungle nations, the Amazonians whose territory is being thoroughly invaded only today. Among them, in a great arc stretching from the upper Amazon through coastal Brazil right round to Paraguay, lay the vast language family of the Tupi and Guarani. Though the Tupi and Guarani were soon terribly reduced by Portuguese and French penetration of their territory from the Atlantic coast, Guarani survives today as one of the official languages of Paraguay. By a strange coincidence, the eastern boundary of the Inca was paralleled in the papal decrees issued in the wake of the 'discovery' of South America in order to ensure its orderly settlement. The line which now separates

Spanish America from Brazil is a result of these decrees, the Pope
having ignored France and entrusted the imperial task to Spain and
Portugal only.

Northern America

Sixteenth-century Spanish penetration of the continent north of
Mexico was more inconclusive and restricted than in Meso- and

Map 4: The Ohio Valley and its surroundings.

South America. While Coronado rode up to Kansas, Fernando de Soto (who had been with Pizarro in Peru) marched from town to town through Florida and the southern Appalachians to the Mississippi. A weighty burden on the food supplies of the Cherokee and the Creek Indians, he noted the architectural splendour of their houses and pyramids and robbed them as he dared. Far to the north in 1534, Cartier visited Hochelaga, which later became Montreal. But it was not until the following century that Europeans – French, English, Dutch, Swedish, German – began a purposeful settlement which was much accelerated when the thirteen states of the Union declared their Independence of Europe in 1776. And only in the nineteenth century did these English-speaking pioneers completely break the power of the Iroquois (northern relatives of the Cherokee) and force a clear passage across the Appalachians to the Ohio and the Mississippi. This was the heartland of the two largest language families east of the Rockies, the Siouan and the Algonkin. By this date, the Sioux were prominent as the horsemen of the Plains (their horses descended from Spanish runaways). The Algonkin were the widest spread, from Nova Scotia to Wyoming, from the Arctic shore to Virginia. Pocahontas was Algonkin, and so were the Indians who had taught the New England Puritans how to grow maize. They dominated the western Great Lakes, home of the Ottawa ('traders') and Ojibwa, and the Ohio valley, a focus for the Shawnee, Illinois, Lenape and others.

Once into the Ohio and the northern Mississippi valleys, the U.S. went on to surround and expel the Cherokee and the Creek, and wrest Texas, the Southwest and California from Mexico; and then from west and east they finally closed in on their earlier purchase of the Plains (the sellers having been the French, not the local owners). They also successfully vied with Mexico and the British in repulsing the Russians in the Pacific Northwest. This is the part of America where Europe, moving out west and east, met itself, and where the circuit of planetary consciousness was definitively closed.

I.1 *Annals of the Valley of Mexico before and during the Spanish Conquest (1516–25)*

Cortés's appropriation of the Aztec empire, centred on Tenochtitlan, in the highland Valley of Mexico, was recorded by many of its citizens, in native and in European script. This account is copied from a screenfold which recorded the history of the metropolitan area from the twelfth to the sixteenth centuries. It is in Toltec writing, used by the Aztecs and many other Mesoamerican peoples as an official script. Like all historical narratives in Toltec writing, it is calendrical. Events are narrated year by year, with the annual dates appearing here in Aztec style, in a row of boxes. The period covered in this extract goes from the year 11 Flint ($=1516$) to 7 House ($=1525$); the Toltec system of dating, explained in Chapter IV, involves the use of four 'Year-Bearer' signs, House, Rabbit, Reed and Flint, with co-efficients from one to thirteen; thus, 1978 is 5 Rabbit, and 1979 is 6 Reed.

In part, Toltec 'writing' is obviously pictographic. We see that there was conflict in the year 12 House because a warrior, holding spears and shield, brandishes a sword (of wood inset with obsidian blades). Two years later, in 1 Reed, the appearance of a horseman with metal shield and sword and a trefoil cross announces that the Spaniards have landed; they are greeted by an envoy of Moctezuma's, whose gift to them shows that the Aztecs were fully apprised of their journey from Cuba. Similarly graphic are: the fight at Tenochtitlan, in which Aztec priests are dismembered by the foreigners' steel swords on the very steps of the main pyramid of the city, topped by twin sanctuaries (2 Flint); Cortés's second and successful attack on the capital (3 House); the surrender of Moctezuma's successor, Cuauhtemoc, in his canoe (4 Rabbit); and the hanging of Cuauhtemoc near the Usumacinta river (6 Flint).

Toltec writing is also ideographic: clothing, weaponry, furniture, buildings, plants, and animals, hand-gestures and many other phenomena all have their precise shapes and meanings. A mummy on a wickerwork throne or seat means a royal funeral (11 Flint); spears and shield mean war (13 Rabbit, 1 Flint, etc.). By occupying a native house or sanctuary, Christian friars usurp the priests of the Toltec religion (4 Rabbit, 6 Flint), just as native royalty, with their seats of authority, are displaced by the introduction of folding chairs of Frankish design (6 Flint to 8 House).

Conventional objects and shapes are also used as numbers, and to identify people and places. Eastern neighbours of the Aztecs, the Tlaxcalans, bear a crescent under the chin as their characteristic: they appear as opponents of the Aztecs both before the Spanish conquest (12 House, 13 Rabbit) and during it, as allies of the Spaniards. Under the year 3 House, we see that Cortés's second attack cost him a hundred of his own men (bearded corpse with 5 banners each having the value of twenty) and four hundred

Codex Ríos, pp. 86v., 87r. (top), 87v., 88r.

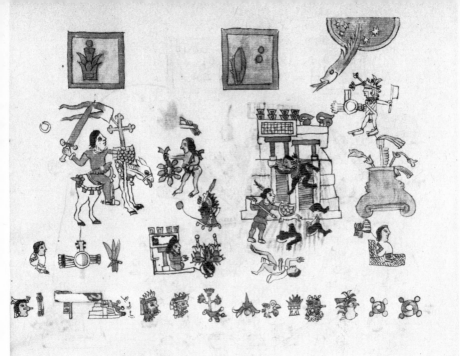

Tlaxcalans (head, with a feather denoting that quantity). In Nahua, the language of the Toltecs and the Aztecs, Cuauhtemoc means 'Eagle Falling': the emperor's name glyph has this bird on a downward trail of footprints (4 Rabbit and 6 Flint). The glyph of the Aztec capital Tenochtitlan (seen in 13 Rabbit, 1 Reed, etc.) comprises a stone (*te-tl*) and a cactus (*nochtli*). Other place names are indicated by a House or by a hill sign, and, like the names of the Aztecs' allies (listed from 1 Reed to 3 House), they can often be read by equivalent elements in languages other than Nahua. That these readings of Toltec writing were phonetic as well as ideographic, however, is shown by the approximate rendering of Spanish sounds by Nahua word-signs. Cortés corresponds to *coatl* (snake) while the Franciscan Juan Tecto (see 5 Reed) is transcribed as *oua-tl* (cane) and *totec* (grown maize).

Annals like these which narrate the 'trauma' of European invasion well illustrate the resilience and adaptability of Toltec writing and of narrative conventions that are inseparable from the year-based calendar of the Toltecs. In fact the presence of 'barbarian' Europeans (*popoloca*) becomes calendrically notable only when they intervene directly in national affairs.

I.2 *The siege of Tenochtitlan, 1521*

At the centre of this design is Tenochtitlan, the island capital of the Aztecs. It is represented by its huge main pyramid, which stood on the site now occupied by the Cathedral of Mexico City. Around it on Lake Texcoco, Aztec warriors in canoes hold shields, clubs and spears and swords inset with obsidian; one of them (lower left) is distinguished by the Jaguar uniform of the military elite. At the corners are four towns, shown by a large House sign; in each of them mounted Spaniards, together with native allies, trample on the dismembered bodies of vanquished local inhabitants (the arrow sticking in Xochimilco, upper right, means 'conquest'). These native allies are the Tlaxcalans, the authors of the document in which this scene appears, which is known as the 'Lienzo' or tapestry of Tlaxcala. After fiercely resisting Cortés when he entered their territory (roughly the modern state of Tlaxcala) on his march from the Gulf Coast, the Tlaxcalans joined him in the Spanish attack on their old enemies the Aztecs and became his stoutest allies. The siege of Tenochtitlan is one of several major campaigns depicted in their Lienzo, which the Tlaxcalans painted *c.* 1550 to celebrate

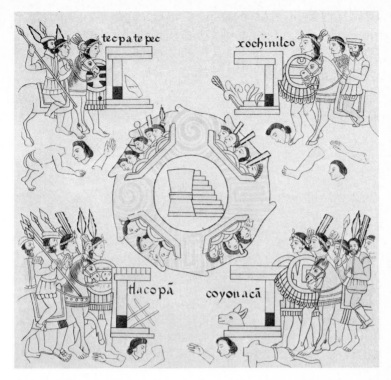

Lienzo of Tlaxcala, scene 42

their prowess and to remind the Spaniards of their indebtedness to them. In this scene we find some of the Toltec recording conventions used in the Valley of Mexico Annals. The circular lake bears the sign Water; and each of the four towns is named in the Roman alphabet and in Toltec writing: Xochimilco (*xochitl* = flower; *milli* = field) and Tecpatepec (*tecpatl* = flint) at the top; Tlacopan (*tlacotl* = twig) and Coyoacan (*coyotl* = coyote) below. (The endings *-co*, *-tepec*, 'hill' or 'pyramid', *-pan* and *-can* are all common in Nahua place-names). Yet, although the historical events depicted in the Lienzo as a whole appear in chronological order, the work is not calendrical, nor even a narrative. Each scene is highlighted separately, in its own right. This is a technique found in Toltec screenfolds concerned more with ritual than with calendrical matters. Indeed, though it records a particular event in

33

space and time, Cortés's siege of 1521, the scene is organized entirely into a ritual pattern. The towns are matched in pairs, with the eastern pair at the top: for their actual, quite asymmetrical positions, see the inset in Map 2 (Tlacopan and Coyoacan guarded the causeways to Tenochtitlan from the west and southwest). In Toltec ritual, this fourfold alignment around a circle may of itself denote pressure on the centre from the surround.

I.3 *Havoc wrought during Cortés's second attack and the three-month siege of Tenochtitlan and Tlatelolco, 1521*

Before being incorporated into Tenochtitlan by the Aztec emperors, Tlatelolco had been an independent community and its inhabitants retained a strong sense of their own identity. But they stoutly supported Cuauhtemoc, and were among the foremost in resisting the Spanish invasion. Their Annals, written in Nahua in the Roman alphabet in 1528–31, only a few years after the capital had fallen, are in part transcribed from originals in Toltec writing beginning in the twelfth century. The entry for 3 House (1521) gives a highly dramatic account of the agonies suffered by the defenders of the capital. The devastating lack of supplies during the siege by Cortés effaced good manners and social distinction, and brought about a collapse of the economy more drastic than in the worst famines of the past. The high intensity of the lament set in the narrative echoes the rhythms and phraseology of Nahua lyric poetry.

> And all this happened among us. We saw it. We lived through it with an astonishment worthy of tears and of pity for the pain we suffered.
> On the roads lie broken shafts and torn hair,
> houses are roofless, homes are stained red,
> worms swarm in the streets, walls are spattered with brains.
> The water is reddish, like dyed water;
> we drink it so, we even drink brine;
> the water we drink is full of saltpetre.
> The wells are crammed with adobe bricks.
>
> Whatever was still alive was kept between shields, like precious treasure, between shields, until it was eaten.

We chewed on hard tzompantli wood, brackish *zacatl* fodder, chunks of adobe, lizards, vermin, dust and worms.

We eat what was on the fire, as soon as it is done we eat it together right by the fire.

We had a single price; there was a standard price for a youth, a priest, a boy and a young girl. The maximum price for a slave amounted to only two handfuls of maize, to only ten tortillas. Only twenty bundles of brackish fodder was the price of gold, jade, mantles, quetzal plumes; all valuables fetched the same low price. It went down further when the Spaniards set up their battering engine in the market place.

Now, Cuauhtemoc orders the prisoners to be brought out; the guards don't miss any. The elders and chiefs grab them by their extremities and Cuauhtemoc slits open their bellies with his own hand.

Annals of Tlatelolco, part 5

I.4 *An Aztec agreement to supply an* encomendero *with goods, 1554*

In the wake of the Spanish military conquest of the Aztecs came the *encomienda* system, by which the Spanish monarchy rewarded its agents in America. Conquered populations were granted in lots to Cortés and the other conquistadors, and to privileged Spaniards, and were obliged to minister to their needs, though not technically as slaves. In the Aztec empire an important distinction had been made between commodity tribute and personal labour, and this was reinforced by the Spanish viceregal courts set up in the 1540s. In this contract (of a kind accepted in the courts until 1600 and later), the Aztecs of Huitzilopochco (now Churubusco, Mexico City), through their representatives, formally accept the demands of their *encomendero* Bernardino Vázquez de Tapia. Reading anticlockwise from the upper left, the Toltec signs specify the tribute due in order of frequency: 100 bushels of maize (per year); 50 *tepuztli* or base metal coins (per quarter); 2 bundles of firewood and 2 bundles of *zacatl* fodder and one turkey (daily). The canoe means that the daily tribute should be brought (by canal) to the *encomendero*'s house. Such documents were part of the normal working of the Aztec state; Huitzilopochco figures in a surviving copy of Moctezuma's tribute list (cf. *VII.10*). The Spanish gloss below dates the agreement at 17 October 1554.

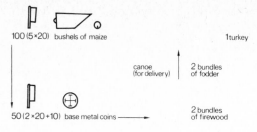

100 (5×20) bushels of maize   1 turkey

canoe (for delivery)   2 bundles of fodder

50 (2×20+10) base metal coins   2 bundles of firewood

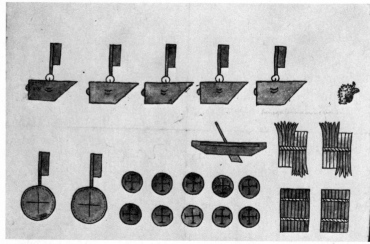

Huitzilopochco, Contrat de Commanderie

I.5 *Evidence submitted to prove cases of Spanish brutality, c. 1529*

Under the *encomendero* system, Spanish abuse was not uncommon. But, in principle at least, redress was possible through the viceregal courts, in which legal evidence was provided by native documents such as this one. It is from Coyoacan (the place name, designated by a seated coyote by a hill, is just below the centre of the page). Cortés

Manuscrito del Aperramiento

himself is indicted here (top left), together with his interpreter Marina (also known as Malinche and Malintzin), who holds a rosary in her hand. The victim of their crime, hands tied and held on a chain, is being savaged by a mastiff, a form of intimidation, indeed a pastime much favoured by the Spaniards. Las Casas wrote that it was not unusual for one Spaniard to say to another: 'Lend me a quarter of a Villaine [an Indian], to give my Dogs some meat, until I kill one next.' Below, the *encomendero* Andres de 'Dabia' [Tapia] is accused of crimes committed in Cholula, where he was given an *encomienda* by Cortés. Cholula's inhabitants had been massacred by Cortés and the Tlaxcalans on the march to Tenochtitlan in 1519: to the right, the enslaving (a decade later) of six surviving leaders is shown, all of them being bound to a chain. Their names are indicated by Toltec signs (note the components Deer, Snake and Dog) and are written out in Nahua. Though the style of drawing on this page is partly Europeanized, it adheres to Toltec writing conventions in its method of naming and in such details as the weight given to hand gestures. In the Indian sign language common to North America, the gesture made by Cortés means 'to meet', which suggests that he had summoned the native leaders under the pretext of offering Christian instruction (Malinche's rosary).

I.6 *A Maya account of the death of Cuauhtemoc, 1524*

After accepting the surrender of Cuauhtemoc, from his canoe on Lake Texcoco, Cortés did not have him killed immediately. Rather he used him, along with other dignitaries from Tenochtitlan and Tlatelolco, as companions in further expeditions, counting on the awe they could be expected to inspire along the road. The passage quoted here tells of their arrival in the border country at the mouth of the Usumacinta river, known in Nahua as Acallan ('Boat-Place'), where, now as then, Maya territory begins. Here Cuauhtemoc's usefulness diminished and, accused by a certain Paxbolonacha of wanting to kill Cortés, he met his end. The quotation is from a Maya narrative written in 1612 to further the interests of Paxbolonacha's descendants under Spanish rule: hence the emphasis on Paxbolonacha's loyalty to Cortés. Paxbolonacha was one of the Mactun or 'Chontal' Maya, who as a border people had no particular reason to love Cuauhtemoc and the Aztecs on the one hand; nor, on the other, did they share that strong sense of cultural identity as Maya which inspired their brothers further east, in Peten or Yucatan proper, to resist the Spanish as foreigners. (Not long before the Spaniards arrived – as the Paxbolon Papers tell – the Mactun had been suppressed by an alliance between the Aztecs at their eastern outpost at Xicalanco and the Maya of western Yucatan.) Accounts of Cuauhtemoc's death, by native and by Western historians, differ in their explanations of *how* the Aztec emperor was killed. The Valley of Mexico Annals (above; *I.1*) show him hanged. Other Nahua sources, like the annals in the Mapa de Tepechpan, show him hanging by his feet from a tree, terribly mutilated and headless. The Mactun account says he was baptized only to be decapitated, or, more accurately, decorporated. This version has a certain Maya edge; and as a motif, the close association between naming and the severed head hanging in a ceiba tree is found in Classic Maya literature.

Cuauhtemoc, the emperor who had come from Mexico-Tenochtitlan with Cortés, was there. He said to Paxbolonacha, the ruler I mentioned earlier: 'My lord, as for these Spaniards, the day will come when they will cause you much trouble and kill your people. I believe rather we should kill them, for I bring a large force and you are many.' So spoke Cuauhtemoc to Paxbolonacha, ruler of the Mactun. On hearing these words of Cuauhtemoc, the other replied that he would first have to think it over. He considered that the word of the Spaniards was good; they did not kill or abuse people. They only asked for much honey, turkeys, maize and fruit, every day. He said to himself: 'I will not be equivocal or double-hearted towards the Spaniards.' Not so Cuauhtemoc, the Mexican leader, who wanted to kill the Spaniards, and urged him on. In view of this, Paxbolonacha went to Cortés: 'My lord Capitán del Valle, this ruler Cuauhtemoc who is with you, watch out for him in case he commits treason against you; three, four times he has told me you should be killed.' Cortés heard this. Immediately the Mexican was seized and put in chains. On the third day that he was a prisoner they took him out and baptized him, whether with the name Don Juan or with the name Don Fernando is unsure. He received a name and was sliced through the neck. His head was hung in the ceiba tree before the sanctuary in Yaxdzan.

Paxbolon-Maldonado Papers, pp. 160–1

39

I.7 *The self-defence of a Maya from Yucatan who collaborated with the Spaniards, 1562*

Even in the heart of Maya territory in Yucatan, not everyone chose to resist the Spanish, and some actively helped them. Nakuk Pech, of Chac Xulub Chen, 'Great Horns Well' (the district on the north coast around Sisal, the port after which that fibre is named), was such a collaborator, and he wrote a Maya chronicle to justify himself and his claims on his new masters. He notes the high status of his family before the Spanish invasion, confined as this was to a few towns. He emphasizes the services he rendered to the conquistador Montejo, and also notes his support of the missionary activities of the Church when the padres arrived in 1552 in his part of Yucatan. In making his case, he defends his right to private property in terms more normal among the Spanish than among the communally minded Maya. And his chronicle reckons time according to the European, not the Maya calendar. Pech thus comes to distinguish himself as an individual from the 'Maya men' among whom he had grown up. However, in stressing obedience to the Christian choirmasters who taught singing, he alludes to the native American custom of valuing song as a form of national self-expression, which any conqueror had the right to adopt or, as here, replace. And though he does not complain directly about European behaviour in Yucatan, there is a good deal of veiled criticism in his chronicle. For example, he refers in detail to the abuses (including the use of mastiffs; cf. *I.5*) which the Spanish Crown attempted to curtail through its own direct representatives, like the auditor Tomás López, and through the system of 'audiencias' or appellate viceregal courts. More noteworthy still, he uses a traditional Maya word to describe the Spaniards: *dzulob*, foreigners. That is, he sees them as alien invaders like the Toltecs and the Mexicans who preceded the Spanish incursion into post-Classic Yucatan by five hundred years.

> When the foreigners came to the towns of this land, there were no Maya men who wanted to pay tax to the first of them to arrive. Hence these first Spaniards made an account of those towns which were to be given to be governed. I, Nakuk Pech, was the first recipient of this town in the district Chac Xulub Chen.
>
> In the year 1552 the padres settled here. In this year they came to teach singing here at Sisal. They came from the west to teach the

chants of mass and vespers, to the music of the organ and flute, and plainsong, which we had not known here before.

In the year 1553 the Auditor Don Tomás López arrived in this land of Yucatan from Castile, as a messenger from the great ruler Rey de Castilla to protect us from the hand of the Spaniards here. He put an end to burning by the Spaniards, an end to savaging by mastiffs, he originated the appointing of chiefs in the towns, by the gift of the yardstick; he also adjusted the rate of tax. Three times we paid tribute to the Spaniards: blankets, beeswax, turkeys, maize, wooden buckets, salt, peppers, broad beans, narrow beans, jars, pots, vases – a list of the tribute payable to the *encomendero* before the auditor turned his attention to these matters.

So too I built my house of stone on the north side of the church. To prevent Maya men saying it belongs to them, this is why I set out what was done by me, Don Pablo Pech Ah Macan Pech, my father, Don Martín Pech Ah Kon Pech, and my lord Don Ambrosio Pech whose Maya name is Op Pech, and Ixil Ytzam Pech, and Don Esteban Pech Ah Culub Pech.

Ah Nakuk Pech, *Chronicle of Chac-Xulub-Chen*

I.8 *Maya objections to the behaviour of the Spaniards and their agents in Yucatan, 1559*

The tone of these Maya references to the Spanish is very different from Nakuk Pech's or Paxbolonacha's. They stem not from an individual or even a family but from one of the community books of the Yucatecan Maya known as the Books of Chilam Balam. Each of these books is named after a village or community, the one quoted here belonging to Chumayel. The objection here is to the uncontrolled abuse of the defenceless population, to the gulf between moral principle and moral practice, and to the lack of solidarity on the part of opportunist, self-seeking, fellow Maya. Robbery and exploitation are so rife that even petty cash is thought worth snatching; the institution of Christian charity turns out to mean the poor making the rich richer, and the viceregal courts meant to protect native Americans mete out summary justice like darts from a blow-gun. Maya people are oppressed by a plague of sub-human creatures who squeeze them and live off them with animal cunning. It is not that these Maya wished to reject the Spaniards out of hand: they were used to dealing with 'foreigners'. Nor did they necessarily refuse to listen to the word of the 'true *Dios*', brought by the padres; and indeed they adapt Christian terminology to their own needs: Antichrist, and *justicia*, for example.

The passage belongs to a specific literary form, calendrical in origin – that of the traditional pronouncements on and for the *katun*, the 7,200 day period of the Maya calendar (20 'years' of 360 days). This pronouncement is for the Katun 11 Ahau, which ended in 1559; its political insight, firm moral tone and overall rhetoric are characteristic of the *katun* texts which, transcribed in part from hieroglyphs into alphabetic writing, are an important element in the Yucatec Community Books. *Katun* texts exist in hieroglyphic form in the thirteenth-century screenfold now in Paris, and these have their origin further back still, in the inscriptions at Tikal and other Classic Maya cities. In drawing on this long tradition, the Chilam Balam Book of Chumayel, the source of this passage, evinces a wholly distinctive sense of what it means to be Maya, historically and politically.

> . . . the true God, the true *Dios*, came, but this was the origin too of affliction for us. The origin of tax, of our giving them alms, of trial through the grabbing of petty cacao money, of trial by blowgun, stomping the people, violent removal, forced debt, debt created by false testimony, petty litigation, harassment, violent removal, the collaboration with the Spaniards on the part of the priests, the local chiefs, the choirmasters, public prosecutors through the agency of the children and the youths of the town, and all the while the mistreated were further maltreated. These were the people who had been reduced to want but who did not depart even when they were so squeezed. It was through Antichrist on earth, the kinkajous of the towns, the vixen of the towns, blood-sucking bugs of the town, those who suck dry the common people. But it will happen that tears will come to the eyes of God the father. The *justicia* of God the father will settle on the whole world, it surely will come from God upon Ah Kantenal, Ix Pucyola, the opportunists of the world.
>
> Book of Chumayel, pp. 14–15

I.9 *The sufferings of the Cakchiquel Maya, in highland Guatemala, 1530–1*

The message of this laconic passage is plain enough. The arrival of the Spaniards led by 'Tunatiuh' (Pedro de Alvarado) brings humiliation and enslavement. ('Tonatiuh' was the name given to Alvarado by his Mexican mercenaries on account of his blond hair; in Nahua it means 'sun'.) Yet this is not enough to destroy the ability or the will to record history. The quotation is from a document written, in their language, by the Cakchiquel Maya, who still live in the southern part of Maya territory, in highland Guatemala. The form of the document is calendrical, events being dated by days and by conventional 'years' of 400 days (*huna*), this being the time between 12 August 1530 and 10 September 1531. The count of *huna* here dates back only to the 'revolution' of 1493; but the system itself is much older and goes back to the Maya Classic period, in being based on the day, not the solar year of the Toltec calendar (also, the *huna* are grouped in cycles of 20, called '*may*', which resemble the *katun* of the Yucatec to the north). As with the Yucatec, the importance of the calendar cannot be over-emphasized. The 400-day *huna* governs the number of slaves required to be sent to build the town of Pangan and to satisfy the Spaniards' greed for gold: day for day, the Cakchiquel Maya themselves are made the substance of 'heavy tribute'. Being Maya, the calendar is also bound up with the system of electing and 'naming' rulers, like 9-Maize (a calendar name). After this ruler died ignominiously slaving away to find gold, Alvarado openly flouted the Cakchiquel system in not holding an election to replace him. It is through 'small' details such as these, meticulously recorded, that the Cakchiquel Maya indicate how the Spanish invasion most affected them.

> On the day 13 Reed [12 August 1530] ended the thirty-fourth 'year' [*huna*] after the revolution.
> During this year heavy tribute was imposed. Gold was contributed to Tunatiuh; four hundred men and four hundred women were contributed to work in Pangan on the construction of the city, by order of Tunatiuh. All this, all, we ourselves saw, oh, my sons!
> On the day 10 Reed [16 September 1531] ended the thirty-fifth 'year' [*huna*] after the revolution.
> During the two months of the third year which had passed since the lords presented themselves, the king 9-Maize died; he died on the day

7 Deer [24 September 1532] while he was panning gold. Immediately after the death of the king, Tunatiuh came here to choose a successor to the king. Then the lord *Don Jorge* was installed in the government by order of Tunatiuh alone. There was no election by the people to name him. Afterwards Tunatiuh talked to the lords and his orders were obeyed by the chiefs, for in truth they feared Tunatiuh.

Book of the Cakchiquel, part 2

I.10 *The dispersal of a local chapter of priests in Peru, 1533*

Only a few native documents deal with the forty-year Spanish invasion of the vast Inca empire. Among the most valuable of these is the sixteenth-century Quechua text known as the Huarochiri Narrative; it consists of oral and written reports gathered by the Franciscan missionary Francisco de Ávila in the area around Huarochiri, Checa and Yauyos (on the road from Lima to Cuzco). The chapter quoted here notes an augury of the Spanish invasion at Yauyos and the dispersal of the group of priests there as a result of the Spanish advance. The Spanish presence is said to become 'news' when Pizarro reaches Cajamarca, the town in which Atahuallpa was 'ransomed' for prodigious quantities of gold artifacts before being killed in 1533. In taking Cajamarca the Spaniards established their power in that part of the Inca Tahuantinsuyu ('Four Districts') known as the Chinchasuyu, which Atahuallpa's father, Huayna Capac, had extended well to the north of Quito. For the priests of Yauyos, who allude to these matters here, the military success of the Spanish poses the question of their own dependence on the secular power of the Inca. As we learn, their worship of Pariacaca, in truth only their own local god and an 'aspect' of the Inca official deity Viracocha, has been controlled by an imperial order from Cuzco and adjusted to the state calendar of 30-day months. Witnessing both the vincibility of the Inca state and the sacrilegious behaviour of the Spaniards in their greed for treasure, they decide in the end that they are facing a change equivalent to that between the 'world ages' of Quechua and American cosmology in general (see p. 149 below). Their response is to return to their separate communities (*llanta; ayllu*), in the like of which millions of Quechua still thrive in Peru, Bolivia and Ecuador.

The Inca ordered that thirty men from Upper and Lower Yauyos should serve the god Pariacaca in the month of Pura. And fifteen men from each district served the god, giving him food. One day they sacrificed one of their llamas, whose name was Yauri Huanaca. As the thirty priests gathered to examine the llama's heart and entrails, one of their number, Llacuas Quita Pariasca, said:

'This is not a good moment, brothers. Before long our father Pariacaca will regress into the past age of the Purun.'

But the others said: 'That's only your opinion', and one went on: 'Why do you say that? Through this heart our father Pariacaca speaks good.' He didn't go near the heart, but still pronounced: 'Pariacaca himself says so, brother.' And they insulted Llacuas Quita Pariasca, saying angrily: 'The stinker, what does *he* know! Our father Pariacaca's realm stretches through the Chinchasuyu, how could he be superseded! What does this man know?'

A few days later they all heard the news: the Spaniards were in Caxamarca [Cajamarca].

Moreover, among the thirty priests was an old man from Checa (*ayllu* Cacasica) who was the wisest of them all; he was called Caxalliuya. When the Spaniards reached here they asked: 'Where is the silver belonging to this god, and his regalia?' Since none of the priests wanted to say, the Spaniards grew furious; they heaped up some grass and put Caxalliuya to burn. The wind whipped the flames up one side of his body and he suffered terribly. Only then were the silver and the regalia given to the Spaniards. All the priests agreed:

'Llacuas Quita Pariasca gave us good advice, brothers. It's best we disperse; this is not a good moment.'

And each went off to his community.

Huarochiri Narrative, chapter 18

I.11 *The killing of the royal Inca, Tupac Amaru, in Cuzco, 1572*

Like his contemporaries, the Quechua authors of the Huarochiri Narrative, the early Peruvian writer Guaman Poma ('Hawk Puma') was preoccupied with the events and the effects of the Spanish invasion of his country. His great work, entitled *New Chronicle and Good Government* and composed between 1585 and 1613, consists of a narrative, part Spanish, part Quechua, regularly illustrated with pictures like this one. It shows the emperor Tupac Amaru ('Shining Snake'), at the tender age of 15, being beheaded by three hatted Spaniards; still wearing the woven imperial Inca belt, he holds the cross of last-minute redemption in his manacled hands. This event, of 1572, marked the end of the military resistance which the Inca had organized from Vilcabamba, after the fall of their capital Cuzco in 1533. Below Tupac Amaru, in Guaman Poma's picture, his people lament their loss, saying, in Quechua: 'Inca Huanacuari, where are you going? Our wicked enemies, without there being any reason of guilt, have cut off your head'. These phrases, which echo Inca funeral liturgy, are included by Guaman Poma to suggest that, while tragic, Tupac Amaru alone suffers less than those who survive him, the helpless and the oppressed who have to go on living. For the decapitation of Tupac Amaru left Peru literally headless, as long as its new conquerors proved unable or

Guaman Poma, *Nueva corónica*, p. 451

46

unwilling to assume the central position of responsibility held by the royal Inca. It is just this responsibility that Guaman Poma aimed to awaken with his work, which grew from a transcription of the official Inca records known as *quipus* (knotted cords), and from a long lonely journey to Huarochiri and places throughout the old Tahuantinsuyu where he could learn about current events. When it was finished he sent his manuscript as a letter to the Spanish king, Philip III, to advise him how Peru could be better ruled. Only in the present century has anyone cared to read or even notice it.

I.12 *A Spanish peace offer rejected in the name of Chibcha integrity, 1541*

Between the Inca Tahuantinsuyu and Mesoamerica a third focus of civilization flourished in the sixteenth century, inferior to none in gold-working techniques and, as the fabled El Dorado, the subject of conflicting and incomplete report. Lying in what is now Colombia, this territory became much desired as the 'third marquisate' of America, after Quesada's conquest of Bacata (Bogotá) in 1536. Highland cities like Cuzco and Tenochtitlan, Bacata and its rival Hunza (Tunja) were centres of Chibcha power, and of a trading system which linked them with linguistic relatives among the millennial gold-workers on the Caribbean coast, among the Cuna and others up towards Nicaragua; and, to the south, among the Paez on the multiple watershed of Las Papas, part of which they still defend. Both Bacata and Hunza accounted themselves heirs of the ancient shrine of Iraca, called Sogamoso by the Spaniards, whose sanctuaries and houses are referred to in the passage quoted here. After the fall of the Zipa (ruler) of Bacata, the Sogamoso area was defended for several years by the author of this speech, Tundama. The behaviour of the Spaniards and their Peruvian mercenaries did not encourage him to accept the offer of peace made by Baltasar Maldonado in 1541 to which he replies here. Tundama's own idea of peace and of Sogamoso as a civilized 'centre' derived from the teaching of Bochica, the culture hero who by Chibcha reckoning visited Sogamoso late in the first millennium B C. Bochica's exit from the city was commemorated by an immense causeway to the eastern Plains, atop which stood a golden house similar to the Coricancha in Cuzco.

Before the Spaniards arrived, Tundama and his fellow-Chibcha had been long standing opponents of the neighbouring Panches and Muzos, Carib-speakers referred to here as barbarians, as well as of the Arawak, the third main language family of the area. At the same time, these peoples traded with each and shared metal technologies, numbering systems, calendars, and iconographic symbols used by their descendants today.

I am not so barbarous, famous Spaniard, not to believe peace to be the centre on which the bounds of this world depend; but do not think I'm unaware that the bland words with which you offer it to me are much belied by your harsh behaviour.

Who will say that Tundama should give to the vassal the tribute due to the king? I cannot serve someone who serves his king so badly. According to your own accounts of the King of Spain's clemency, it is not credible that he should send you to kill and rob us so.

More barbarian than the Panches and the Muzos, you bathe your horses' mouths in our blood, which they drink out of hunger and thirst and which you spill to display your cruelty. You desecrate the sanctuaries of our gods and sack the houses of men who haven't offended you. Who would choose to undergo these insults, being not insensitive? Who would omit to rid himself of such harassment, even at the cost of his life?

You well know that my people were bred with no fewer natural privileges than yours we now know that you are not immortal or descended from the sun. Since your people refuse tax and tyranny you cannot be surprised that mine do, with determination.

Do not take as examples the Zipas, killed sooner through your treachery or their bad government, or because they fought with less right, than because of the valour you claim for yourselves.

Note well the survivors who await you, to undeceive you that victory is always yours.

Tundama's speech

I.13 *A Tupi taunts French missionaries on the Brazilian coast, 1612*

In this emphatic speech, the warrior-priest Cettvy-ci, a Tupi-Guarani, challenges Europeans as they approach South America from the Atlantic to explore the coasts of his country, Brazil. It was heard, and recorded (though only in part in Tupi), by the French Capuchin, Yves d'Evreux, on a mission begun in Brazil in 1612. The Europeans, Portuguese and French, who first visited Brazil sixty or so years before, were generally well received, especially if they were traders with European weapons. In fact, as here, they were thought, and spoken, of as 'Caribs', that is the foreign tribe to the north of the Tupi (near the sea now named after them), who were famous as seamen, metalworkers and arms dealers. Conflict arose partly because of inter-European rivalry, and because of the Church's strict missionary efforts against customs which, through the writings of Montaigne and others, provided the Western world with the idea of the 'Noble Savage'.

The defiant rhetoric of Cettvy-ci's speech is that of a conventional form or 'carbet' used by Tupi braves to taunt their rivals with examples of their own prowess. Speeches like it formed part of the repertoire of the groups of Tupi shipped to Rouen to entertain French royalty in the late sixteenth century. Though he got little response from Yves d'Evreux, who refused to rise to such a challenge, Cettvy-ci emphasizes the differences between himself and the Frenchman. He presents himself as a *pagy* or shaman, and the other as a *pai* or Christian father (*pãe* in Portuguese). He boasts of having killed a Christian at Yves d'Evreux's parish of Yuiret and of being able to rot the manioc (this being one of the staple crops of tropical America) grown there. As a professional priest he demeans the foreigners' ways of serving God, *Tupã* in Tupi, not just out of bravado, but because in certain respects Christian teaching seemed inadequate to Tupi-Guarani theologians. In conversation with Yves d'Evreux, his fellow *pagy* compared, for example, the biblical Genesis with the Tupi-Guarani liturgy of creation which has survived to our time under the name Ayvu Rapyta or 'Origin of Human Speech' (cf. *V.10*).

I I I   the brave.
I I I   great pagy.
I I I   pai-killer.
I killed the pai who is dead and buried at Yuiret the home of the great pai to whom I send every evil and whom I'll kill as I did the other one.
I shall torment the Carib foreigners with disease.
I shall cause worms to infest their feet and legs so that they will have to go home.

I shall cause the manioc in their fields to rot so that they perish from
  hunger.
I was near them once; I have often eaten with them.
I observed their ways when they served Tupã the God.
I saw they knew nothing compared with us pagy.
We should not fear them.
I will go in front when we attack.
I the brave.

Cettvy-ci's challenge

I.14 *An Algonkin account of whites entering northern America, seventeenth century*

One of the few extant native records of European arrival on the
eastern coasts of North America is found in the Walam Olum ('Red
Score') of the Lenape-Algonkin. Comparable with the screenfolds
of Mesoamerica, it falls into two parts, dealing respectively with
cosmogony and national history. This quotation is from the end of
Part 2, in which narrative continuity is given by the list of successive
Lenape *sachems*, or chiefs, over several centuries. The first
appearance of the whites under Sachem He-Makes-Mistakes (164)
may be dated to the sixteenth century, when they began to have an
impact on the affairs of the Atlantic seaboard. At that time, having
driven a wedge between the Iroquois League to the north and the
Cherokee to the south, the Lenape had governmental residences in
the mid-Appalachians, Pennsylvania (Sassafras Land; 160) and
New Jersey (the Shore; 161, 175). The viewpoint on events,
however, remains that of a central Algonkin group with strong
connections with the ancestral Ohio Valley. This is where the
Sachem Saluted (178) protected Lenape towns (e.g. Coshocton;
Chillicothe), and where the Walam Olum was copied by the
antiquarian Rafinesque in the early 1820s (together with the
accompanying oral text). The 'closing in' from north and south in
the last symbols (183–4) corresponds to the English pincer
movement in the seventeenth century, down from New England
and up from Virginia, on the Atlantic coast.

The Lenape were regarded as a senior nation by fellow Algonkin,
and were respected by such Iroquoians as the Hurons, and by the
Creeks, who called them grandfather. An effect of white intrusion

was to increase their activity as diplomats and arbitrators. After fighting the Cherokee they take care to re-establish peace with them (169), as well as with the Hurons. And in order to resist the combined threat of the Iroquois League and their English allies in New York, they cement a close alliance between the Illinois, Shawnee and Kanawha (or Convoy) divisions of the Algonkin (170), and send a high-level mission to the 'junior' Ottawa on the Great Lakes (173). The pattern of this policy was closely followed in the preparations for the rising led by the Ottawa Pontiac in 1763.

The symbols in the Walam Olum derive from the pictographic fund used by the Algonkin, Iroquoian and Sioux nations alike. On their pipe-stems, weapons and other articles, these peoples all used similar conventions to render such elements as national hair-style; rank of head-dress; gesture (friendship, fear etc.); place-names, like the mound or pyramid for Cherokee country (169); and various flora and fauna. (The so-called 'effigy' mounds of the Sioux in Wisconsin themselves represent such creatures as fox, turtle and beaver.) There were also agreed signs for abstract concepts like speed, a spiral (163); war, a diagonal cross (167, 177); and prosperity, a triple vertical cross (165). Among the Algonkin, these signs were fully articulated as compound symbols according to the ritual of their Midewiwin or Grand Medicine Society, which still exists. Each symbol of the fourfold lines of the Walam Olum occupies its 'house' (a box like the houses aligned by the Sachem Friend-to-all; 162) and these were originally the four 'houses' of ritual initiation. Moreover, as in that ritual, they are oriented along an east-west line, originally the path of the initiate through these houses. Being to the right of the 'shore' in symbols 164 and 184, the whites' ships thus come from the east (the word 'east' in Lenape by coincidence also means 'white'); and the Great Lakes, to the left in 171, are westward. This device is integrated with the principle of inversion either side of the line to express the concepts 'above' and 'below' (sea and lakes being below), of north and south, the directions from which the whites come the second time, and of negation and opposition (for which parallels may be found in Iroquoian, Sioux and in Toltec iconography). These final symbols of the Walam Olum complete the total of 184. This equals the numbers of days from the beginning of the Midewiwin year at the spring equinox to the autumn equinox, the turning-point into winter. In the cosmology of many native north Americans, this is the half of the year and of ritual time in which the gods, stirring momentarily at the solstice, are lost in sleep.

160

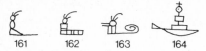
161   162   163   164

Great Beaver was sachem, remaining in Sassafras land

White-Body was sachem, at the Shore
Friend-to-all was sachem, he did good
He-Makes-Mistakes was sachem, he arrived with speed
At this time whites came on the eastern sea

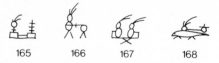
165   166   167   168

Much-Honoured was sachem; he was prosperous.
Well-Praised was sachem; he fought in the south;
he fought in the land of the Cherokee and Koweta
White-Otter was sachem; an ally of the Hurons

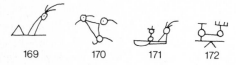
169   170   171   172

White-Horn was sachem; he went to the Cherokee
To the Illinois, the Shawnee and the Kanawha
Coming-as-a-Friend was sachem; he went to the Great Lakes
visiting all his children, all his friends.

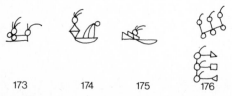
173   174   175   176

Cranberry-Eater was sachem, and ally of the Ottawa
North-Walker was sachem; he made festivals
Slow-Gatherer was sachem, at the Shore;
the three clans were chosen, Unami, Minsi and Chikini

177   178   179   180

Man-Who-Fails was sachem; he fought the Iroquois
He-is-Friendly was sachem; he scared the Iroquois
Saluted was sachem; over there
on the Scioto river, he had foes

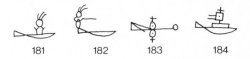

181   182   183   184

White-Crab was sachem; a friend of the shore
Watcher was sachem; he observed the sea
At this time, from north and south, the whites came
Their large ships went easily, wherever they pleased.

Walam Olum, part 2

I.15 *A wampum belt commemorating a Pennsylvania treaty, 1682*

Wampum is made of two kinds of shell, white, and light and dark purple, drilled and cut into small tubular beads. The Walam Olum shows the Lenape making wampum on the New Jersey coast before the arrival of Europeans. Strings and belts of these beads were used internationally in diplomacy and trade between the eastern Algonkin and the Iroquois, and, later, the white settlers. William Penn made his famous treaties with the Lenape by means of belts like this one (which has eighteen rows.) They showed tribal boundaries and symbolically commemorated the political attitudes of the parties concerned. In this belt, which dates from 1682, a white man (with hat) clasps the hand of a Lenape in friendship, while territorial and other information is given in the diagonal

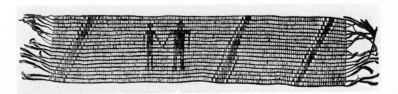

stripes on either side of them. The shell (rated first against sterling and later the dollar) was used as currency by whites and Indians in New Jersey until the late 19th century. Strings of wampum also served as an integral part of the rituals and the diplomacy of the Iroquois Great League (cf. *I.15*).

I.16 *Diplomacy of the Iroquois Great League towards the French and the British, 1684*

The Great League, Peace or Commonwealth of the Iroquois, founded by Hiawatha in the fifteenth century, united Five Nations: the Cayuga, Seneca, Onondaga, Oneida and Mohawk. Tightly knit, the League held firmly on to their territory at the headwaters of rivers flowing from the northern Appalachians, an Iroquoian strategy also practised by the Cherokee at the southern end of the same range. While the more loosely allied Algonkin and fellow Iroquoians like the Huron and Erie generally traded with the French, the main connections of the League were with the Dutch and English, though they never compromised their political independence. In 1684 the French massed troops in Fort Cadaracki, Quebec, with a view to beating the Five Nations into submission and severing their links with the recently installed English commander at Albany, New York (here called Corlar, after the Dutch governor Arent van Curler who concluded the first European treaty with the League in 1642). However, the French were plagued by sickness and fatigue, and when they finally reached the Five Nations at Kaihohage on the north shore of Lake Ontario, the French captain, M. de la Barre, had to bluff. His noisy threats were answered by an Onondaga, the spokesman nicknamed Grangula ('grande-gueule'), who addressed his words not to de la Barre but direct to the French Governor of Canada (called Onnontio, or 'big hill' in Iroquois after the first incumbent, de Montmagny).

The first four invocations to Onnontio make up the exordial response, full of ironic geniality and speculation, on the motif of the calumet or ceremonial pipe. The friendship between the Five Nations and the French, once sealed by the calumet held by Grangula, should indeed be honoured; fire and flood and natural forces have not been too much for the Iroquois who are unmoved by the visitor's threat. The hatchet should not be dug up because it would be to French disadvantage: the weakness and sickness of the

French troops have in fact saved them and their 'great captain', de la Barre.

Next come the hard political facts, recorded explicitly in three wampum belts. The Five Nations have more arms than could be paid for in the beaver currency of the fur trade: these they have taken from an alliance of Algonkins who had invaded Iroquois territory and had committed a capital crime as hunters. M. de la Barre's violent protest at the Iroquois dealings with the Algonkin is shown to be irrelevant, because they are part of the strategies described in the Walam Olum and belong to Indian not French affairs. And the French are reminded that their access to the Five Nations depends on the Algonkin no more or less than English access to the Algonkin and the Huron in the Ohio and on the Great Lakes depends on the Five Nations. Here Grangula's irony gives way to sarcasm: the French should go ahead and treat their allies like slaves if they cannot think of any better way to act.

In the third and final part of his speech Grangula invokes Onnontio twice more and refers to two further wampum belts, of signature and authority. To the calumet of the exordium is added the motif of the tree of peace. The French should not so crowd themselves into Fort Cadaracki because it could be bad for the roots of the tree of friendship between the two sides which had been planted there, over their buried weapons, according to Hiawatha's custom.

> Onnontio! I honour you, and the warriors that are with me all likewise honour you. Your interpreter Akonessan has finished your speech; I now begin mine. My words make haste to reach your ears. Harken to them.
>
> Onnontio! – You must have believed when you left Quebec, that the sun had burnt up all the forests, which render our country inaccessible to the French, or that the lakes had so far overflown the banks, that they had surrounded our castles, and that it was impossible for us to get out of them. Yes, you must have dreamed so, and curiosity to see all that burnt or flooded country has doubtless brought you so far. *Now* you are undeceived. I and the warriors here present are come to assure you that the Senecas, Cayugas, Onondagas, Oneidas and Mohawks are yet alive. I thank you in their name, for bringing back into their country the calumet, which your predecessor received from their hands. It was happy for you that you left under ground that murdering hatchet, so often dyed in the blood of the French.

Hear, Onnontio! I do not sleep. I have my eyes open. The sun, which enlightens me, discovers to me a great captain at the head of a company of soldiers, who speaks as if he were dreaming. He says that he only came to the lake to smoke on the great calumet with the Onondagas. But *Grangula* says that he sees the contrary; that it was to knock them on the head, if sickness had not weakened the arms of the French. I see Onnontio raving in a camp of sick men, whose lives the Great Spirit has saved by inflicting this sickness on them.

Hear, Onnontio! Our women had taken their clubs, our children and old men had carried their bows and arrows into the heart of your camp, if our warriors had not disarmed them, and kept them back, when your interpreter came to our castles. It is done and I have said it.

Onnontio! We plundered none of the French, but those that carried guns, powder and balls to the Miami and Illinois, because those arms might have cost us our lives. Herein we follow the example of the Jesuits, who break all the kegs of rum brought to our castles, lest the drunken Indians should knock them on the head. Our warriors have not beaver enough to pay for all the arms they have taken, and our old men are not afraid of the war. This belt preserves my words.

We carried the English into our lakes, to trade there with the Ottawa and Hurons, as the Algonkin brought the French to our Five Nations, to carry on a trade, which the English say is theirs. We are born free. We depend neither on Onnontio nor on Corlar. We may go where we please, and carry with us whom we please, and buy and sell what we please. If your allies be your slaves, use them as such, command them to receive no other but your people. This belt preserves my words.

We knock the Miami and Illinois on the head, because they had cut down the trees of peace, which were the limits of our country. They have hunted beaver on our lands. They have acted contrary to the customs of all Indians, for they left none of the beavers alive – they killed both male and female. They brought the Shawnee into their country, to take part with them, in their Algonkin alliance against us. We have done less than either the English or French that have usurped the lands of so many Indian nations, and chased them from their own country. This belt preserves my words.

Onnontio! What I say is the voice of all the Five Nations. Hear what they answer. Open your ears to what they speak. The Senecas, Cayugas, Onondagas, Oneidas and Mohawks say that when they buried the hatchet at Cadaracki, in the presence of your predecessor, in the middle of the fort, they planted the tree of peace in the same place, there to be carefully preserved: that in the place of a retreat for soldiers, that fort might be a rendezvous for merchants: that in place of arms and ammunition of war, only beavers and merchandise should enter there.

Hear, Onnontio! Take care for the future that so great a number of soldiers as appear there do not choke the tree of peace planted in so small a fort. It will be a great loss if, after it had so easily taken root, you should stop its growth, and prevent its covering your country and ours with its branches. I assure you, in the name of the Five Nations, that our warriors shall dance to the calumet of peace under its leaves. They shall remain quiet on their mats, and shall never dig up the hatchet, till their brother Onnontio, or Corlar, shall either jointly or separately endeavour to attack the country, which the Great Spirit has given to our ancestors. This belt preserves my words, and this other the authority which the Five Nations have given me.

Grangula's speech

I.17 *A scene from the Battle of Little Big Horn, or 'Custer's Last Stand', 1876*

By the last decades of the nineteenth century, Indian territory in northern America, the last free band of Plains and Rockies, was being squeezed between east and west. In this predicament the nations of the area settled old differences and regrouped, together with the mass of refugees from the east. Eastern Algonkin like the Lenape joined western and both allied with their ancestral Siouan neighbours from the Ohio and Mississippi. Militarily, the most effective alliance was between the Cheyenne Algonkin and the Sioux, who fought at Little Big Horn. In June 1876, Lt-General Custer, known to the Cheyenne as 'Squaw-Killer', and to the Sioux as 'Long Hair', attacked the Sioux in the Black Hills of Montana and died with all his men. Many native accounts of the victory exist. One of the most complete is by Red Horse, who fought in the battle alongside Sitting Bull and others. His pencil illustrations evoke the style of pictography with developed with the horse-borne way of life on the Plains. The Sioux are identified by hair-style and braves by the long feather tails on their war bonnets, while their horses, with tails braided for battle, show the tactics and movement of the fighting. The U.S. cavalry have hats, jackets and striped trousers; arrows, gunfire and wounds are conventionally rendered, like the bugles and the U.S. flag (inverted). The priority of Plains pictography is movement: this is true of the swirling narratives painted on the tipi and on buffalo-skin robes, and even of the spiral calendars of the Sioux (e.g. *IV.1*).

Red Horse, *The Battle of Little Big Horn*

I.18 *Chief Skowl's ridicule of Russian Orthodox missionaries in the Pacific Northwest, mid-nineteenth century*

A fitting last item in this chapter is provided by the graphic art of the peoples of the Pacific Northwest, where invading Europe met itself. Even before the U.S. existed, Russia made its presence felt in America. Traders (*promishleniki*), soon followed by missionaries and government agents, spread east across Asia and thence to Alaska and down as far as California, there to come face to face with the Spanish. There are many signs of their activities in 'Russian America', one of them being this totem pole from the Haida town of Kasa-an, on Prince of Wales Island. The Haida are Athapascans (like the Navajo and Apache who, however, had long ago migrated south to Pueblo territory), one of several language groups of the

Totem pole, Kasa-an

Pacific Northwest. This culturally homogeneous region comprises Alaska below the southern frontier of the Eskimo, British Columbia, and the state of Washington. A practice exclusive to the region is the carving of totem poles out of the trunks of red cedars. The poles had a variety of functions, as free-standing mortuary posts for chiefs and shamans, for example, or as door-posts in buildings. Most were heraldic in nature: the word 'totem' itself is Algonkin for 'clan' or 'domain'. The poles, which are to be read as columns from top to bottom, also commemorate ritual and historical events. This one, which belonged to Chief Skowl (d. 1882), is a ridicule or 'discredit' pole, and stood at the back of the chief's house; he is represented here by his eagle crest, which surmounts a Russian making a pious gesture. Below are a winged angel and the Russian Orthodox priest, with folded arms, who had made an abortive attempt to convert the chief and his people. The eagle appears again in the pair of symbols at the base of the pole, above one of the traders who worked the same routes as the missionaries.

II Defence of traditional values and forms

THE invasion of the New World by the heirs to the Old has traditionally entailed wholesale loss of goods and territory, 'removal', forced labour and even total extermination. The momentum of these processes has meant that over the centuries, few of its victims have had the opportunity to evaluate their experience philosophically. Yet such evaluations do exist, which provide a context for the records of actual historical events quoted in the previous chapter. In contrasting native with imported values and forms, these texts clearly have enormous interest, since they bring out the priorities of pre-Columbian or 'pre-contact' America. Four such texts are brought together here, authoritative commentaries from four major cultures in the continent: the Toltec and the Maya in Mesoamerica, with the Inca to the south and the Algonkin to the north. Some of the issues they raise are best understood regionally; others have a continental dimension.

When they took over the Aztec empire, the Spaniards aspired also to spiritual conquest. Their efforts to convert the native people began in earnest with the arrival in Tenochtitlan of a group of Franciscans, known as the 'Twelve Apostles', emissaries of the Pope and the Holy Roman Emperor (Charles V). The dialogue held in 1524, between these Christian missionaries and the members of the Aztec priesthood who received and answered them, stands as the first of several exchanges of its kind in America. Points made by the Aztecs were made again and again, by the Tupi in Brazil, for example, before the French and the Portuguese; and by the Algonkin and the Iroquois in northern America, before the Germans (Moravians) and the English. Why should your rituals and your ideas of divine power be better than ours? How can you *know* you represent the true God? These are questions regularly asked of Christian missionaries in all parts of the world. In America they were sharpened by a special understanding of shamanistic ritual, of chronology, and of cosmogony – all subjects which will be discussed in the following chapters. Much of the ritual is alive still, so that the modern religious practices of the Southwest, for example, aid our interpretation of the screenfolds used by the Aztec priests. Chronology and calendars were deemed crucial, not least because, like rituals, they lay at the origin of the skill – literacy – which the Christians made the most of when pressing their evangelical claims. For the heirs to the Toltec, the Maya, the Inca and the Algonkin traditions alike, the argument that God had revealed Himself through Holy Scripture could in itself only provoke rather than resolve a debate.

With their fundamental belief in the Bible, the Christian colonizers of America, right up to this century, have tried to fit the American Indians into a biblical version of world history. That the first inhabitants of the New World were one of the lost tribes of Israel was a hypothesis urged by the earliest missionaries; and today the Mormon Church still spends much money seeking to prove it through archaeological and other research. When asked, the Indians themselves have rarely found this account of their origins satisfactory, preferring their own oral and written traditions. In one of the first examples of Old and New World comparative historiography, the Aztec annalist Chimalpahin pointed out discrepancies between the Christian and the Toltec datings, which undermined the missionaries' claims. With the Maya, the calendrical masters of the continent, the 'correlation problem' was even more severe from the start. Here we find not just disagreement with European datings but a temporal perspective so grand that in it the Europeans appear only as one in a series of invaders of Maya territory. At this point what is usually termed the 'Discovery of America' must be seen to entail the problem of who is entering whose history. Indeed, in terms of biblical dogma which dated the beginning of the world at around 4000 BC, the New World had every reason to consider itself as ancient as its 'Old' World invaders.

In commenting on the Christian invasion the Maya, in the Book of Chumayel, make it clear that their calendar in itself provides a reason for resistance not just as the written memory of the past, but as the means of articulating the present, socially and politically. It serves as the conscious expression of a way of life beside which that practised by the Europeans seems blinkered and self-contradictory.

Appreciating the strong rivalries between the religious and the secular powers within the nations who attacked them, American Indians (notably the Aztecs) tried to profit from them. Yet few succeeded for long in getting the various representatives of the Church to disown their national or worldly masters. Most often, from Las Casas on, the Church has played a charitable role, there can be no doubt. But not to the extent of refusing ultimately to validate the colonizing enterprise and hence (since they were not to be controlled) all the evils of secular exploitation. This is the root of the hypocrisy objected to not just by the Maya but by other American peoples for whom government, demography, and the distribution of food and wealth have been matters of prime importance. Several of these societies have the distinction of having defended their principles against enormous odds, notably in the wave of full-scale military risings which marked the eve of independence movements in America: the Algonkin Pontiac in 1763; the Maya Canek in 1761; and Tupac Amaru II in Peru in 1780–1. (In South America the Independence fighters relied so heavily on Indian support that they were called 'tupamaros' after Tupac Amaru II.) Further, with the Inca and the Algonkin as salient examples, these societies have much affected the growth of secular political philosophies in the West.

II.1 *The Aztec Priests' Speech, 1524*

The Franciscan missionaries known as the Twelve Apostles began their work by urging the Aztec priesthood, or what was left of it, to convert to Christianity. Their efforts provoked this considered reply during the discussion held in 1524. It opens on a note of great humility and courtesy: the welcome offered is very like that offered by Moctezuma to Cortés when they first met. The speaker then rehearses the claims made by the Christians made on their own behalf, which gives them an ironic air. No outright objections are pressed, however, for the Aztecs' concern is professional. They no more want to demolish the Franciscan friars than they themselves want to be demolished. Though they see that their epic encounter is witnessed by 'the trustees of this entire world', they would prefer not to unsettle things 'with what we say amongst ourselves'; later they warn the new arrivals: 'If you want peace, do not force this population to see that we are put aside.' They refer to religion and its rituals as artifacts which have a carefully tended and necessary function within society. Upon this follows a strong and conscious self-defence: the Christians can hardly judge their religion since they know nothing about it. They offer their words as jewels from the treasure caskets used in their rituals. The renewed humility at the end scarcely conceals their sarcasm and, since nothing could be done, a suicidal arrogance. These priests had fought the conquistadors on the steps of the Great Pyramid at Tenochtitlan and had been 'cast in a corner' by Cortés ('our sovereign here'), and now the Franciscans could not or would not hear them as peers.

In presenting their religion, the Aztec priests refer to its rituals and to their own theocratic role in society. Their understanding with the gods makes possible the three kinds of 'gifts' they mention: those appropriate to themselves as theologians and cosmographers, and those due to the two complementary professions of the planter and the hunter-warrior. In each case the source is specified in official toponomy. From the 'place of the eldest darkness' they receive the first gift: the law of ritual itself, the 'whole service'. From Tlalocan, the abode of the thunder-rain god Tlaloc, they pray for agricultural bounty, on behalf of the planter: 'maize and beans', which are among the continent's oldest staple crops. For the hunter-warrior, the priests ensure the success emblemized by the Aztec war-god Huitzilopochtli, whose sanctuary stood next to Tlaloc's on the Great Pyramid at Tenochtitlan. The warrior's 'gifts' – woven clothing, featherwork, food, precious metals and stones – are listed in the sequence found in the records of tribute kept by the Aztec emperors. In this tradition, Tenochtitlan itself is not mentioned, only its glorious antecedents, among them Tula and Teotihuacan.

Like Rome, Tula is invoked as both a spiritual and a worldly centre. As the capital of the Toltecs (and later the Chichimecs) it was the home of the Toltec calendar and writing, and the bastion in whose name the Aztecs claimed preference over fellow Nahua-speakers and over the older-established Otomanguan peoples of Mesoamerica, like the Mixtec at Tilantongo. The Aztecs were especially proud of sharing the Toltecs' language, Nahua, which is used to superb effect in this speech. Tula was also the city of the famous ruler Quetzalcoatl, the 'Feather Snake' or 'Precious Twin', whose heart became the planet Venus and who wore the mask signifying Wind. 'Quetzalcoatl' is in fact the title of the priest who delivers this speech, in which the Omneity or god claimed by the Christians as their own is esoterically referred to here as 'the night, the Wind'. Before Tula came Teotihuacan, the highland metropolis which flourished *c.* AD 600. Its Nahua name means 'the place where gods are made'. In Toltec religion, in the ritual screenfolds, we see gods being consciously shaped to exist in mutual dependence on each other and on man. The 'world-makers' at Teotihuacan also established the symbols of state authority. Among the few early glyphs at Teotihuacan is that for the 'knotting of the mantle', a sign of high rank, found also at Palenque and in the Maya area. In summing up this tradition, the priests refer to the three 'laws' of the Triple Alliance which constituted their empire, with their own 'Toltec-Chichimec' law dominating that of the Colhua to the east at Texcoco and that of the Otomi-speaking Tepanecs to the west at Azcapotzalco or Tlacopan.

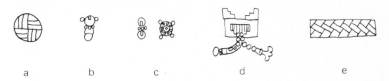

a   b   c   d   e

Fig. 1. Toltec symbols: (a) *tlalpiloni* (knot in mantle); (b) *teocuitlatl* (gold); (c) *chalchiuitl* (jade); (d) *petlacal* (treasure casket, upturned); (e) *petatl* (mat – of power or authority).

Through their response to Christianity, the Aztec priests invoke a complex historical tradition, at once glamorous and imperial, bloody and exquisite, of which the subtlest inner testimony is found in the ritual screenfolds of the Toltec faith. Attenuated yet resilient, this tradition lives on today among Nahua speakers in central and northern Mexico, and among the peoples of the Southwest (Arizona and New Mexico) whose sandpaintings are related to the Toltec screenfolds.

What we say here is for its own reason
beyond response and against our future.

Our revered lords, sirs, dear ones,
take rest from the toil of the road,
you are now in your house and in your nature.
Here we are before you, subjected,
in the mirror of yourselves.
Our sovereign here has let you come,
you have come to rule
as you must in your own place.

Where is it you come from,
how is it that your gods have been scattered
from their municipal centres?
Out of the clouds, out of the mist,
out of ocean's midst you have appeared.
The Omneity takes form in you,
in your eye, in your ear, in your lips.
So, as we stand here,
we see, we address,
the one through whom everything lives,
the night, the Wind,
whose representatives you are.

And we have felt the breath, the word
of our lord the Omneity,
which you have brought with you.
The speaker of the world sent you because of us.
Here we are, amazed by this.
You brought his book with you, his script,
heaven's word, the word of god.

And now what? How is it,
what are we supposed to say,
what shall we present to your ears?

Can it be said we are anything at all?
We are small subjects.

We are just dirt,
no good,
pressed, reduced to want;
furthermore our sovereign here
mistook us consistently
and has cast us into a corner.

But we refute the logo of the Omneity.

We are down to our skulls in this and we fall over
into the river, into the abyss.
Anger and wrath
will be attracted to our behaviour.
Maybe this is our moment; perhaps this is ruin.

In any case, we shall be dispirited.
Where do we go from here
in our subjection,
reduced, mortalized?
Cut us loose,
because the gods have died.
But you don't have to feel any of this.

Our dear lords,
we share some of it all.
Now we open a little
the store, the treasure casket,
for our sovereign here.

You say
that we don't know
the Omneity of heaven and earth.
You say that our gods are not original.
That's news to us
and it drives us crazy.
It's a shock and it's a scandal,
for our ancestors came to earth
and they spoke quite differently.

They gave us
their law
and they believed,
they served, and they taught the honour among gods;
they taught the whole service.
That's why we eat earth before them;
that's why we draw our blood and do penance;
and that's why we burn copal and kill the living.
They were the Lifelord
and they became our only subject.
When and where? – In the eldest Darkness.

They gave us
our supper and our breakfast,
all things to drink and eat,
maize and beans, purslane and sage.
And we beg them
for thunder-Rain and Water

on which the earth thrives.
They are the rich ones
and they have more than simply what it takes;
they are the ones with the stuff,
all ways and all means, forever,
the greenness of growth.
Where and how? – In Tlalocan
hunger is not their experience
nor sickness, and not poverty.

They gave also
the inner manliness, kingly valour
and the acquisitions of the hunt:
the insignia of the lip, the knotting of the mantle,
the loin-cloth, the mantle itself;
Flower and aromatic leaf, jade,
quetzal plumes, and the godshit you call gold.
When and where? – It is a long tradition.
Do you know
when the emplacement of Tula was, of Uapalcalco,
of Xuchatlappan, of Tamoanchan,
of Yoalli ichan, of Teotihuacan?
They were the world-makers who founded
the mat of power, the seat of rule.
They gave
authority and entity,
fame and honour.
And should we now destroy the old law,
the Toltec-Chichimec law,
the Colhua law,
the Tepanec law,
on which the heart of being flows,
from which we animate ourselves,
through which we pass to adulthood,
from which flows our cosmology
and the manner of our prayer?

Oooh! Señores Nuestros,
do nothing;
don't do anything to your population.
It can only bring more ruin,
it can only bring more ruin to the old ones,
our elders, from whom man and woman have grown.

Let us not
anger the gods;
let us not invite their hunger.
Do not unsettle this population.
Why should we agitate them
with what we say amongst ourselves?
If you want peace
don't force the people
to see that we are put aside.

Let's think about this.
At heart, there is no satisfaction for us.
We don't believe, nor do we mock.
We may offend you,
for here stand
the citizens,
the officials,
the chiefs,
the trustees and rulers of this entire world.

It is enough that we have done penance,
that we are ruined,
that we are forbidden and stripped of power.
To remain here is to be imprisoned.
Make of us
the thing that most suits you.
This is all we have to reply,
Señores.

The Aztec Priests' Speech

II.2 *Mankind's ideal course, according to the Maya,* c. *1550*

Like the Aztecs, the Maya viewed the conquistadors as newcomers to an old-established world. Just as Tula and Teotihuacan stood for the Aztecs as proof of a great highland Mexican tradition, so the cities of lowland Peten, rich in hieroglyphic inscriptions dating back to the first centuries AD, reminded the Maya of their Classic past. However, in reacting to the Christian invaders, the Maya tended not to glorify sheer 'emplacement' (to use the Nahua term) in this way. Nor, in opposing the Christians, did they insist, as the

Aztecs did, on differences in ritual. Rather, they mounted a whole moral-philosophical argument, in which their Classic values are meticulously compared with those professed by the new arrivals.

In part a transcription of Maya hieroglyphic texts into the Roman alphabet, this passage sums up the opening section of the Book of Chumayel, which deals with such matters as land ownership and the problem of whether to enter into agreement with the newly arrived foreigners and pay them tribute, or to resist them militarily. As foreign invaders, the Christians are compared with the Itza and the Toltecs who preceded them. Indeed, from the Maya point of view the impression of three invasions is so clear that a joke is made of it (lines 39–40). Since the third lot of invaders, the Spaniards, legally exempted old men, over sixty, from tax and tribute it occurred to the Maya, with their vigesimal arithmetic, that for them each invasion amounted to a score, or twenty Maya years (*tun* or *hab*) of tribute paying, as if next time they would have to be eighty to obtain exemption. According to this text, things began to go wrong not with Europeans like Cortés or Montejo, nor yet with the Itza, but with Nacxit Xuchit. This is the debased Nahua name (4-Foot Flower) of the Toltec leader who invaded Yucatan from Tula long before the Spaniards (an event recorded in Nahua poetry; cf. *IX.4*). Although this figure is revered as the imperial dispenser of insignia and status in the Book of the Cakchiquel and the *Popol vuh* of the Quiche Maya, works from the highlands to the south, to the north, in Yucatan, he is said to have initiated a regrettable change in attitudes and behaviour. In the Book of Chumayel, he and his companions are accused of causing mortal sickness (*cimil*) where previously there was none. The particular diseases he brought may be deduced negatively from the first half of the passage (lines 20–24). They afflict the body politic as a whole, this body being federal, like the cities of the Classic Maya, and not subject to a single capital. Further, the health of Maya society is not just a matter of internal politics, but depends on the sky. The coursing of breath and blood corresponds to astronomical movement. The good days which vanished with the Toltecs' coming were assured by the correct calendrical reading of the reign (*ahaulil*) of good stars. What had been sound and whole was afflicted and eclipsed, 'chibil' serving for both meanings.

Of course, similar connections between the terrestrial and the celestial may be found in ancient cultures other than the Maya. The Maya, however, formulated the relationship of earth to sky in a way peculiar to them, in the Classic period; and the moral history in the

Chumayel is best understood with this in mind. The main link between our alphabetic text and the cosmology of the Classic period is in fact calendrical, and is provided by the hieroglyphic 'Katun-Round' texts discussed in chapter IV. Here the Maya literary tradition itself is made to indicate its own point of origin and inspirational source in the Classic period, in times prior to foreign intrusion, when 'everything was good'. The dates given, in the 360-day year (*hab* or *tun*) of the Maya calendar, take us back to the fourth century BC, the time of the earliest constructions at Tikal and at the 'Olmec' capital, La Venta. At this later site a monument commemorates exactly the three lineages mentioned in the Chumayel text: bird, stone and jaguar (lines 4–6). With their 'great priests and speakers', these founding fathers knew 'the rhythm of the days in themselves' (line 9), in contrast to the foreigners led by Nacxit Xuchit, who introduced a '2-day chair' and a '2-day rule' (references to the leap-year or 'double-day' in the Toltec calendar, which unlike that of the Maya was based on the solar year and was arithmetically inconsistent; see p. 123). Further, the great priests ensured that 'the course of mankind was ciphered clearly' (line 25), the main term, *tzolombil*, being charged with connotation: *tzol* means to set in order, or count or make clear, and describes exactly the arithmetical logic characteristic of the calendar and the hieroglyphic writing of the Maya. In this logic are found the 'rhythm' and the 'wholeness' of the Classic age, when there was harmony between cycles counted in day-units: lunar, menstrual, solar, dynastic, planetary, moral and so on. Ratio is of things in time, measured from moment to moment, from rest (bed, mat, throne) to rest in time. The numerical astronomy of the Maya, and the script which conveyed it, may in turn be held responsible for the

Fig. 2 (*Left*) Stone, Jaguar and Bird emblems on Monument 13, La Venta; (*above*) Jaguar roar, with inset teeth, Teotihuacan.

71

concept *cuxolalob* (line 19), preserved in Maya philosophy from the Classic period to the present day: a sound or living knowledge, a science that is rational yet animate.

In assessing the invasion of their territory in the sixteenth-century, the Maya authors of the Book of Chumayel drew on a literary tradition, calendrical in origin, which antedated Christianity itself. Passages like this one were copied and added to in subsequent centuries, in this and other of the community books of Yucatan, to justify where necessary the policy of military self-defence alluded to in the closing lines, the story of which is not yet over.

> They didn't want to join the foreigners
> Christianity was not their desire
> they didn't want another tax
>
> Those with their sign in the bird
> 5   those with their sign in the stone, flat worked stone
> those with their sign in the jaguar – three emblems –:
> four times four hundred *hab* was the period of their lives
> plus fifteen score *hab* before that period ended
> because they knew the rhythm of the days in themselves.
>
> 10   Whole the moon whole the *hab*
> whole the day whole the night
> whole the breath when it moved too whole the blood too
> when they came to their beds their mats their thrones;
> rhythm in their reading of the good hours
> 15   rhythm in their search for the good days
> as they observed the good stars enter their reign
> as they watched the reign of the good stars begin
> Everything was good.
>
> For they kept sound reason
> 20   there was no sin in the holy faith of their lives
> there was no sickness they had no aching bones
> they had no high fever they had no smallpox
> they had no burning chest they had no bellyache
> they had no chest disease they had no headache
> 25   The course of mankind was ciphered clearly.

Not what the foreigners arranged when they came here
Then shame and terror were preferred
carnal sophistication in the flowers of Nacxit Xuchit and his circle
no more good days were shown to us
30   this was the start of the two-day chair, the two-day rule
this was the start of our sickness also
there were no good days for us, no more sound reason.
At the end of the loss of our vision and of our shame
    everything will be revealed.
There was no great priest no lord speaker no lord priest
35   with the change of rulers when the foreigners came
The priests they set down here were lewd
they left their sons here at Mayapan
These in turn received their affliction from the foreigners called the
    Itza.
The saying is: since foreigners came three times
40   three score *hab* is the age to get us exempted from tax
The trouble was the aggression of those men the Itza
we didn't do it we pay for it today
But there is an agreement at last to make us and the foreigners
    unanimous
Failing that we have no alternative to war

Book of Chumayel, pp. 19–21

II.3 *The good government of the Inca state, 1613*

These pictures have been selected from Guaman's Poma's *New Chronicle and Good Government* to suggest the overall argument of that work. The upper row is of pictures taken from Part 1, which are matched below with pictures from Part 2. For, moving from the early history of the world, its 'ages' and generations, to the political conquests of the Inca and the social administration of the Tahuantinsuyu, the ten main sections of Part 1 provide the premise of Part 2, in which Guaman Poma suggests how Inca principles can and should be adopted under Spanish rule.

The first pair of pictures brings out the importance attached by the Inca, as by the Maya, to the calendar as a means of social organization. Taking advantage of the fact that the Inca and the Christian years both have twelve months, Guaman Poma correlates them, technically modifying the former to fit in with the latter in deference to the Spaniards' rights as conquerors. He also removes months named after the festivals and other pagan activities of the Inca (like the sacrifice of llamas), replacing them with others dedicated to 'harmless' agricultural work. Here, being originally agricultural, the Inca 'Field Planting' month (*chacra yapui quilla*) survives almost unchanged as August, in the Peruvian spring. This month marks the start of the sowing season, a time of gaiety when *chicha* beer (made from fermented maize) is brought out to community work-teams in the fields, where they sing and dance as well as plant. (A work-song or 'haylli' is written out in Quechua in 1b: the women ask the men if there are any flowers and red peppers in their 'garden' and the men reply: 'Yes, here they are, princess, here I've seeded them'). In both pictures the digger nearest to us has a superior tunic and wears shoes; he is a local inspector of agriculture. It is notable that, while he digs along with the rest in 1a, in 1b his foot-plough (*taclla*) remains out of the soil and he concentrates instead on the *quipu* held in his other hand. Guaman Poma seems to suggest that in post-Columbian times there is a need for extra surveillance of the workforce.

Accepting the Spaniards' right as conquerors to impose their calendrical system on the Inca, Guaman Poma shows in his work how the Inca in their turn had imposed their calendar and laws on the territories they had conquered in the previous century, notably the Chimu on the north coast and other heirs to the Tiahuanaco and Chavin cultures of the highlands, which date back to the first millennium BC: a feat ascribed mainly to the emperor Pachacuti.

The next pairs of pictures (2 and 3) are both concerned with that basic means of administration without which an empire as large as the Tahuantinsuyu could not have functioned as it did. This is the *quipu*, a system of knotted cords still used today on a reduced scale among the Quechua (and among their neighbours to the north). Like the hieroglyphic system of the Maya, the *quipu* appears to have been calendrical in origin (*quipu* is related to *quilla*, month), and also used place-value notation: see the counting board in 3a and the explanation of its meaning in Table 4. *Quipu* cords, of four main colours and variously twisted, expressed main items or 'nouns'. In Inca times the categorization implicit in the system lay not just within a single *quipu* but in the range of *quipus* used for different subjects or topics, the date of their compilation and their place of origin. (Under the Inca the *quipu* appears to have been developed to incorporate the ideographs – *timehri* – used independently of it by peoples to the north.) *Quipu* literacy was a subject taught to the sons of the nobility in a four-year course at the 'Yacha huasi' or

Instruction House at Cuzco. Because of the complexity and extremely abstract nature of the total system, the few surviving Inca *quipus* can no longer be read. But the *quipu* can safely be assumed to be at the root of the categorization in Guaman Poma's work, and he himself said that it was largely a transcription of that legacy. The male and female population, each ranged in 'rows' by age and employment; the months of the year, subdivided into weeks of fifteen days (see p. 44 above), the seasonal duties and festivals attaching to them and how these are financed; the stocking of the communal food stores; even Inca history and ritual and the policing of the state: all are recounted and structured by Guaman Poma according to *quipu* norms.

In the Tahuantinsuyu, regional and local administrators communicated at regular intervals with the capital by means of runners, *chasqui* (2a), who travelled the excellent roads and bridges of the empire. In Cuzco, this information was collated and assessed by the Sapa Inca's adviser-secretary, who took part in decisions of policy; executive power lay with the treasurer of the whole Tahuantinsuyu, shown in 3a with his counting board. With unquestioning faith in the continuing rightness of this form of administration, and pointing up the equivalence of *quipu* and alphabetic literacy, Guaman Poma then shows how it should be adopted in his day (lower pictures). The *chasqui* runner is seen carrying a letter rather than a *quipu* and blows a horn rather than a conch (2b); and the *quipu* treasurer is replaced by a clerk scribe (3b) 'appointed by his Majesty'.

The connection between the last pair of pictures (4a and b) is less direct. In 4a we see a *zancay*, one of the underground prisons used in Inca times. The criminal struggles to survive among dangerous and noxious beasts, cruelly reminded of the need for social control. That the Spanish conquest entailed the loss of just this social control is made clear in the lower picture, for here we see a poor Indian ('pobre de los indios') beset by beasts who are his new masters. Pleading in Quechua, 'May they not strip me bare, for the love of God', he is attacked by the three main arms of Spanish power in America and their agents: the corregidor-serpent and the pressgang-tiger, both secular servants of the Crown (top); the *encomendero*-lion or puma and the doctrinal priest-fox (middle); and the minor figures, often of native origin, who aid them in their work, the cacique-mouse and the scribe-cat (bottom). These are the 'six animals who eat and feed on the poor Indians of this realm'. In so clearly identifying all the main forces of Spanish colonial rule and

Guaman Poma, *Nueva corónica*, pp. 250, 350, 360, 302 (top); 1153, 811, 814, 694 (below)

CÕTADOR MAIOR I TEZORERO
TAVANTINSVIOQVIPOC
CVRACA·COÑ⸱DOR·CHAVA

con taβas y quipos   contador

CASTIGO INSTICIA
SANCALI NOVICIO

yaya pachacamac
ñanpazacyaya
caysonchuay
payunyas
cansui

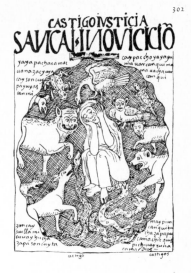

caypachoyayapi
maxiarcanquima
maxaxhuaman
canqui

zancau
suella mi
cunay hi ñay
zapa sonchuy ta

maypim
canquichi
chazapasa
xma chie quie
pushuayxuña
camarxios

castigo   castigos

ESCRIVANODECABIL DO
NOMBRADO·DESV·M⸱

quilcaycamayoc

en el Reyno   escriuano

POBRE DELOSIÑS
DESEISANIMALESÕCO
mente men. los pobres selos yñs enesii reyno
amallapallay que tigreespanoles selvabo
collatanauayiño poramos de
pora mor de dios raysio
dios rayio

caxesar
xerpe

leon
comanzeo

zorra
xabito to teyna

gato
ezcriuano

rralon
cacíq̃ prunipal

es los 9 años animales q̃
no temen dios de quellos
a los pobres selos yñs
enes fii reyno y nauay
reme dio

pobre de jesu cristo   quelos

the rivalries between them, Guaman Poma's manuscript resembles the Yucatec Chilam Balam books, as it does in pointing up the gulf between the theory and the practice of the invaders and their essentially destructive influence. The manuscript has become a reference point for politicians concerned with Indian affairs in the Andean republics.

Fig. 3. Cotton page design, Ancon (after Wiener).

The pictures in Guaman Poma's work are integral to it. Though Europeanized, they continue a pre-Columbian tradition of illustration: they rely heavily on set types and scenes and are always attributed to a calendar time, a place or a social function. Messages encoded in *quipu* knots or incised beans were amplified in this way. Examples of such illustrations are found in the framed pages of biography in tombs on the Peruvian coast, and on the pottery and textiles of the Chimu.

II.4 *The shaping of the alliance led by the Algonkin Pontiac, 1763*

The rising organized by the Ottawa leader Pontiac against the British in 1763 is usually referred to as his 'conspiracy'. Centred on the Ohio heartland, it was in fact a movement to defend and recover territories west of the Appalachians threatened by the British after their defeat of the French in the Seven Years' War. It coincided with major risings elsewhere in the continent at this 'pre-Independence' period. At the same time it falls within the tradition of specifically Algonkin resistance, which began in the early seventeenth century with the battles of Powhatan in Virginia and Metacom (King Philip) in New England, and which was continued by Tecumtha in 1812, whose continental vision and policies followed Pontiac's, and by Black Hawk at Saukenuk in 1832. Commemorated by a wampum belt six feet long, Pontiac's alliance was truly international. Following strategies described in the Walam Olum, Pontiac banded together the Ottawa (his own nation), the Ojibwa and the Pottawatami, and was soon reinforced by the Lenape and the Shawnee. He also drew in Iroquoian sympathizers like the Huron and the Erie, even managing to win over the Seneca who, as members of the Iroquois League and guardians of its 'western door' to the Ohio, had hitherto remained aloof from such alliances.

At a crucial moment early in his campaign (27 April 1763), Pontiac won over the core of his alliance by means of a speech, in which he recounted the experiences of Wolf, the name by which the Lenape were known to their neighbours. As a hunter, Wolf is also the first to feel the effects of encroachment on land used in fact for agriculture as well as hunting by the nations addressed by Pontiac. The Wolf of Pontiac's speech devotes himself to finding the way to meet the Master of Life, the source of truth and moral values. True, Pontiac makes this figure recognizable as the Christian God, not wanting to preclude the support of the French or to contradict unnecessarily the teaching of the Jesuits among the Huron or of the Moravians among the Lenape (the Moravians were the first to print the Bible in America, in German, in 1743). Also, Wolf undergoes a form of baptism before entering heaven's 'gate'. But these details do not affect the principle of the story, which has a very different source in American shamanism. The Master of Life, in the speech quoted here, discreetly plays down the practices of the 'jugglers', or *jessakid*, a lower order of the Mide. But, as a whole, Wolf's experience thoroughly reflects that of the Mide shaman Pontiac himself.

Throughout the shamanistic literature of America, journeys like Wolf's give form to accounts of the rising into true life, in the texts of the Sioux, the Nahua and the Maya alike. Moreover, Wolf's journey takes eight days, eight being a ceremonial number taken from the period during which the planet Venus disappears at inferior conjunction, as it 'journeys' from west to east. And when he arrives in the east, Wolf is met by the moon, in the form of a woman of 'dazzling beauty in snow-white garments'; her role is to show him how to 'measure his footsteps' so as to climb to the home of the Master of life. This is 'heaven's heart', at noon or midway (*nauwequa* in Algonkin) along the sun's path. For his part, before instructing Wolf, the Master of Life describes himself as the Manito or Great Spirit in terms found in Mide texts and in the cosmological part of the Walam Olum (cf. *V.11*). In short, through his journey Pontiac's Wolf is able to distinguish between 'all you have seen on earth and all you see now' with the heightened understanding of the shaman's trance, whose truth was implicitly believed by Pontiac's audience.

Through the Master of Life's words, Wolf and hence the Indians are alerted not so much to the cruelty and depredation of the whites as to their own weakness and dependence on ways and materials imported from Europe. *This* is the reason why hunting has become difficult: a moral weakness which it is in Wolf's power to make good. Only by consciously valuing their previous way of life and economy will the Indians live 'wholly' and find the strength to resist and to reclaim the land intended for and settled by them. This was exactly the lesson taught later (1808) by the Shawnee Prophet, Tecumtha's brother, and later still by the visionaries of the Ghost Dance, who promised to bring back the buffalo. The Master of Life also gives Wolf a prayer which summarizes the speech, forbidding adultery, alcoholic drink, internecine fighting and affirming common ownership of land and goods. The prohibitions (which echo those of the Maya and Inca) were meant particularly to counteract the effects of liquor and even of drugs like laudanum brought in by traders. The imperative of the prayer, as of the speech, is: drive out the 'dogs in red uniform' who 'have come to trouble your country', that is, the English. (Unless they resisted, the French – the 'children of your Great Father', Louis XV – were to be left alone for the moment.) Pontiac went on to record that the prayer was given to Wolf in writing, to be taken back to his people, to the elders of the Lenape who were known to be adept and authoritative in such matters. (Written prayers were to play a similar role in the Shawnee Prophet's movement.) The Walam Olum itself sets up the same sort of opposition as Pontiac's text does, between Manito, the creator of sky and earth, and the 'evil spirit' in life. Pontiac concluded by saying that news of Wolf's experience had spread, eventually reaching him, thus vouchsafing his message at least within the Algonkin tradition. It is significant that when the Lenape went to the Great Lakes to join their 'Ottawa children' they assessed Pontiac's claims and performance, in council with the Ojibwa. At first they were sceptical and criticized him for too much reliance on the French; but then they agreed to support him and further his cause.

Still a strategist and a Mide shaman, Pontiac was killed in 1769, possibly by a British agent, in Cahokia (now part of St Louis, Mo.), one of the great towns of the Mound Builders. Among those who supported his cause some, like the Seneca and the Ojibwa, held on to part of their territory in New York State and Canada and have kept their traditions; others, like the Lenape, crossed the

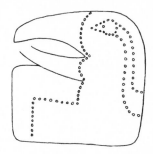

Fig. 4. Eagle (punched copper token), Ohio, *c.* AD 200(?).

Mississippi, going on back to Mexico. The native evacuation of the Ohio, a civilized centre since before AD 100, effectively ended when the Shawnee left their capital Wapokenota in 1825.

I am the Master of life, and I know you want to meet and talk to me. Listen well to what I am going to say to you and all the Indians.

I am he who made sky and earth, trees and lakes, rivers and all men, all you see now and all you have seen on earth.

Because I have made all this and because I love you, you must do what I say and like and not do what I hate.

I do not like you to drink until you lose your reason, as you do, or to fight each other. I do not like you to take two wives or to run after the wives of others. You behave badly; I hate that. You must have but one wife, and keep her until death.

When you want to go to war, you juggle, you sing the medicine dance believing that you speak to me. You are mistaken that it is

Manito that you speak to. It is a bad spirit who whispers nothing but evil to you and whom you listen to lacking knowledge of me.

This land, where you live, I have made for you and not for others. How do you happen to suffer the whites on your lands? Can't you do without them? I know that those you call the children of your Great Father supply your wants, but if you were not bad, as you are, you would well do without them. You might live wholly, as you did before you knew them. Before those whom you call your brothers came on your lands, did you not live by bow and arrow? You had no need of gun nor powder, nor the rest of their things, and nevertheless you caught animals for food and clothing. When I saw that you went to the bad, I called back the animals into the depths of the woods, so that you had need of your brothers to have your wants supplied and cover you. You have only to become good and do what I want, and I shall send back the animals to you to live on. I do not forbid you, for all that, to suffer amongst you the children of your Father. I love them, they know me and pray to me, and I give them their necessities and all that they bring to you. But as regards those who have come to trouble your country, drive them out, make war on them! I love them not, they know me not, they are my enemies and the enemies of your brothers! Send them back to the country which I made for them! There let them remain.

Pontiac's speech

III Ritual

As the 'prescribed order' for performing religious and other devotional service, ritual articulates chance with logic, the desired with the actual, and in so doing specifies where, with whom and what, when, and even why this or that ceremony is performed. This explicit formal quality of ritual makes it important as a factor not just within a given culture but in its image-making. Beginning at the northern edge of the New World, and going back in time from the present to the classic periods of the Toltec and the Maya, this chapter attempts to show how rituals practised by native Americans have produced shapes, signs and figures used conventionally by them, in some cases over large geographical areas. The birchbark scrolls of the Midewiwin, the painted buffalo skins of the Plains, the sandpaintings of the Southwest, and the parchment and paper screenfolds of the Toltecs prove to have much in common iconographically, and they contain elements which may be further related to those incorporated arithmetically into the hieroglyphic writing of the Maya. Over half the texts quoted here belong to the corpus of ritual screenfolds once owned by the priests of the Toltec faith, and which includes the Borbonicus from Tenochtitlan; the Borgia from the Tlaxcala-Cholula region; the Laud and the Fejérváry, which closely resemble each other; and two major Mixtec works, the Vienna and the Nuttall, which deal with calendrical as well as ritual matters. Coming from the bibliographical heart of pre-Columbian America, in far greater numbers than the three extant screenfolds of the Maya, these works serve as an invaluable term of reference and are one of the continent's greatest treasures.

Frame
First of all, ritual defines the area of its activity, putting an edge between itself and the surrounding world. This 'definition' of ritual

is evident archeologically at the cities named by the Aztec priests, the avenues, stepped platforms and pyramid tops at Teotihuacan, for example, being as much stages for ritual in this respect as was equivalent architecture among the Mound Builders, or in the pre-Inca cities of northern Peru. Within such frames, on a greater or a lesser scale, the random and the circumstantial are given order and significance, in the forms of ceremonial objects and structures, and of actors with given positions, gestures and dress. To worship or exorcise, to encourage or negate, these participants behave like dancers on a stage or teams in a game whose rules and boundaries are conventionally recognized. In alliance or opposition they make patterns within the frame, the logic of which is perceived in plan as linear, binary or concentric.

On occasions when darkness is needed the ritual area may be more closely defined as a sanctuary, a sacred lodge or house to which light and people have restricted access (the Maya sign 'darkness' and the Toltec sign 'House' are equivalent in the Twenty Signs – see Table 2 below). In such cases the edge between the inner ritual space and its surroundings may be isomorphic or identical with the body. The Borgia screenfold shows sanctuary entrances as mouths with tooth-steps and exits as vaginal or anal. Similarly, the single entrance-exit *kiva* and *hogan* sanctuaries of the Southwest are typified in the cradling body frames of Navajo sandpaintings, with the head to the left of the eastern door and the foot stretched round anticlockwise to the right.

This capacity of ritual to define its area of meaning acquires paramount importance through its effect on the graphic conventions according to which it is represented or described. The 'house' symbols of Midewiwin scrolls, the sandpaintings of the Southwest and the squarish pages of Toltec screenfolds all derive conceptually from the actual arrangements and physical context of ritual. (The Maya screenfolds, to which this kind of ritual 'plan' is alien in principle, correspondingly have a different format, being taller and narrower.) As representations of ritual, these Mide, Southwestern and Toltec designs presuppose the same choreographic conventions in their internal reading order – anticlockwise – and in their orientation, with east at the right or the top. Moreover, the four- or eight-symbol stanzas of Mide script correspond to the intercommunicating lodges constructed for initiation and other ceremonies, and to the days which these last; similarly, the single-entrance sandpaintings of the Navajo are made on successive nights in the *hogan* as stages in the 'Ways' or paths of their ritual.

The Mesoamerican sets of Figures, Numbers and Signs

While for the Midewiwin and in the Southwest, the ritual area itself alone or in sequence provides a principle of co-ordination, in Mesoamerica the situation is more complex. In the Toltec ritual screenfolds, reading order depends also on sets of 'characters' (some of them not unlike those from which the Roman alphabet derives). The chief of these sets, the Nine Figures, the Thirteen Numbers and the Twenty Signs, are listed in Table 2; throughout, they are referred to respectively by cardinal numbers (1st–9th), ordinal numbers (1–13), and Roman numerals (I–XX). Of the utmost significance in ritual and all other aspects of pre-Columbian life, these sets may be traced back at least to the first millennium BC; they are among the defining characteristics of the Mesoamerican cultural area, though as hieratic knowledge they now survive only in diminished form. Several of the elements in these three sets are readily recognizable to north and south, especially in masks and artifacts used for ritual purposes, and in the designs based on such objects, like the bird and fauna petroglyphs of northern South America, for example. And we find numerous parallels with the *kachina* and other dolls of Southwestern ceremonial. Yet only in Mesoamerica did these Figures, Numbers and Signs become finite sets of words and designs in their own right, with a firm internal sequence, which could be systematically correlated with each other.

The Nine Figures are most sharply defined in the set used in Toltec ritual, with which the Maya (and the Zapotec) versions may be compared. The nine embody origins, places of birth and re-birth, or primary parental forces, like the set of nine 'mothers' found in Chibcha cosmogony. This is clearly true of the two women in the set, Lust-Goddess (7th) and her companion Jade Skirt (6th) who, like the Navajo Changing Woman, belong to the west. Obsidian (or Flint; 2nd) is the material from which the hero Quetzalcoatl was born, terrestrially, while in the Maya tradition at least Maize (4th) is the substance of the American Adam. For his part, Dead Land Lord (5th) guards the 'bones' from which men are created, according to Toltec teaching. The house of Tlaloc (9th) at the zenith is the place from which reborn and transformed beings descend as by an umbilical rope. The caves inside the wild Hill Heart (8th) recall the seven-chambered womb, 'Seven-headed earth snake' in Zapotec, from which several tribes claimed to originate, not just in Mesoamerica but among the Navajo and among the ancestors of the Chibcha-speaking Paez in Colombia.

Royal Lord (or Sun; 3rd) is often invoked as a royal ancestor. First place is reserved for the Fire- or Year-Lord, fire kindling being the means of inaugurating calendrical eras, and of clearing the ground at the start of the agricultural cycle; among the Zuni, it is the Fire god who literally leads the dance of the Council of Gods.

As a set of nine, the figures will recall the Ennead of the ancient Egyptians, worshipped at Heliopolis, or the nine muses of genesis and divination discussed by Hesiod. Yet their identity is strongly American, not just as individual phenomena (e.g. Maize) but as a set which hinges on its central 5th member, turning in ritual from the virtual to the actual, the emetic to the affirmative, like the nine Mothers of Chibcha creation and the nine nights of the Navajo Ways. This internal logic and its relationship to the Venus-cycle is discussed under 'Timing' below.

The Thirteen Numbers are much harder to perceive as 'characters' than the Nine Figures. Indeed, they are often represented just in arithmetic by bars (five) and dots (one), or simply dots, apparently devoid of individual significance within the set as a whole. Yet the thirteen constituent numbers are shown to have properties of their own, as lucky and unlucky, and certainly as odd or even. In Maya hieroglyphs they appear as thirteen heads, each with a distinctive eye, nose, cheek or head-dress, this last evoking the numbered runners depicted on pre-Inca pottery (cf. *IX.9*). The Toltec equivalent to these heads is a set of Birds (or 'Fliers'). There appears to be little correspondence between the two sets, though the protuberant nose of the head for 13 recalls the beak of the Parrot (13); and the dots and beard of 9 recall Turkey (9) – the seeds given for comfort from under that bird's wing and its beard from which the Navajo pluck a hair to safeguard the properties of their Nine-Night Ways. The Toltec Birds offer a clue to the origin of the set, for they are very like the birds recognized by the Chibcha in their calendar of lunar months, models of which survive in gold. At the Huan festival of the Chibcha, when adjustment was made to the solar year, twelve red dancers would be joined by a thirteenth, in blue, all of them bearing distinctive bird emblems on their heads. The twelve and thirteen lunar months of northern American calendars are also often identified by birds, Hawk and Eagle commonly occupying third place, for example, as in Mesoamerica. This likely lunar origin would certainly explain the significance of the transition from 12 to 13 within the set, as it is brought out in both Toltec and Maya texts (e.g. *III.12* and *V.14*). Once established, the set was very widely employed, notably for example to number the stages in the growth of the maize plant, for which special words exist in Nahua, Maya, Chibcha, Quechua and other American languages.

As for the Twenty Signs, they match the total of man's digits and fit in with the vigesimal arithmetic which is typical of Mesoamerica and which left its mark on the ritual number signs (1–10, 20) of the Chibcha, exemplified in the Sopó Calendar Stone (fig. 5). There is evidence that this set was specially constructed with arithmetic in mind, with borrowings from the Nine Figures (Tlaloc's mask, Rain XIX) and the Thirteen Numbers (Eagle XV). Nevertheless, as the

Fig. 5. Chibcha number signs on the Calendar Stone from Sopó (north of Bogotá): Mica, 3; and Gueta, 20.

'patrimonium commune' of Mesoamerica, it is of great antiquity, and may be associated with the sun in the way that the Thirteen Numbers and Nine Figures are with the moon and Venus; the period of twenty days or 'suns' is recognized in ritual from the Pacific Northwest (Nootka) to the south Caribbean. The five pairs of signs in the first decimal half of the set tell a cosmogonical story which is echoed through America (see chapters V and VI); the signs in the second half, which serves as a counterpoint, include phenomena exclusive to the tropics (Ape XI and Jaguar XIV) and vary more in detail between the areas and languages of Meso-america.

In the Toltec screenfolds, all three sets of Figures, Numbers and Signs have wide-ranging uses in co-ordinating and patterning ritual. They are used to mark out positions in choreography involving actor-deities, where they should stand or walk to; and to create icons of major deities. They are also used in divination and soothsaying, as 'stoicheia', like the suits and numbers of playing cards and the figures of the tarot pack. And they are found similarly 'dealt' into the four- and fivefold patterns proper to the cosmic 'maps' of shamanism. In all this, these three ritual sets of Mesoamerica exist as a resource which is systematic and rich in permutation.

Timing

By far the most frequent use of the ritual sets of Mesoamerica, in both the Toltec and the Maya screenfolds, is for counting of time-units during and between ceremonies. For this purpose, nights are numbered by the Nine Figures, and days by a combination of the Thirteen Numbers with the Twenty Signs (260 units in all). It is probable that the Nine Figures, known as *yohualtecutin* or 'Night Lords' in Nahua, were time-units in this sense by their very origin, for they commemorate the all-important period of Venus's passage from the western horizon as evening star to the eastern horizon as morning star. In American astronomy this was deemed to be nine nights with eight days between (Venus's cycle as a whole is exemplary for the shaman's trance journey and for the soul after death – see below p. 258). This time count also underlies the full ceremonial periods of cultures to either side of Mesoamerica: the Ikala or Ways of the Chibcha-speaking Cuna in Panama (see p. 254), and to the north, the Navajo Ways and the Midewiwin initiation rituals of nine nights and eight days respectively. Further, as the 5th of the Nine Figures, the Dead Land Lord marks the half-way point between west and east, which is also recognized as such by the Cuna, and is commemorated in the 'half' ceremonial period of five nights and four days found in the Southwest and in Midewiwin ritual. As a means of counting nights, the Nine Figures were incorporated into the calendars proper of the Toltec and the Maya, though in slightly different ways.

As a means of counting days, the 260-unit combination of the Thirteen Numbers and the Twenty Signs known as the 'Sacred Round' was also incorporated into the Toltec and Maya calendars, though once again in different ways. For ritual purposes, the Numbers and Signs served in the same way to identify days and the correct intervals between them, 1 Snake (V) for example coming twenty-seven days after 13 Flint (XVIII). Several of the surviving screenfolds, Toltec and Maya, contain tables for the correct timing of umbilicus-cutting and burial of the dead, hunting and maize-planting, victory celebrations, curing, and 'everyday' tasks like weaving, net-making, and tending bees.

Predominant in Mesoamerica, this development of ritual iconography into a timing system was discouraged in principle, from the very start, in a graphic form like Southwestern sandpaintings. In the context of the Navajo *hogan*, sandpaintings are part of a total experience, with claims not just on the eyes but on other senses like smell (through incense, for example) and touch. An ingredient like pollen, which lends colour and shape to the design, may be taken from it and applied to the body, therapeutically. This immanent quality of sandpaintings is jealously guarded: once their 'moment' in the ceremony has passed, they are destroyed. By contrast, the priesthoods of Mesoamerica fixed their ritual texts on paper and parchment, drawing up tables from which the right days and intervals of days could be read off as required.

In certain of the Toltec screenfolds, this concern with timing is taken a step further. Ritual dates and intervals are expressly stated as dates in the year calendar of the Toltecs (which is discussed in the next chapter). As a guide to the Fire-Drilling ritual, for example, the Vienna screenfold relates the orthodox practice of the present to the past, drawing out the significance of the Signs and Numbers which identify major dates in tribal history and by which historical characters are named. In such cases the screenfold takes on another format: a reading 'stream' in boustrophedon (Table 6), unconfined to synchronic single-page designs or to tabular arrangements of the Sacred Round. Like the technically simpler ritual narratives of the Midewiwin to the north, based on fourfold stanzas of 'day' symbols, these priestly epics of Mesoamerica are exegetical and explain the why of this or that practice through recorded precedent.

In the hieroglyphic texts of the Maya, the incorporation of ritual matter into calendrical form was taken to its limit. With the Maya, all writing, for ritual or any other purpose, was regularized and encoded according to the arithmetical norms, found in pure and abstract form in the Inca *quipu*, which shaped the day calendar of the Classic period. Many of the elements in Maya hieroglyphic writing come from the Mesoamerican sets of ritual Figures, Numbers and Signs, and from images of ceremonial and other objects recognized by the Toltecs and to some extent further north. Yet within the Maya system they were all made uniform, interchangeable and adaptable to the spoken language. Unlike that of the Toltec screenfolds, the format of Maya requires neither page 'frames' nor boustrophedon sequence. Sufficient to itself, writing is clearly separable from picture or illustration, the scribe and the artist each finding a freedom of his own. This is true both of the carved inscriptions of the Classic Era and of the three post-Classic paper screenfolds. Yet what Maya hieroglyphic writing gains in conciseness and phonetic precision it loses in flexibility of focus and scale, in spatial logic and the syntax of componental forms. These qualities are highly developed in Toltec script, along with the

Table 2. RITUAL SETS AND THE SACRED ROUND
OF MESOAMERICA

(a) **The Nine Figures**
(Nahua: Yohual-tecutin = Night Lords; Maya: Bolon ti ku, or Dzacab = Nine gods or ancestries)

	1st	2nd	3rd	4th
Toltec sign*				
Nahua name	Xiuh-tecutli Fire- or Year-Lord	Itztli or Tecpatl Obsidian or Flint	Piltzin-tecutli Royal Lord (the sun)	Cin-teotl Maize-God
Maya glyph**				
Yucatec name			Kin Sun	Maize

This correlation of the Toltec and Maya sets (which revises that of Kelley 1976: 90–1) relies on the common identity of the 3rd (never disputed), 4th and 6th figures (seen, then neglected by Thompson), and on the reading of the Maya *xaman* (9th) as zenith (i.e. Tlalocan) and not north. In the Zapotec set, which has been firmly correlated with the Toltec, the 8th figure is Mbaz, a 'Seven-headed earth-snake', to which the glyph here corresponds; cf. also the Nahua Chicomoztoc, the Seven Caves of the mountain as the tribal womb of the Chichimec (below, p. 196).

(b) **The Thirteen Numbers**
(Nahua: Quecholtin = Fliers; Maya: Oxlahun ti ku = Thirteen gods)

Number	1	2	3	4	5	6
Toltec sign*						
Nahua name (13 is tentative)	Huitzilin Humming-bird (white or blue)	Huitzilin Humming-bird (green)	Huactli Hawk	Zozoltin Quail	Cuauhtli Eagle	Chicuatli Screech owl
Maya 'head' glyph**						
Yucatec name	*hun*	*ca*	*ox*	*can*	*ho*	*uac*

* after Borbonicus screenfold; ** after Thompson

5th	6th	7th	8th	9th
Mictlan-tecutli Dead Land Lord	Chalchiuh-tlicue Jade Skirt	Tlazo-teotl Lust-Goddess	Tepe-yollotli Hill Heart	Tlaloc Thunder-rain
	Mol Jade	(Moon)	(Seven Caves)	Xaman Zenith

*after Borbonicus screenfold; **after Thompson

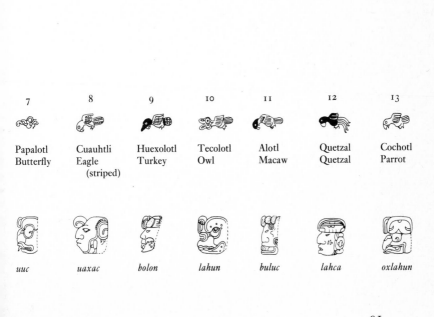

7	8	9	10	11	12	13
Papalotl Butterfly	Cuauhtli Eagle (striped)	Huexolotl Turkey	Tecolotl Owl	Alotl Macaw	Quetzal Quetzal	Cochotl Parrot
uuc	*uaxac*	*bolon*	*lahun*	*buluc*	*lahca*	*oxlahun*

Table 2. (*continued*)

(c) **The Twenty Signs**

	I	II	III	IV	V	VI
Toltec sign*						
Nahua name	Cipactli Earth-beast or Ground	Eecatl Wind	Calli House	Cuetzpalin Lizard	Coatl Snake	Miquitzl Death
Maya glyph**						
Yucatec name	Imix (reptile)	Ik Wind	Akbal Night or Darkness	Kan Maize	Chicchan Snake	Cimi Death

	XI	XII	XIII	XIV	XV	XVI
Toltec sign						
Nahua name	Ozomatli Ape	Malinali Grass (Teeth)	Acatl Reed	Ocelotl Jaguar	Cuauhtli Eagle	Cozca-cuauhtli Vulture
Maya glyph						
Yucatec name	Chuen Ape	Eb Teeth or Stairway	Ben Reed	Ix Jaguar	Men	Cib Beeswax

(d) **The Sacred Round** – 260 (13 × 20) units of combination
(Nahua: Tonalpohualli)

Note the 'doubling up' of the 8th and 9th of the Nine Figures at the end of the Sacred Round; this occurs only in the Toltec system. In the Maya system the Nine Figures are not normally so incorporated into the Sacred Round, and calendrically they provide a separate night count correlated rather with the 360-day *tun* – see Table 3.

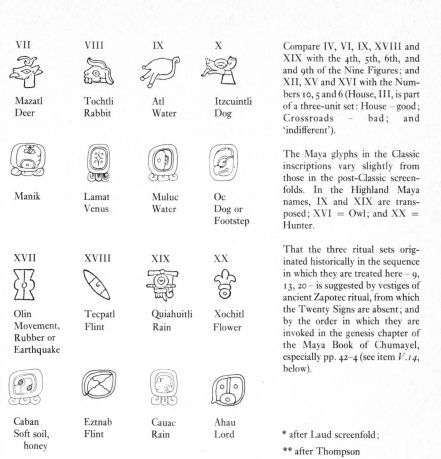

VII	VIII	IX	X
Mazatl Deer	Tochtli Rabbit	Atl Water	Itzcuintli Dog
Manik	Lamat Venus	Muluc Water	Oc Dog or Footstep

XVII	XVIII	XIX	XX
Olin Movement, Rubber or Earthquake	Tecpatl Flint	Quiahuitli Rain	Xochitl Flower
Caban Soft soil, honey	Eztnab Flint	Cauac Rain	Ahau Lord

Compare IV, VI, IX, XVIII and XIX with the 4th, 5th, 6th, 2nd and 9th of the Nine Figures; and XII, XV and XVI with the Numbers 10, 5 and 6 (House, III, is part of a three-unit set: House – good; Crossroads – bad; and 'indifferent').

The Maya glyphs in the Classic inscriptions vary slightly from those in the post-Classic screenfolds. In the Highland Maya names, IX and XIX are transposed; XVI = Owl; and XX = Hunter.

That the three ritual sets originated historically in the sequence in which they are treated here – 9, 13, 20 – is suggested by vestiges of ancient Zapotec ritual, from which the Twenty Signs are absent; and by the order in which they are invoked in the genesis chapter of the Maya Book of Chumayel, especially pp. 42–4 (see item *V.14*, below).

* after Laud screenfold;

** after Thompson

1 I	2 II	3 III	4 IV	5 V	6 VI	7 VII	8 VIII	9 IX	10 X	11 XI	12 XII	13 XIII
1st	2nd	3rd	4th	5th	6th	7th	8th	9th	1st	2nd	3rd	4th

1 XIV	2 XV	3 XVI	4 XVII	5 XVIII	6 XIX	7 XX	8 I	9 II	10 III	11 IV	12 V	13 VI
5th	6th	7th	8th	9th	1st	2nd	3rd	4th	5th	6th	7th	8th

. . .*[lines 3–19]* . . .

1 VIII	2 IX	3 X	4 XI	5 XII	6 XIII	7 XIV	8 XV	9 XVI	10 XVII	11 XVIII	12 XIX	13 XX
5th	6th	7th	8th	9th	1st	2nd	3rd	4th	5th	6th	7th	8–9th

ingenious deployment of colour and line; feathery Water, Snake-like plough, star-eyes, mist of down, and the heart as fish or Flower.

The ceremonies to which the following texts are devoted cannot all be fully understood. Their meaning has sometimes been eroded by time and by the effects of invasion from beyond the New World, especially in the case of the socially and architecturally elaborate rituals of Mesoamerica and Peru. Even so, a lot can be learnt from them. They show unequivocally the power of ritual in a variety of societies, small and economically complex, theocratic and secular. Moreover they allow us to deduce how ritual is connected with the graphic and literary image, with representation and writing.

III.1 *The seance of an Eskimo shaman in Alaska*

The Eskimos are not Indians; but they exist as a link between them and Asia, the probable home of shamanism. Their clear, pictographic carvings, one of which is copied here, well illustrate some basic shamanistic practices. In this text, three drummers sit opposite the single door of the subterranean house, while the rest of the congregation lines the other walls. In the centre is the fire and a 'T'-shaped pole supporting two lamps, ceremonies normally being

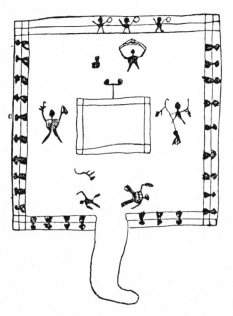

held at night. The shaman himself is shown at three separate moments during the ritual. First (top), in front of the drummers, chanting before the crouching patient; then, to the right of the fire, driving the 'bad spirit' out of the patient's head; and last, to the left of the fire, fetish in hand, sending the bad spirit towards the door where his two assistants wait to knock it out of the house. The ritual is shown to demand the participation of more actors than just the shaman and his patient; there is a definite location and choreography for the repertoire of acts and chants appropriate to the exorcism.

III.2 *The path followed by the candidate of the Midewiwin society*

In agreeing on the standard performance of particular ceremonies in their Midewiwin society, shaman-priests of the Algonkin (and the Sioux) built up an elaborate system of initiation, in all probability prior to European arrival. Over much of their lifetime, fee-paying candidates, male and female, progress along a carefully defined path of knowledge, through a series of houses or degrees. This knowledge is transmitted as orthodox, but the meaning and conduct of ritual are also discussed exegetically by master priests. For these purposes, Mide shamans have a repertoire of literary documents, which was extensive at least up to the end of the last century. Birchbark scrolls like the one depicted here show the plan of major initiation rituals. Within the house, two lines of shaman priests face each other, four to four, their characteristic round heads, faces and arm positions being found also in sandpaintings. Above are the sun and another celestial disc (Venus?); below, two underworld monsters. These scrolls reveal how ritual provided the principles of Midewiwin writing exemplified in the Walam Olum. First, a symbol in that text occupies a space equivalent to a 'house' of initiation. Some symbols are in fact identical with a house, their meaning residing in such details as seating arrangement, each internal position always being read in the same anticlockwise order. Moreover, Midewiwin texts of the Ojibwa Algonkin show 'external' phenomena like rare, magic or dangerous beasts being put into a house, formally, by the power of the priest's mind. The journey of ritual initiation co-ordinates the diverse elements of Algonkin writing, otherwise found separately as petroglyphs or incisions on wood; the candidate's west-east path both gives a standard

Midewiwin scroll

orientation to the symbols and provides the thread of sequence from one 2-door house to the next. Corresponding to Venus's journey to or through to the east, houses of initiation total four or eight: lines of Midewiwin writing normally have four (or eight) symbols. One of the *sachems* listed in the Walam Olum is called 'Olumapi', which means inciser or writer; his symbol is four houses with the west-east path running through them.

Fig. 6. Lenape literary sachems: Olumapi, Scribe; and Walamolumin, Painter Scribe (after the Walam Olum).

III.3 *A Sioux revelation*

A veteran of the battles of Little Big Horn and Wounded Knee, Black Elk (Hehaka Sapa), dedicated his life to defending the traditions of his people, the Sioux, as they had evolved on the Great Plains. His *Memoirs* record his history as a 'keeper of the sacred pipe and rites' of the Oglala Sioux. Anyone aspiring like him to know the

Great Spirit, to discover his own secret name and to join the council of holy men in the tipi lodge, had first to have his lifetime vision of the universe. While Black Elk's vision is an intensely individual experience, the imagery through which it is recorded verbally by him belongs to North American ritual generally. This fact, true for other Plains visions, is emphasized in the illustrations, appended to the first edition of Black Elk's text, by his friend Standing Bear (a fellow Sioux, who also fought at Little Big Horn). Initiation into Sioux ritual begins as here, with the entry, through the door with its two guardians, into the sacred enclosure, where six elders each impart their secrets. Sets of magic animals lend their strength and give encouragement, speaking and singing through the 'voice line' from their hearts. The first gifts Black Elk receives are water and the bow, emblems respectively of the primary professions of the planter and the hunter. Some details of his account, like the rainbow frame and the wooden bowl of water, correspond exactly to the iconography of Southwestern sandpaintings (cf. *III.4*; *VI.4*). Even so, the dominant quality of Black Elk's prose is kinetic; neither Standing Bear's drawings nor the swirling pictography ('a whole skyful of horses dancing') of the Plains could fully capture these rapid metamorphoses and brilliant shifts of pace and focus.

Then the bay horse spoke to me again and said: 'See how your horses all come dancing!' I looked, and there were horses, horses everywhere – a whole skyful of horses dancing round me.

'Make haste!', the bay horse said; and we walked together side by side, while the blacks, the whites, the sorrels, and the buckskins followed, marching four by four.

I looked about me once again, and suddenly the dancing horses without number changed into animals of every kind and into all the fowls that are, and these fled back to the four quarters of the world from which the horses came, and vanished.

Then as we walked, there was a heaped up cloud ahead that changed into a tipi, and a rainbow was the open door of it; and through the door I saw six old men sitting in a row.

The two men with the spears now stood beside me, one on either hand, and the horses took their places in their quarters, looking inward, four by four. And the oldest of the Grandfathers spoke with a kind voice and said: 'Come right in and do not fear.' And as he spoke, all the horses of the four quarters neighed to cheer me. So I went in and stood before the six, and they looked older than men can ever be – old like hills, like stars.

The oldest spoke again: 'Your Grandfathers all over the world are having a council, and they have called you here to teach you.' His voice was very kind, but I shook all over with fear now, for I knew that these were not old men, but the Powers of the World. And the first was the Power of the West; the second, of the North; the third, of the East; the fourth, of the South; the fifth, of the Sky; the sixth, of the Earth. I knew this, and was afraid, until the first Grandfather spoke again: 'Behold them yonder where the sun goes down, the thunder beings! You shall see, and have from them my power; and they shall take you to the high and lonely center of the earth that you may see; even to the place where the sun continually shines, they shall take you there to understand.'

And as he spoke of understanding, I looked up and saw the rainbow leap with flames of many colors over me.

Now there was a wooden cup in his hand and it was full of water and in the water was the sky.

'Take this', he said. 'It is the power to make live, and it is yours.'

Now he had a bow in his hands. 'Take this', he said. 'It is the power to destroy, and it is yours.'

Then he pointed to himself and said: 'Look close at him who is your spirit now, for you are his body and his name is Eagle Wing Stretches.'

Black Elk, *Black Elk Speaks*, pp. 25–7

III.4 *The principal sandpainting of the Navajo Night Way*

Athapaskans who emigrated from the Pacific Northwest, like the Apache, the Navajo are not the oldest practitioners of Southwestern sandpainting. That privilege belongs more likely to the Hopi and other relatives of the Nahua-speakers in the area. But this art plays an indispensable role in Navajo rituals or 'Ways', which developed from shamanistic curing and other practices. The designs, linear or concentric, are made the tamped floor of the *hogan* with dry paints of sandstone, charcoal, pollen and other powdered substances which themselves may have therapeutic qualities. This painting is used in the 'Night Way', a major ceremony which fully embodies the logic of the nine-night Southwestern ritual as a form, moving from the emetic during its first half, the way down from the west, to affirmation during the second, the way back up to the east. Made on the fifth night, this painting in fact marks the turning point in the

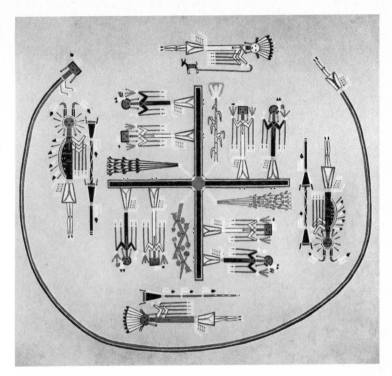

'Whirling Logs' sandpainting

journey. At the east, conventionally placed uppermost as in the Toltec screenfolds, stands a figure known as 'White Body', who is faced by 'Yellow Body' in the west. They have the same feather head-dresses and are the maize forms of Speaker god (*hastshe yalti*), of the dawn and the eastern sky, and his companion the domestic Hogan god (*hastshe hogan*). Using maize of these colours Speaker god is credited with having made the race of men of this world age. By the lasso-like 'finding rope' in his hand, he holds two sources of man's food, from hunting and planting, in the single symbol of the mountain sheep filled with seeds. The two figures to either side, blue and black, also with pouches at their waists, are more elaborate versions of this creature, having horns and seed-filled hunchbacks. In concert the four figures steady the four rainbow 'logs' which touch the centre of the painting, the lake of innermost earth, represented by an actual bowl of water set in the floor of the *hogan*, on which herbal leaves and then sand are laid. Amongst other things the logs are the magic conveyances for shamanistic journeys of soul heroes. Together with their square- and round-headed travellers they form a swastika (cf. the Toltec design in *IV.3*) which is prevented from 'whirling' by the pairs of gods – White and Yellow Body and the blue and black hunchbacks – who steady them. Balance is also given by the four plants that grow between them. As in the Toltec tradition these start with maize, upper right, followed here, anticlockwise, by tobacco, squash and beans. The whole is framed by a rainbow body, encircling like the *hogan* itself, which meets head to foot at the eastern door of the painting.

III.5 *The forces of Tlaloc oppose those of Quetzalcoatl*

This page is part of the magnificent central section of the Borgia screenfold (pp. 29–46) which shows the choreography and the architecture proper to Toltec ritual as it was practised in Mesoamerica prior to the arrival of Christianity. It comprises a sequence of sanctuaries, specifying their shapes, entrances and exits, the paths between them, and their disposition relative to one another. A sanctuary in plan often corresponds to a page of the screenfold, as it does here, where the enclosing frame is anthropo- or theriomorphic. Enclosing the darkness or night necessary to ritual are the belly walls of a mammal, human or bestial, the passages from and to the outer world being oral or anal-vaginal. The creature of this sanctuary has an outer skin of clouds and stars, with hand claws on the upper and foot claws on the lower corners of her body. In its context, the page is read from top to bottom: entrance is via the tooth-steps in the open jaws of the tilted head; exit is from below.

The page design deals with Rain-making and inherent in it is the logic of the opposition it makes between the centre and the four corners. Exactly like the four towns besieging Tenochtitlan in the Lienzo of Tlaxcala (cf. *I.2*), four priests, with the thunder Rain mask of Tlaloc and incense pouches and penance bones in their hands, exert pressure on the central disk, a huge jade. Identified by four different trees set at intervals by four encircled signs – Ground (I), Death (VI), Ape (XI), Vulture (XVI; the ring of Twenty as a whole runs in normal anticlockwise sequence) –, they are opposed by

Borgia screenfold, p. 30

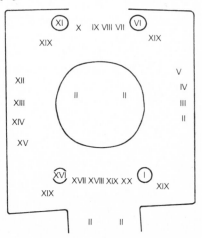

a team of four priests with the Wind mask of Quetzalcoatl. These are being forced out of the jade area: two are swallowed by snakes, the other two are expelled through the exit below. There is also a numerical conflict between Wind (II), the second of the Twenty Signs, and Rain (XIX), the second from the end. For Tlaloc's thunder rain to fall the atmosphere must be humid and still and free from Quetzalcoatl's drying wind.

III.6 *The Twenty Signs and Tlaloc*

On this page of the Laud screenfold, Tlaloc is shown in ritual stance and in full regalia. Wearing a jaguar hood and appropriately armed, he kneels between the clouds above and the waters below. His might reunites these two watery regions and obliterates contrasts, as is shown in the long Snake-lightning in his left hand; in the Water (IX) by the fire-axe in his right; and in the Jaguar (XIV) roar of thunder rising straight from his mouth to its House (III) above, against which the Wind (II), trapped near his nose, is powerless so that the rain, far left, falls as a deluge. This process is helped on by his assistants: the frog-like Lizard (bottom left) who pours water from a calabash and spits lightning; and the aquatic creatures frothing up the water below, crustacean, jade alligator and shellfish. (The frog, as a water bringer, a common glyph or *timehri* in South America, is the first of the Chibcha number signs.) Tlaloc, the last of the Nine Figures, also owns the sign Rain (XIX) which appears above his head-dress and as his mask or 'persona'.

This master of rain and water is ancient not just in Mesoamerica but further afield. Obtaining and controlling his favour was a practice at least as old as agriculture itself: that this design had such a purpose is suggested by the maize plant (lower right), and by the Lizard representing fruit and abundance (bottom left). He may be seen in the murals at Teotihuacan and, as a rain-giver, he is intimately related to the 'Thunders' of the Southwest, to the *cocijos* of the Zapotec and to the long-nosed Chacs of the Maya. Iconographically he may be found in some of the earliest known carving and weaving in northern South America. With his goggle eyes and toothy mouth, Tlaloc is identical with the thunder-rain *kachina* doll of the Hopi (whose ritual vocabulary incidentally preserves the same classic Nahua terms once used at Tula). His axe of copper or base metal (*tepuztli* – cf. p. 35) suggests that like Jove

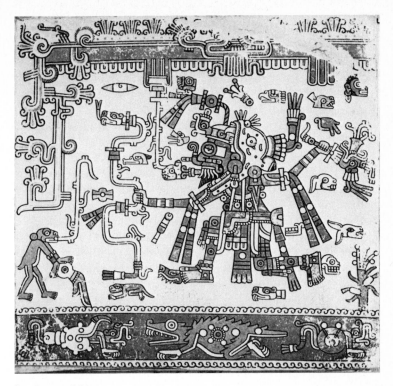

Laud screenfold, p. 2

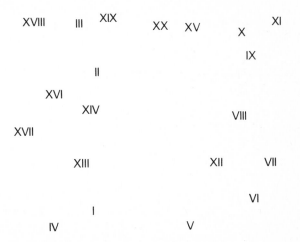

he was held responsible for meteoric thunderbolts, as an expert in smelting techniques imported (in this case) from South America.

III.7 *Tlaloc's hymn*

In Toltec religion, screenfolds depicting ceremonies and gods were complemented by oral liturgy, and early Christian missionaries in Mexico were careful to obtain samples of both types of ritual text. Working in Tepepulco not far north of Teotihuacan in 1559, the Franciscan Bernardino de Sahagún received copies of the Twenty Sacred Hymns to the Aztecs' gods, which constitute the highest form of Nahua poetry and which echo the screenfolds in their subject matter and imagery. This hymn to Tlaloc is the third in the series. It requires several speakers: chorus, officiating priest, sacrificial victim and Tlaloc himself. The request made of Tlaloc is for rain, and the payment offered is the blood of victims, whose weeping 'at the time for weeping' is a form of sympathetic magic. (Gold masks with tears were used for this purpose by the Chibcha and the Inca.) The reciprocity between men and gods is here made especially obvious when Tlaloc acknowledges the priesthood as his 'fathers', the elders who have given him his 'Jaguar-Snake', i.e. his thunder and lightning. The priests' 'blood-thorns' are for self-laceration, and the 'offerings' to Tlaloc are copal.

Two of the participants are named as characters, but their identity is obscure: Acatonal who comes to fetch the victim in the insidiously beautiful jade or stone boat mentioned throughout North American ritual, and Tozcuecuexi, whom the victim addresses as his elder brother and one who has already travelled, shaman-like, beyond death. The 'frightening prince' in the 'place of the unfleshed' is the Dead Land Lord who must be passed in his underworld before the passage up to Tlalocan, with its quetzal plumes, high in the sky and the mists of the hill Poyauhtlan. The period of four days or 'years' it takes to reach the abode of the Dead Land Lord (the 5th of the Nine Figures) is still widely observed in native wakes, while the correlation of days and years in itself, of immediate and entranced time, is to be explained by the Venus cycle (below, p. 149) and may not implausibly be connected with the formative experience of American shamans in and near the Arctic, where the day is a year.

CHORUS   In Mexico the god is being asked for a loan
          among the paper banners in four directions
          now is the time for weeping

PRIEST   I am prepared   I take to the courtyard
the bundles of bloodthorns of my god
you are my commander magic prince
and you are the one who makes our flesh
you are the very first one   the offerings
can only cause you shame

TLALOC   But if someone causes me shame
it is because he didn't know me
you are my fathers my elder priesthood
the Jaguar Snake
the Jaguar Snake

PRIEST   From Tlalocan in a jade boat
Acatonal comes out
extend yourself in Poyauhtlan
with rattles of mist he is taken to Tlalocan

VICTIM   *My brother, Tozcuecuexi,*
I am going forever it's the time of weeping
send me to wherever it is
under his command   I have already said
to the frightening prince I am going forever
it is time for weeping
over four years we shall be carried on the wind
unknown to others by you it is told
to the place of the unfleshed
In the house of Quetzal plumes
transformation is effected
it is the due of the one who vivifies men

CHORUS   Extend yourself in Poyauhtlan
with rattles of mist he is taken to Tlalocan

'Tlaloc Icuic'; Twenty Sacred Hymns, 3

III.8 *'Curing' the sun of eclipse*

The purpose of the activity shown on this page of the Laud
screenfold is to save the sun (centre) from eclipse. A phenomenon
more frequent in the tropics than elsewhere, eclipse was feared like
Tlaloc's Flood as a catastrophe which had brought the world to an
end in a past creation (see chapter V). In Toltec religion the sun
was 'cured' on such occasions by a practice basic to shamanism: the

sucking out of 'afflicting darkness' from the body of the patient. Here, the priest-figure performing the cure is the skeletal Dead Land Lord, 5th of the Nine Figures. Offering the heart of a sacrificial victim as sustenance for the sun, he sucks the darkness from it, back down to his gloomy underworld. On his own behalf the sun, Royal Lord – the 3rd of the Nine Figures – orders the darkness down out of the solar disk in which he sits (centre). Encouraging him from above (left) is the high–flying Eagle (number 5 of the Thirteen Birds and XV in the Twenty Signs). Assisting from east and west at ground level (note the sign Ground in the strips along the edges) are two teams of priests in the guise of other major deities, equipped with penance bones, incense pipes and pouches, musical instruments, staves, and other cult objects. They are grouped in four pairs, each 'located' by one of the Twenty Signs spaced at twenty-five places (counted as dots) from one another. At the top, east, reading inwards from left then right, are Quetzalcoatl and the club-footed warrior Tezcatlipoca with the sign Ape (XI) between them, faced by Xipe, whose coat of flayed skin signifies renewal in the vegetal world, and another Tezcatlipoca, with Vulture (XVI). The doubling of Tezcatlipoca, brought face to face with himself in white and red-stripes is explained by the fact that warfare was also a main antidote to eclipse, as was the sound of the musical instruments held by two of the four deities below at the western horizon. These four deities are all members of the Nine Figures (reading inwards from right then left): Tlaloc (9th), with his snake-lightning and fire-axe, and 'Hill Heart' (8th) walking backwards (to mislead, like the woodland monsters of South America) and holding a rattle, who have the sign Ground (I) between them; they are faced by Royal Lord (3rd), here blowing his solar trumpet, and Obsidian (2nd), with Death (VI).

In other words the positions of these four pairs of actors at each horizon or edge of the page are indicated respectively by signs from the second and the first decimal half of the Twenty Signs: Ape (XI) and Vulture (XVI) at east, and Ground (I) and Death (VI) at west. From these positions they are moving together to provide points of support for the sun at the signs characteristic of east and west, specifically as 'Year-Bearers' of the Toltec calendar (see p. 139 below; note also how the seven 'bulges' rising from the Ground implicitly join to support the two sets of seven marks on the sun's disk). These signs are: Reed (XIII), the shaft of light thrown by Quetzalcoatl as the planet Venus rising in the east; and House (III), the western entrance to the darkness of the underworld Dead Land,

Laud screenfold, p. 1

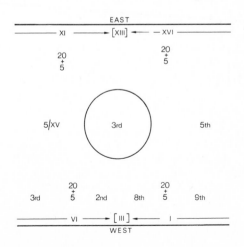

EAST

—————— XI ————→ [XIII] ←—— — XVI ——————

20
+
5

20
+
5

5/XV

3rd

5th

3rd

20
+
5

2nd

8th

20
+
5

9th

—————— VI ————→ [III] ←——— I ——————

WEST

through which the path back to the east leads. We may deduce this because Reed (XIII) is separated by one Sign from Ape (XI) and by two from Vulture (XVI) and these 'distances' are marked respectively by the downward-pointing fingers of the Tezcatlipocas in the pairs at Ape and Vulture. In meeting at XIII in the east and at III in the west, the two pairs in each team will contribute a decimal set of signs to the ailing sun, from the fives of their twenty-five positioning dots, which will be superfluous as such. The sun will thus have restored to him the full set of Twenty Signs, XI–XX from the east and I–X from the west, which characteristically surrounds him when he is at the height of his power (cf. *V.1*).

III.9 *The Twenty Signs and Tezcatlipoca*

Unlike Tlaloc, the Toltec god Tezcatlipoca has few counterparts outside that culture and religion; indeed he is difficult to describe at all adequately. There can be no doubt about his importance: in one or more colours or aspects of himself he is the offspring of the original cosmic pair, with Quetzalcoatl for a brother or a rival. His name means 'mirror' or 'glinting' (*tezcatli*) smoke (*poca*), a quality shared by the 'mirage' gods of the Southwest but proper to him as the shaman who 'sees all' and can therefore instigate the direst strife. He is club-footed, because as the Great Bear constellation his 'leg' came to dip below the horizon, in the view of the Nahua as they moved south into the tropics; on this page of the Borgia his deformity is covered up by the mirror-smoke of his name. His hanging umbilicus reminds us that he was born just as he appears here, fully armed, the paragon of the Toltec warrior. In his right hand (behind him) he holds his spears and his down-tufted wooden shield, as well as a 'pantli' banner; in his left, his spear-thrower. He has a warrior's face-paint (banded, as in sandpaintings – cf. *V.13*), a splendid head-dress, a bundle of quetzal plumes at his back, a shell pendant on his breast and a finely woven cloth about his loins.

More important still in this celebration of Tezcatlipoca's might are the Twenty Signs, which serve to define him closely as a single figure in profile and to specify his particular powers. His spears are sharp like Dog's (X) teeth and deal Death (VI), his spear-thrower has the force of lightning and thunder Rain (XIX). At his extremities the Deer (VII) of his head-dress and the Wind (II) of his loin-cloth suggest speed. His eye is keen like a Reed (XIII) arrow, the hinge of his jaw has the Movement (XVII) of an earthquake; his

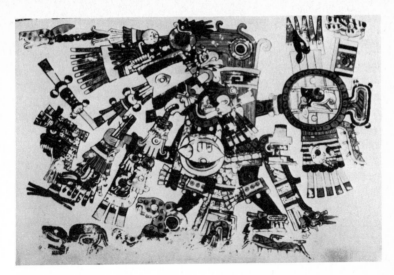

Borgia screenfold, p. 17

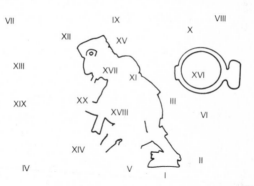

mouth utters lordly or Flower (XX) sounds and his left foot makes
the Ground (I) tremble. The Snake (V) of potency protrudes from
his loins. His head-dress is woven (XII) with the Ape's (XI) artifice
and shimmers like Water (IX). The Eagle (XV) at his head and the
Jaguar (XIV) at his right foot are the emblems of the two military
orders of the Toltecs. He has the sacrificer's Flint knife (XVIII) on
his breast; and Rabbit (VIII), the sign of the captive victim, on his
banner. His shield protects Vulture (XVI), emblem of merchants
and of trade; behind him, the House (III) or sanctuary of the settled
community is safeguarded. (The remaining sign IV has the
eccentric quality it has in Tlaloc's picture; cf. *III.6*.)

III.10 *Prognosis of marriage by Numbers*

Certain of the major Toltec ritual screenfolds have a chapter devoted to the divination or prognosis of marriage. The means of prognosis is two sets of the Thirteen Numbers; in any one case, the numbers allotted respectively to the man and the woman are simply added together. Their fate as a couple is then read from a table of 25 pairs, running from 2 to 26. This extract from the table in the Borgia is for the totals 23 and 24. As an uneven (masculine) number, 23 is marked by a sun (top centre), while as an even (feminine) number 24 has sun and darkness together. Below are bowls with prophylactic offerings for cases of misfortune. In 23 (right) the pair, sitting on stools covered with jaguar skin, each hold 'bleeding hearts' (also found in Algonkin script) in their hands; with gestures of authority they match and complement each other. The conjugal balance is less perfect in the next prognosis, for the total 24 (left), where (top right) the 'arrows and shield' sign denotes strife. The erring husband, a long 'snake' protruding from his loins, has to be held by his wife, in warrior-fashion by the hair, as he attempts to fondle the 'other woman'.

Borgia screenfold, p. 59 (detail)

III.11 *A Sacred Round table for timing funeral ceremonies*

In those screenfolds used as reference works for the timing of rituals, the correct moments and intervals were deduced and read off from tables based on the Sacred Round. The example here, from the Laud screenfold, concerns burial. The ceremonial may be understood by comparison with other screenfolds and, not least, thanks to the survival of traditional beliefs in the Southwest. In the lower register various prerequisites are listed (left to right): firewood, copal, blood, flowers, jewels, plus prayersticks laid in patterns like those still used in the Southwest. The start date is 1 Water. In the upper register, from left to right, the actual ceremonies are depicted. Here we see that the fire on which the corpse is burned should be quenched on 1 Water (IX). The sign here is also incorporated into the water flowing from the woman's pot, and in each case is fused with the sign Ground (meaning well-water?). Steam rises from the embers like Tlaloc's mist (above, p. 102). Twenty days later, on 8 Water (right), the ashes are to be placed in a hole in the ground. Using a sharp bone, the woman does

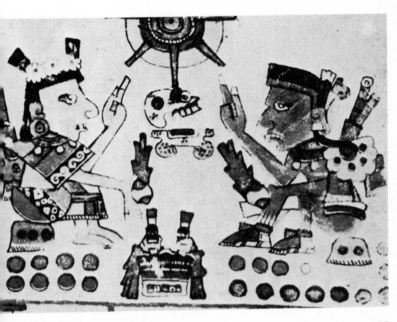

penance so that the deceased may set off on his journey – note the footsteps. As companions he has the two domestic creatures of the Twenty Signs and the Thirteen Birds respectively: Dog (X) and Turkey (9th). The Turkey drops four seeds from under its wings: maize, squash, bean and melon. This gesture is explained in Navajo ritual still alive today, where the Turkey gives the visionary Self-Teacher exactly these four seeds, for comfort on his journey into the life beyond. In other words, there is a complete concordance between this document, prepared in Mexico around the fourteenth century, and modern religious belief in an area over a thousand miles to the north.

Laud screenfold, pp. 26, 25

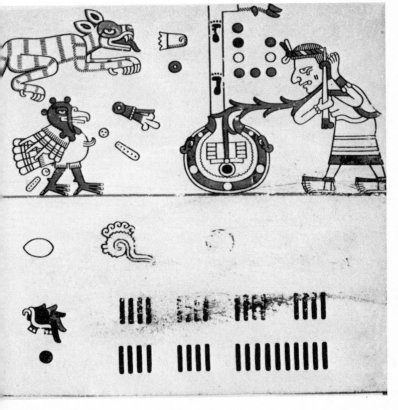

VII

8   IX   X (Dog)   8

1
IX   9
(Turkey)

Bundles of firewood   Blood   Flower

Copal

Prayer sticks   IX
                         1   Prayer sticks

III.12 *Activities for and during the New Fire ritual*

With this brief chapter from the Vienna screenfold, we enter a further dimension of Mesoamerican ritual literature: the calendrical. The whole of the obverse of the Vienna is in fact dedicated to the 'New Fire' ritual peculiar to the Toltec calendar. In regions using this calendar (the Vienna belongs to the Mixtec town of Tilantongo), each new period of 52 years (known as the 'Calendar Round') began officially with the spreading of new fire from the source depicted here (middle column): a fire-drill held between the palms of an elaborately attired high priest. Regular new kindlings of this kind were practised to the north by the Iroquois (in their 'Condolence Ritual') and the Algonkin; and to the south by the Inca, who once a year spread fire out through the Tahuantinsuyu, from the capital Cuzco. (Among the Toltecs the fire-drilling equipment depicted here, the *mamalhuatzli*, gave its name to the constellation Orion, which was named 'Council-Fire' by the Algonkin.) As a specifically calendrical ritual of the Toltecs, these fire-drillings became quite awesome occasions. While shaman-like priests elsewhere may have kept their ceremonial props in boxes or portable 'medicine bundles' and needed only a minimum of physical labour by others, the choreographers of the Toltec New Fire ritual counted on arsenals of material supplies and on the skills of a host of artisans: dress-makers, distillers, scribes (who carefully listed their own contribution of brushes and paints), architects, masons, and thatchers.

This chapter opens, bottom right, with such a list of requirements: baskets of incense and jars of honey: fringed mantles for the performers; chisels and paint brushes; agave and other fibrous plants for making an alcoholic drink and possibly rope and paper; cocoa pods and so on. Details of building activity are also given: rough, coloured stone is fetched (on feet); pyramids and stairways are erected, as well as four sacred houses each with a cult object inside (cocoa beans, blood, bird and starry eye). The work goes on for a year: next to the men with the measuring rope is the 'A' shaped solar year sign with a dot for 'one', representing this period. After the fire kindling comes a series of place names (left) conjoined in a multiple 'hill' sign, and a long list of buildings erected. Those shown here include the H-shaped Ball Court (lower left) found as far north as Arizona and in the Caribbean; the bird courts are of the quetzal and parrot, 12 and 13 of the Thirteen Birds. Steam-baths were another frequent item, a more luxurious version of the baths

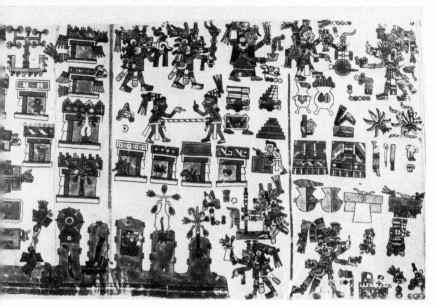

Vienna screenfold, pp. 18–17

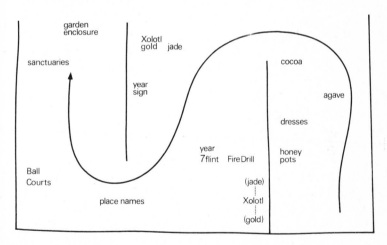

used before rituals by shamans throughout northern America. Archaeology confirms that the New Fire rituals were celebrated by large-scale building activity and the results of these activities still dominate landscapes today in Mesoamerica.

In all, the obverse of the Vienna contains ten chapters, each concerned with a Fire-Drilling ritual, of which this is the fourth, and of which the first is by far the longest. As well as listing material prerequisites, these chapters explain who should perform the ceremony, at which date, and who from among the Mixtec nobility should act as assistants. The Driller in the first chapter is Quetzalcoatl himself (i.e. his priest impersonator); in this chapter it is his 'dog twin', Xolotl, who is identified by his canine mask. Decorated in jade and gold, Xolotl appears previously (at the top of the middle column) carrying a torch and blowing a conch. Other officiating priest-gods burn copal and sacrifice a Quail (4 in the set of Thirteen Birds; the conch and the Quail are mementos of Quetzalcoatl's epic journey as Venus (see below, *V.3*). The year date, 7 Flint, is shown by the 'A'-shaped solar sign near the drilling. Finally we should note that in this dated narrative we have a new format, the boustrophedon. Unlike the 'synchronic' tables and pages in the Borgia and the Laud, this chapter has a linear reading order, from right to left.

Fig. 7. Toltec and Mide steam-bath symbols.

III.13 *Consecration of the sanctuary of Quetzalcoatl*

The Nuttall screenfold, from which this page is quoted, is closely related to the Vienna, in being also both calendrical and ritual, and in belonging to Teozacoalco, a Mixtec town not far from Tilantongo. However, it places more weight on the dynastic history of the Mixtecs. Here (bottom right) we see Lady 3-Flint (her birthday or calendar name) and her royal consort 5-Flower consecrating the sanctuary of Quetzalcoatl, after the introduction of Toltec religion to the area in the tenth century. The date '5 Rain in the year 10 Reed [AD 931]' is shown beside the thatched roof of the sanctuary. Behind (above) them in the right-hand column stand two pairs of priests. The senior pair (uppermost; note the 'old-man' mouths), 10-Rain and 10-Grass, contribute firewood and incense. Their juniors, 10-Reed and 10-Vulture, carry medicine bundles (standard shaman's gear) on their backs and bear standards decorated with feathers and flowers.

Because the ceremony itself is of especial importance, the boustrophedon reading line is made to open out into a 'synchronic' area around the pyramid: a good example of the adaptability of Toltec writing. With his name 9-Wind like a mask before him, Quetzalcoatl looks out of a Flint wrapped in a medicine bundle in the sanctuary (his terrestrial birth from a Flint on a day – 9 Wind – in the distant past is recorded in the Vienna). Above, a Feather Snake (Quetzalcoatl) is entwined in the roof. Before the pyramid steps, Lady 3-Flint censes a load of sand brought for the occasion (note the feet), which is laid in patterns (the smaller dots are no longer random) in the walled enclosure alongside the pyramid, and inset with inverted stars to show depth. In the Pool below, attired in a Feather Snake, she burns more incense. Behind her is a Ball Court that is swallowed, i.e. partly below ground level, and covered with thatch. Top left, 5-Flower pierces his ear with a sharp bone; 10-Reed and a companion, incense pouches in hand, bring offerings of branches and a Quail.

Nuttall screenfold, p. 15

III.14 *Maya worship of maize*

At the Classic Maya city of Palenque there is a group of three
sanctuaries each named after the finely carved panels found in
them: the Sun, the Cross and the Foliated Cross; the last of
these is shown here. Between the priest and his assistant stands the
object of veneration: a maize plant, in the form of a man with

Fig. 8. Mide vision symbol: Tree-man.

outstretched arms. Maize and men are shown to be intimately
related throughout Classic Maya iconography, in the post-Classic
screenfolds and in post-Columbian texts from both Yucatan and
the Guatemalan highlands, notably the Quiche genesis in the *Popol
vuh*. Four double columns of hieroglyphs, two either side, explain
the origin and form of the ceremony. The left-hand columns,
beginning with a Maya Era date (see below p. 126), deal with events
in the third millennium BC, including the emergence of deities
('birth' glyph, C5), and the major astronomical phenomena with
which they were synchronized. The time period of the right-hand
columns, the seventh century AD, is roughly contemporaneous with
the carving of the panel. Here these precedents are linked to
political figures and to the place Palenque itself (L14). Deities
appear as the 'Triad' specific to that city (N9–O10) and ceremonials
are given definite directions, plans and participants. The commentary, then, deals with the kind of historical consecration we
found in the Nuttall screenfold and as exegesis of ritual both texts
make use of the Sacred Round to locate events and people in time.
Yet the types of writing involved, Maya and Toltec, differ crucially,
Maya hieroglyphic being encoded as in arithmetic and quite
separable from illustration as such. Note how the square glyph-
spaces follow the writing convention given typically by the
numerical affix and the main sign in the Sacred Round dates: 2
Ahau (XX) at C8, 1 Ahau (XX) at D14 and 2 Cib (XVI) at L1. The
Thirteen Numbers appear as main signs in the form of 'heads', as in
the 'Axe-eye' deity 6 (D9) and in the opening Maya Era date: 1.18
[10 +8]. 5.4.0. (A3–A7). The sign at B9 is the 2nd of the Nine
Figures, part of the night count. Other signs and affixes convey

information determined by actual position, gesture, colour and so on in the Toltec screenfolds: 'offering to or of the Maize God in the west' (B14–B15); blood-letting as penance (L12); 'step, walk or count to' (C12 – *xoc ti* in Yucatec); 'green' or 'new' (affix D12). The hand sign for holding the heart as a fish occurs twice (C9 and M10), indicating the importance of that act in maize culture; the sign in fact also serves to designate the Maize-God as the 4th of the Nine Figures. As columns to either side, these hieroglyphs provide the design as a whole with a frame, but one which (unlike the Toltec theriomorph) is open, theoretical and erect.

Foliated Cross panel, Palenque

III.15 *Two prayers in worship of Viracocha*

In the Inca state, ritual was the responsibility of the official 'priest-poets' known as *haravek*, who were highly trained in the use of the *quipu*. By this means ritual texts in Quechua were 'regularized', much as they were in Maya by hieroglyphic writing. The first prayer or hymn quoted here was actually transcribed from a *quipu*, and we may be sure that the formulaic phrases in both texts ('peace-safety', 'established-made', 'light-illumine', etc.) correspond to specific knots in that now indecipherable device. Also, the reference to 'shepherding' reminds us that one of the chief uses of the *quipu* under the Inca, and numerically still today, is for counting flocks, pastoral activity in pre-Columbian America having been most developed in the Andes. Both texts are entirely measured in their cosmological allusions and entreaty: everything is subject to the supreme authority and intelligence of Viracocha, whose earthly representative is the Sapa Inca himself. Within his established order requests for its continuing welfare can only be 'reasonable' in tone and argument. (It is noteworthy that Guaman Poma presents as dispensable if not dangerous to 'Good Government' ritual practices which retained too much shamanistic force of their own.) In the first text (a) Viracocha is said to have assigned to the thunder-rain gods the *duty* of providing rain. In the second (b), the Sun has been given the task of enlightening the state in its three social divisions: aristocratic Inca, common people and servants. In the Coricancha, the main sanctuary at Cuzco, the breath of the congregation uttering prayers like these, rising as mist in the cold air of dawn, was shot through as the gold-covered walls caught the light of the new 'illuminating' sun, to produce a rainbow brilliance.

(a)
Fair princess,
your brother has broken your jar
that is why
it thunders and lightens

so princess
you give us falling rain
or else hail and snow

Viracocha
earth-establisher, earth maker
for this duty
has established you, has made you

(b)
Viracocha, you say
may the sun be, may the night be
you say
may it dawn, may it grow light
you make your son to move in peace, in safety
to give light and illumination to the people
you have created oh Viracocha:

peacefully, safely
sun, shine on and illumine
the Incas, the people, the servants
whom you have shepherded
guard them from sickness and suffering
in peace, in safety

Zithuwa ritual

IV Calendars

No complex society can get along without some sort of calendar, that is, a means of naming and numbering periods of time. A calendar fixes the cycles of religious and economic life (the word itself was coined by Roman accountants) and establishes political eras. Judaism, Christianity and Islam, each have their own calendar. In the China of the Warring States (as Joseph Needham notes) one expressed loyalty to a conqueror by accepting his way of reckoning time; and one of the more conspicuous acts of the French revolutionaries was to rename the months of our year.

When they reached America, prior to the Gregorian Reform of 1582, Europeans still had to produce a calendar as satisfactory as those they found there. Calendrical science is in fact inseparable from the major intellectual achievements of the New World. Historical and astronomical time were systematically correlated there long before they were in the Old World. And in Mesoamerica the principles on which these correlations were based were deemed ideologically so significant that a standing philosophical debate went on between the Maya, who espoused the day, and the Toltecs, who chose the solar year as their basic unit of time.

Year calendars

In temperate latitudes, an annual pattern of seasons is everywhere similar and unmistakable, at least as far as winter and summer are concerned. In the northern Plains, the Sioux mark the passage of time by winters, often in cycles of 70, naming each year after some event which occurred during it. As we have seen, the Algonkin celebrate the emergence from these northern winters by consecrating the spring equinox as the start of their year, the time of the major Midewiwin ceremony. Elsewhere in these extra-tropical latitudes in both North and South America, the year also took precedence. Months or lunations (notoriously difficult to calculate at an average of 29·53 days) were fitted into it by various means. And where necessary, adjustments similar to our leap year were made to allow for the extra day produced every four years by the fact that the earth spends roughly $365\frac{1}{4}$ days on its annual journey around the sun.

Coming into tropical Mexico from the north as they did, early in their history, the Nahua-speakers of Mesoamerica maintained a strong allegiance to the notion of the solar year. A fundamental feature of the Toltec calendar is that it names each year by means of the Sacred Round of Twenty Signs and Thirteeen Numbers. These year names were indicated in the screenfolds by the 'A'-shaped solar sign, or by boxes, as in the Huitzilopochtli screenfold. Each year was in fact named after the Sacred Round name of the day on which it began; and, in order to maintain a harmonious ritual pattern of the signs involved, the year was fixed at a conventional 365 days. This produced the sequence of year names shown here in Table 3, the four of the Twenty Signs after which years could be named being known as 'Year-Bearers'. Since the solar year is not exactly 365 days, the Toltecs added an extra day every four years, much as we do. However, they did not name these extra days separately: had they done so, the set of four Year-Bearers would have constantly changed. After 52 years the names of the years, four Year-Bearer signs multiplied by the Thirteen Numbers, began to repeat, and a new period of 52 years or Calendar Round (*xiuhmolpilli*, or tying of years, in Nahua) was inaugurated with a Fire-Drilling ritual. This all means that the Toltec calendar was arithmetically irregular, since of the 18,992 actual days in a Calendar Round of 52 years only 18,980 (365×52) were individually named (when the Nine Figures of ritual were incorporated, as a night count, the irregularity was aggravated by the 'doubling up' of the 8th and 9th Figures at the end of each Sacred Round; see Table 2d, p. 92). It could also be ambiguous because, 260 being less than 365, there were sometimes two days with the same Sacred Round name in any one year. Nevertheless the pattern of four Year-Bearers were found ritually satisfying. And in providing a ready means of counting and internally dividing years the method was socially convenient. In cultures influenced by the Toltecs, people were customarily named after their birth date, and their lives were in some degree affected by their 'sign', Ape (XI) denoting skill and craftsmanship, for instance. Temporal events generally tended to be interpreted with the ritual properties of the calendar signs in mind: for example 'Rabbit' years meant famine.

Table 3. THE SACRED ROUND CORRELATED WITH THE NUMBER 365

	1	2	3	4	5	6	etc
(1)	1 VIII	2 IX	3 X	4 XI	5 XII	6 XIII	
(2)	2 XIII	3 XIV	4 XV	5 XVI	6 XVII	7 XVIII	
(3)	3 XVIII	4 XIX	5 XX	6 I	7 II	8 III	
(4)	4 III	5 IV	6 V	7 VI	8 VII	9 VIII	
(5)	5 VIII	6 IX	7 X	8 XI	9 XII	10 XIII	
(6)	6 XIII	7 XIV	8 XV	9 XVI	10 XVII	11 XVIII	
(7–48)	etc.						
(49)	10 VIII	11 IX	12 X	13 XI	1 XII	2 XIII	
(50)	11 XIII	12 XIV	13 XV	1 XVI	2 XVII	3 XVIII	
(51)	12 XVIII	13 XIX	1 XX	2 I	3 II	4 III	
(52)	13 III	1 IV	2 V	3 VI	4 VII	5 VIII	

Toltec calendar dates
The conventional 365 days of the year are named by Sacred Round Numbers and Signs, as
set out above; nights are named by the Nine Figures, correlated with the Sacred Round
(Table 2d). Years are named after their 'Year-Bearer' days, in the left-hand column (52
differently named years, or one 'Calendar Round' in all), together with a year sign:

| | Aztec | | Mixtec, Cholulan | | Laud and Fejérváry screenfolds |

Extra days and nights intercalated in leap-years are *not* separately named.

Maya calendar dates
Each unit of the Sacred Round, used with place-value arithmetic, always names one day and
each of the Nine Figures names one night: see Tables 4 and 5.

The intimate connection between Toltec calendrics and ritual is
superbly described in the Fejérváry screenfold; and there is no
clear-cut distinction between the two categories even in narrative
screenfolds like the Vienna and the Nuttall. Other surviving
narratives, however, are predominantly just calendrical like those
which record the genealogy and conquests of the Mixtec royal
families. The Bodley and the Selden screenfolds are of this type.
They have a more regular boustrophedon format within which
names, dates and events are arranged in straightforward chronological order. The Year-Bearer calendar thus becomes the
informing principle of a whole literary genre of annals kept up in
native script well into the 17th century. These are the model for the
many annals written in Nahua, after the Spanish conquest, using
the Roman alphabet, often combined with elements of Toltec
writing. In some cases the dates given are, or have subsequently
been, correlated with our calendar, and in the pre-Columbian
examples these dates range back as far as the 7th century AD. Such
correlations must be tentative, however, because one Calendar

361	362	363	364	365
10 VIII	11 IX	12 X	13 XI	1 XII
11 XIII	12 XIV	13 XV	1 XVI	2 XVII
12 XVIII	13 XIX	1 XX	2 I	3 II
13 III	1 IV	2 V	3 VI	4 VII
1 VIII	2 IX	3 X	4 XI	5 XII
2 XIII	3 XIV	4 XV	5 XVI	6 XVII
etc.				
6 VIII	7 IX	8 X	9 XI	10 XII
7 XIII	8 XIV	9 XV	10 XVI	11 XVII
8 XVIII	9 XIX	10 XX	11 I	12 II
9 III	10 IV	11 V	12 VI	13 VII

Round may be unambiguously distinguished from another only by its serial position, and because different groups and localities had different signs for the same year (so that 1 Reed on one screenfold might equal 3 Flint in another).

Day Calendars

In the tropics proper, in contrast to the temperate and polar regions, the sun's daily course, constantly at or near the zenith, is always close to its own mean length in time and, over the annual 365·225 days, it does not at all differentiate a latitudinal set of yearly seasons. Here, the seasons, such as they are, depend far more on such factors as altitude and very local rainfall patterns. In these circumstances, calendars based on the solar year are likely to lack the obvious general validity that they have in more temperate latitudes. It is with this in mind that we best approach the calendar of the Maya, in which the basic unit is not the year but the day – Helios, not Apollo, to recall the distinction made in antiquity by the Greeks and the Egyptians. Like the Toltecs, the Maya used the Sacred Round of Mesoamerican ritual as an essential ingredient of their calendar, but on a truly diurnal not an annual basis. As we have seen, the Maya actually resented and rejected the Toltec 'double-day' leap-year adjustment as inelegant and arithmetically confusing. Their priorities had less to do with ritual patterns than with astronomical curiosity: they wanted a system which would enable them to explore the secrets of time itself with arithmetical ease.

Two inalienable features of the Classic Maya calendar, whose significance cannot be overstated, are: (a) that it rests on a base date,

'4 Ahau 8 Cumku' – probably 10 August 3113 BC – the start of the Maya Era; and (b) that days counted forward and back from this date are written out not additively in simple accumulation but by means of place-value notation, and hence with the concept of zero as 'absence' (see Table 4). Now, both these features, the base date and the place-value notation, are present in inscriptions (often called 'Olmec') found in and near Maya territory, which date to 300 BC or earlier. Whoever the 'Olmec' were, they must have been extremely close to the Maya since they acknowledged the same Era; also, they very probably spoke Mixe-Zoque, which is akin to Maya. As for place-value arithmetic, this was widely practised in Indian America, from the Algonkin of New England, whose dexterity with counting boards astonished the Puritan Roger Williams, down at least to the southern end of the Inca empire. But a *notation* for this kind of arithmetic appears not to have been developed north of the limit set by the first Olmec/Maya calendrical inscriptions. It is entirely absent from the Toltec calendar. In fact, throughout the world the only other acknowledged source of notational place-value arithmetic is Mesopotamia, at roughly the same period. In turn, the dependence of the Maya calendar on place-value notation, which could not have worked without the formula '1 day = 1 unit', strengthens the hypothesis of their intimate connection, during the first millennium BC, with northern South America. For the knots in the *quipu* are used with place value. *Quipu* knots, and the statistical and calendrical counters of the Inca abacus, placed decimally in a vertical scale, are in principle exactly like the various combinations of bars and dots used vigesimally on the vertical scale of the stone columns of the Olmec and the Maya. How exactly the Inca calendar worked in practice is now unclear; but there can be no doubt that the day-unit, decimal place value and quantities of 360 days (like the Maya '*tun*') were involved. (In their intermediary position between Inca and Maya, the Chibcha had a calendar which was both decimal (Inca) and vigesimal, with months, '*zocams*', of 30 (10 × 3) days and 'years' of 20 *zocams*.)

The Maya calendar proper came into being around AD 100 when the Sacred Round names of days and other information were incorporated into columns of text formerly dedicated just to place-value calculations of elapsed time. This marriage of arithmetic with iconography occurs and is synonymous with the designating of the third unit of place-value calendrics as not 400 but 360, the *hab* or *tun* divisible by 9 (where the 400-day year was retained, as among the Cakchiquel, hieroglyphic writing proper is absent; a further link

Table 4. ARITHMETICAL SYSTEMS

(a) **Inca place-value arithmetic** (decimal):

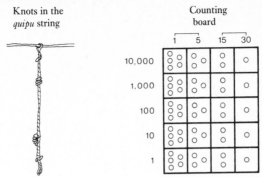

Knots in the *quipu* string

Counting board

	1	5	15	30
10,000	OO OO	O O O	O O	O
1,000	OO OO	O O O	O O	O
100	OO OO	O O O	O O	O
10	OO OO	O O O	O O	O
1	OO OO	O O O	O O	O

Note that the quantities in the first two columns of the counting board (ones and fives) are purely statistical, while those to the right correspond to divisions of the Inca calendar; cf. pp. 126, 141–2. Based on Wassen (from the Handbook of South American Indians, 5: 615–6) and on Acosta's contemporary notes on the distinctive feature of the board, namely the transforming of one unit from the extreme right into three units on the extreme left, one line up ('pasarán un grano de aquí, trocarán tres de allá . . .'; cf. Purchas xv: 378).

(b) **Maya (and Olmec) place-value arithmetic** (vigesimal), where one is represented by a dot and five by a bar, e.g.

For calendrical use, see Table 5.

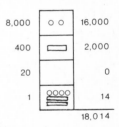

8,000	O O	16,000
400	▭	2,000
20		0
1	OOOO ═══	14

18,014

(c) **The Toltec system**, instead of place value, uses the following signs for 20 and multiples of 20, which are always quite separate from the calendar:

banner 20   feather 400   pouch 8,000

---

between the Cakchiquel and the Olmec is the use of the Mixe-Zoque word *may*, 'count', for the period of twenty 400-day 'years', which became the *katun* of the Yucatec – twenty 360-day years). In the Maya inscriptions proper, each hieroglyph has its own clearly defined arithmetical place or area, usually in a double column,

Table 5. MAYA DATES, AND OTHER GLYPHS

(a) Dates:

In the hieroglyphic texts, dates are counted from the beginning of the Maya Era in the following quantities of days:

kin	*uinal*	*tun* or *hab*	*katun*	*'baktun'*
sun or day	20 days	360 days	20 *tuns*	400 *tuns*

Note that the *tun* (and its multiples) replaces the 400 (and its multiples) of pure place-value notation, used in non-hieroglyphic Maya calendars like the Cakchiquel (see above, p. 126), and possibly the 'Olmec'. The need to specify the *tun* as 360 days (which number, unlike 400, is divisible by 9) by a written sign is thus an important step in the development of hieroglyphic writing as such.

Dates also expressed by the day in the Sacred Round (e.g., 4 Ahau) and by the day in the 365-day cycle of weeks (e.g., 8 Cumku). The nineteen weeks, the first eighteen each of 20 days, the last of 5 days, are shown (glyphs after Thompson – Classic forms), with names in Yucatec. Note the colour combinations, green and yellow, with *kin* (sun) at 7 and 14.

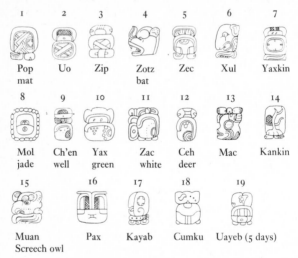

1	2	3	4	5	6	7
Pop mat	Uo	Zip	Zotz bat	Zec	Xul	Yaxkin
8	9	10	11	12	13	14
Mol jade	Ch'en well	Yax green	Zac white	Ceh deer	Mac	Kankin
15	16	17	18	19		
Muan Screech owl	Pax	Kayab	Cumku	Uayeb (5 days)		

(b) Colours and directions (post-Classic forms):

 chac red or big
 ek black or star
 zac white or virtual
 kan yellow
 yax green or new

In the set of four colours, when the emphasis is on the *new* growth *kan* is replaced by *yax*, which then 'opposes' *chac*, as *ek* does *zac*.

 lakin east
 chikin west
 xaman zenith (north)
 nohol nadir (south)

Table 6. FORMAT OF CALENDRICAL SCREENFOLDS AND HIEROGLYPHIC TEXTS

(a) Toltec calendrical screenfolds:

Vienna; Nuttall   Selden

(b) Maya hieroglyphic texts:

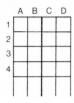

Read: A 1, B 1, A 2, B 2, A 3, B 3, A 4, B 4,
C 1, D 1, C 2, D 2, C 3, D 3, C 4, D 4

Read: A 1, B 1, A 2, B 2, C 1, D 1,
C 2, D 2, E 1, F 1, E 2, F 2

Typical arrangement of chapters in the screenfolds,
in three registers

e.g. as seen in *III.14*. A typical calendrical statement, counted from the start of the Maya Era (4 Ahau 8 Cumku), first noted the number of days which had elapsed since that time, in the quantities listed in Table 5 (*uinal*, 20 days; *tun*, 360 days, etc.). This was followed by the Sacred Round name of the day arrived at (always a true day); the day of the week (see Table 5); the name of the night as one of the Nine Figures (which were never 'doubled up' in the Maya calendar and always equalled one night); and the age of the moon. This arrangement led to the creation of Maya hieroglyphic writing itself. Calendrical mathematics provided the grid, as it were, an ordering principle for the whole range of signs and pictographs used for ritual and other purposes in Meso-america: artifacts and architecture, flora and fauna, parts of the body, personal and place names, and the actions expressed by body position and hand gesture. As we have seen (above, p. 110), in Toltec writing many of these were used ideographically (e.g. arrow and shield for war; sun and night for timeless or even), and even phonetically, especially in place names. But only in the Maya system did they acquire a regular and standard format. Indeed, the Maya calendar produced the three categories of formal expression which characterize Maya script: first, 'main signs', nouns and verbs like those just mentioned; second, affixes, originally just numerical co-efficients and later prepositions and other particles of grammar; and third, the precise area in which glyphs (that is, combinations of main signs and affixes) were placed. This point becomes quite clear when Maya hieroglyphic writing, with its obvious regularity, is compared with other early examples of Mesoamerican script (see below, p. 229).

The calendrical calculations of the Maya sometimes range over thousands of millions of days forwards and backwards in time. Always using the day-unit, the classic Maya synchronized lunar months, solar years, planetary phases, eclipse periods and other phenomena, and correlated them with the events of dynastic and political history. They were the first people in the world to integrate celestial and terrestrial time in a single system and on so comprehensive a scale. Their day calendar, modified by use, endured throughout Maya territory, both in Peten and in the southern highlands. In the Book of Chumayel account of 'Mankind's ideal course' (*II.2*) we noted the profound effect of this heritage even at much later stages of Maya civilization in Yucatan. It is the source of specifically Maya concepts of 'rhythm' (between the 'reigns' of the sky and those of the earth) and 'wholeness', and indeed of hieroglyphic writing itself, through which the 'course of mankind was ciphered clearly'.

As a mode and a stimulus to literacy, calendrical records in the New World are deeply enmeshed with ritual on the one hand and with arithmetic on the other, particularly in Mesoamerica. The stories narrated according to the Toltec Year-Bearer calendar often resemble those in Maya hieroglyphic texts, and many of the signs used in them, besides the Sacred Round, may be traced to the same source. But the two kinds of writing differ in logic, articulation and format, Maya hieroglyphs being set out according to the place-value arithmetic which enabled its authors to test the boundaries of temporal consciousness.

IV.1 *A Sioux Winter Count, 1800–70*

The Sioux calendars known as Winter Counts are simple annual tallies. They mark the passage of the year, which begins in spring and is defined by the long northern winter, by a pictograph of a memorable event which occurred during it. Normally the pictographs are painted in red and black on buffalo skin, in either a boustrophedon or a spiral pattern. Some of the older counts go back over several generations to the eighteenth century; they are kept as the personal property of the author, his family or clan, but are exhibited and known to the community as a whole. Starting dates vary but many counts, including this one by Lone Dog, adhere to the 70-year cycle found *in extenso* in the calendar of Brown Hat, alias Baptiste Good, which covers cycles from AD 930 to 1700. Actual events depicted also vary from one count to another but fall into discernible categories. These are well exemplified in the count (beginning in 1800) made by Lone Dog: ritual events, symbolized by the albino buffalo head of Plains 'medicine' (1810, 1843); the erection of buildings like native fortified lodges, and timber stores of white traders (1815, 1817); celestial events, like the solar eclipse of 1869, the meteor of 1821 and the meteor showers of 1833; food supply, like the good buffalo year of 1845 which shows pemmican meat hung out to dry; battle, amnesty and horse stealing (shown by hoof prints); health, like the smallpox epidemic of 1801 and whooping cough of 1813; and other miscellaneous events, like the trading in Mexican blankets in 1853. The drawings are typical of Plains pictography; note the different hair-styles in the calumet exchange of 1851, the hat of the whites, the various types of horses, weapons and wounds. They were often transcribed from other 'texts', e.g. the painted and beaded shirts and robes of warriors, which showed numbers killed in battle and tactics used (dead are numbered in graves in 1800 and 1805). Some of the events recorded in Lone Dog's calendar appear only in it, while certain other events also specify the same years in other Winter Counts. Events widely agreed upon as characteristic of certain years tend to concern astronomy, war and health. Thus, Black Elk – though a Dakota Sioux (rather than Yankton like Lone Dog) – recorded (in his *Memoirs*) his own year of birth, 1864, as the 'Winter When-the-Four-Crows [another Sioux tribe]-Were-Killed', which is the same as the description given to that year here. An event which is found in all Sioux calendars is the first appearance of the U.S. army in 1822 when they attacked the Pawnee (Western relatives of the

```
                    60    59  58
             62 61
          63   39    38 37        57
                         36     56
       64    40    16 15 14    35       55
                17        13  34
       65            1800    12
       66   41    18        11    33      54
                19      1
      67    42   20    2        10   32
                   21      3      9    31    53
       68   43                8      30
               22      4              52
                            7    29
       69   44    23    5  6      28   51
              45  24                50
             46        25 26  27
                  47  48    49
```

IV.2 *The 52-year Calendar Round*

On these two pages (21 and 22) of the Borbonicus screenfold, from Tenochtitlan, the 52-year cycle of the Toltec calendar is set out as if to illustrate its basic principles. The 52 years follow each other in two spirals of 26, which read anticlockwise (like the spiral of Lone Dog's Sioux calendar) and begin, lower left of p. 21, with the year 1 Rabbit (VIII). This is the year with which the Calendar Round began among the Aztecs: AD 1506 was such a year, as were 1454 and 1402 before it. The years run in their normal sequence, 1 Rabbit (VIII), 2 Reed (XIII), 3 Flint (XVIII), 4 House (III), 5 Rabbit (VIII), etc., and they are 'guarded' by the Nine Figures, one of which is placed open-armed to the right of each year. The complex sequence in which the Nine Figures appear derives from their being both a continuous night count and subject to the 260 units of the Sacred Round (see Table 2d); it begins with the Dead Land Lord.

Each spiral of 26 years borders a pair of deities. On the first page we see Oxomoco, and her husband Cipactonal who is named after the first of the Twenty Signs, *cipactli* or Earth Beast (which appears behind his head). With and without her husband, Oxomoco plays a major role in Toltec cosmogony and also appears in the Quiche-Maya story of creation in the *Popol vuh* (cf. *V.6*). Her genius is for divination with the maize kernels which here she casts like dice from her bowl, while Cipactonal gives her ritual support, burning

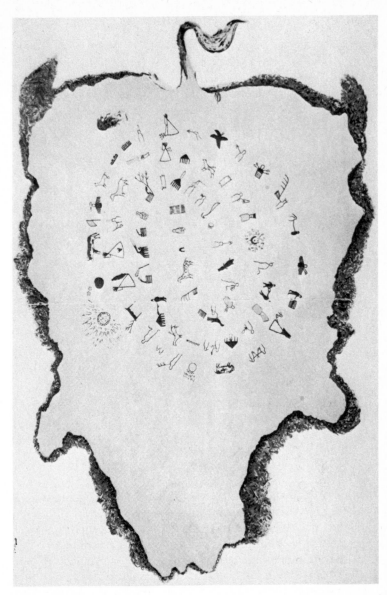

Winter Count by Lone Dog

copal and holding his penance bone ready. The animal-headed staves above them, carved from reed roots, are still used in calendrical ceremonies by such survivors of the Aztecs as the

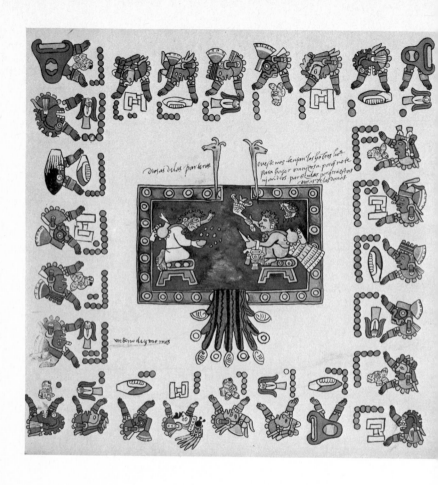

Huichol. As a diviner, Oxomoco is the patron of the Sacred Round and hence of the calendar which derived from it.

On the second page, two 'younger' deities face each other: Quetzalcoatl (left) with his Wind mask, and Tezcatlipoca (right) with his huge shell pendant (cf. *V.6*) and a neck adornment of stars. In the ritualized political history of Tula, Quetzalcoatl the 'culture bearer', the writer and the teacher in his round hat, acts as the great rival to the warrior Tezcatlipoca. They were also patrons respectively of the two types of school in the Aztec education system, the priestly *calmecac* and the military *telpochcalli*. As calendrical patrons and the sons of Oxomoco and Cipactonal, the two are here set in balance.

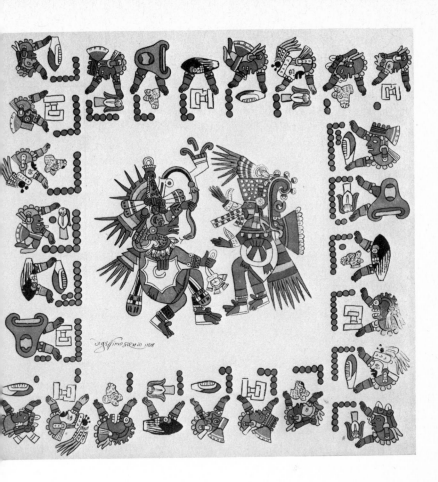

Borbonicus screenfold, pp. 21–22

Sequence of years and order of 'guardian' Figures from the set of nine (both pages
are read anticlockwise, starting at bottom left):

p. 21 – 1 VIII 5th, 2 XIII 3rd, 3 XVIII 9th, 4 III 7th, 5 VIII 4th, 6 XIII 1st, 7
XVIII 8th, 8 III 5th, 9 VIII 3rd, 10 XIII 9th, 11 XVIII 6th, 12 III 4th, 13 VIII
1st, 1 XIII 8th, 2 XVIII 5th, 3 III 3rd, 4 VIII 9th, 5 XIII 6th, 6 XVIII 4th, 7 III
1st, 8 VIII 8th, 9 XIII 5th, 10 XVIII 2nd, 11 III 9th, 12 VIII 6th, 13 XIII 4th;

p. 22 – 1 XVIII 1st, 2 III 7th, 3 VIII 5th, 4 XIII 2nd, 5 XVIII 9th, 6 III 6th, 7
VIII 3rd, 8 XIII 1st, 9 XVIII 7th, 10 III 5th, 11 VIII 2nd, 12 XIII 8th, 13 XVIII
6th, 1 III 3rd, 2 VIII 1st, 3 XIII 7th, 4 XVIII 4th, 5 III 2nd, 6 VIII 8th, 7 XIII
6th, 8 XVIII 3rd, 9 III 9th, 10 VIII 7th, 11 XIII 4th, 12 XVIII 2nd, 13 III 8th.

Annals of the Valley of Mexico, 1506–58, arranged in a fourfold pattern

This page is the last of a three-page screenfold made of native paper, which deals with the fifteenth- and sixteenth-century history of the Valley of Mexico. Each page covers a Calendar Round of 52 years, which are arranged swastika-like in four rows of 13, read from the centre outwards. Beginning like the Borbonicus screenfold with 1 Rabbit, and moving through the usual anticlockwise sequence, each row of years starts and ends with the same Year-Bearer sign: Rabbit (VIII), Reed (XIII), Flint (XVIII) and House (III). Events noted as occurring during most (but not all) years include conquest, funerals and royal accessions in towns round Lake Texcoco, notably Texcoco and Tenochtitlan (note the stone-and-cactus glyph, e.g. in 1523), as well as such other phenomena as famines and freak storms.

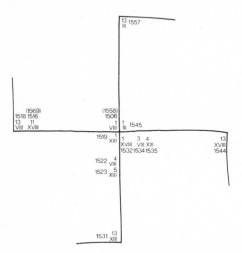

On this page, in 1518 (13 VIII) on the eve of the Spanish arrival, two armed Spaniards are clearly visible, still at sea, with their Cross aloft. Four years later in 1522 (4 VIII) a Franciscan friar appears. The full-scale construction work of the Spanish in the 1530s is noted by European buildings under 1534–5 (3 VIII and 4 XIII), and the latter date also records, pictographically and in the Roman alphabet, the arrival of the first viceroy of New Spain, Antonio de Mendoza. A remarkable feature of the fourfold pattern here is that it is used not once but twice. For the information appearing as glyphs and alphabetic glosses at the further end of some year slots refers to events occurring from 1558 onwards, a full Calendar Round after the events shown further in. For example, the (English) sailing ship and the head of a Señor Enriquez noted under 11 XVIII belong to this later Calendar Round and the year 1569. Apart from simply saving paper, this conjunction of two Calendar Rounds enhances the inherent qualities of the Year-Bearers, conferred on them by their respective Signs and Numbers.

Annals of Texcoco, p. 3

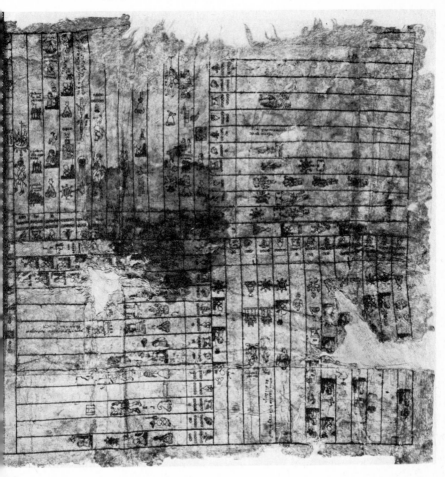

IV.4 *Episodes in the early married life of Lady 6-Ape, 1035–8*

In the annals of the Mixtecs, among the calendrical details of genealogy and political history, we sometimes find vivid accounts of the lives of prominent individuals. The most famous of these is the eleventh-century figure 8-Deer (2nd ruler of the second dynasty of Tilantongo), whose deity ancestors and earthly conquests are noted, at varying length, in the Bodley, the Selden and other screenfolds. This page of the Selden tells part of the story of his relative, Lady 6-Ape, and can be read almost as a cartoon strip. The page is read, from bottom left, along four levels in boustrophedon fashion. On the first date, 10-Wind in the year 10 Reed (AD 1035) there is a dance around the *teponaxtle* drum, involving four men and three women holding 'heart' and 'flower' rattles. This is in celebration of

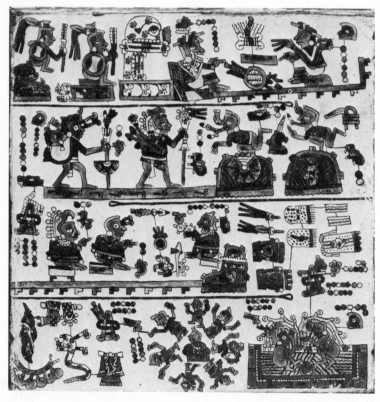

Selden screenfold, p. 7

marriage of Lady 6-Ape to 11-Wind who, on 7 Flower in the year 12 House (1037), are seen bathing ceremonially together; above them is a consignment of mantles and other clothing, quetzal plumes, jade and gold. On the next level, within the walls of a place called Cloud Pattern Hill, a certain 11-Lizard engages two men to accompany 6-Ape on a journey. They are 2-Flower and 3-Ground, and on 9 Snake in the year 13 Rabbit (1038), they set off, 2-Flower carrying her on his back; their path is clearly shown along the second level from the top. On the way they are insulted by 6-Lizard of Moon Hill and 2-Ground of Bee Hill: their cutting words are shown by the Flints on their speech (a convention also used by the Algonkin). On the top level, inside the walls of Death Place, 6-Ape consults its ruler Lady 8-Grass, evidently a powerful woman, for 6-Ape offers her various gifts in return for military aid. The warriors standing behind Lady 8-Grass later help 6-Ape to defeat the people who had insulted her.

The graphic details in these episodes in Lady 6-Ape's life give the narrative a certain power of its own. Nonetheless, the story and the characters are still firmly subject to the calendar, each important event being specified by a Year-Bearer date.

IV.5 *The four Toltec Year-Bearers*

In this opening page of Fejérváry screenfold, the calendrics and the ritual of the Toltecs are subtly wedded. The unbroken outer band consists of the 260 positions of the Sacred Round, with the Twenty Signs at intervals of 13. Inset into it, at the tips of the diagonals, are the four Year-Bearers, Rabbit (VIII), Reed (XIII), Flint (XVIII) and House (III). To the left of each of the diagonals are five of the Twenty Signs; read anticlockwise, the spirals they make plot the 'double-day' mechanism of the Toltec year calendar. The figure in the centre is the Fire- or Year-Lord Xiuhtecutli, 1st of the Nine Figures; the other eight stand in pairs around him. The Year-Bearers, the Twenty Signs and the Nine Figures are related in turn with the Thirteen Numbers or Birds, with four plants and four trees and other ritual emblems and artifacts. Inherent in the whole pattern, as in sandpaintings, is a complex logic of opposition and interchange. Just as the four plants at the diagonals grow out from the centre, with maize upper right as in the sandpaintings, so life-blood flows into it from the four parts of human anatomy (Tezcatlipoca's?) placed to their right, head and hand at the top, club-foot and ribs below.

The opposition most fixed, spatially, is in fact between the top and the bottom of the page, between the sun rising over the pyramid in the east, above the Year-Lord's head, and a crescent moon facing it over the platform in the west, this being the normal arrangement of religious architecture in Mesoamerica. In harmony with this arrangement are the two pairs of the Nine Figures at east and west (Obsidian 2nd, and Royal Lord 3rd; Jade Skirt 6th, and Lust-Goddess 7th) who complement each other sexually, while those to the sides do not, being all male. False analogies with Old World cosmology have caused this page to be described as a 'Maltese Cross' representing the 'four world quarters' or the 'points of the compass'. Rather, the place allotted to Tlaloc between east and west

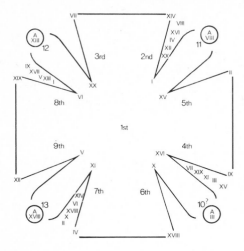

is his place *above*, in 'heaven's heart', just as the Dead Land Lord opposite, between west and east, has his place *below*. The emblem from which the tree between Tlaloc and his partner Hill Heart grows is a bowl, like that shown to Black Elk, with the sky reflected in it, while that opposite, between Dead Land Lord and Maize-God, is the sign Ground positioned to show a deep hole. The unbroken path round the whole design is, then, that of the shaman on his trance journey. Moreover, if we look closely we see that east and west are not simply two of a set of four but have priority. They are continuous with the central area, in a way that the upper and lower regions are not. East and west are shown to be the two basic terms of the unceasing movement of time through the Numbers and Signs of the Sacred Round, and through the four Year-Bearers, two at each horizon.

Fejérváry screenfold, p. 1

IV.6 *An early Olmec calendar date, 31 BC*

From the Gulf Coast site known as Tres Zapotes, this fragment of a stela records a calendar date by means of place-value notation: each element in the vertical scale has its exactly defined position. As in the sexagesimal system of Babylon, and in the Inca and our own decimal systems, quantities are denoted not just by numbers of units (bar for five, dot for one with absence as zero), but by their position in a scale of multiples. In the vigesimal scale of Mesoamerica used here we have (or can reconstruct) the following figures, reading from the top: [7].16.6.16.18. Counting in days from the start of the Maya (or Classic) Era, 10 August 3113 BC, we arrive at the date recorded in the glyph below: 6 Flower(?), which may be correlated with a day in the year 31 BC. As such it is contemporaneous with other dates and carvings of the culture known as Olmec, which stretched from the Gulf Coast to the Pacific coast of Guatemala, and whose most striking artifacts are the colossal six-foot-high heads, chiselled from imported basalt, found at La Venta. The mask beside the uppermost number, 16, has Olmec features. The regularity given by the place-value notation on early fragments such as this was essential to the development of Maya hieroglyphic writing.

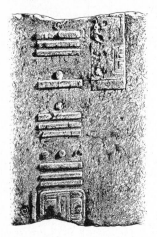

Stela 'C', Tres Zapotes

IV.7 *Maya Era inscriptions on commemorative stelae, AD 692 and 736*

In all the major cities of the Classic Maya period, finely carved stelae were erected to honour rulers and to record important public events: royal births, marriages and deaths; alliances and victories; and astronomical phenomena. Most of these stelae begin their announcements by specifying the date in question in the Maya Era. That we must expect to count days from the start of that Era is made clear by a special opening glyph, which can be seen in both examples here, and in the Palenque panel (cf. *III.14*). These Maya Era calculations have a characteristic grandeur of their own: satisfaction is taken just as much in being able to record time so precisely, in days, weeks, nights, moons and yet other cycles, as in noting the events themselves. Indeed, stelae were frequently erected just to commemorate the passing of certain periods of time, particularly the *katun* (a practice which produced the 'Katun Round' calendar of post-Classic Yucatan: cf. *IV.8*).

1
2
3
4
5
6

A   B

Left

Stela 'C', Tila

A1–B2 Maya Era Glyph

A3	9 *baktuns* (400 *tuns*)	}
B3	13 *katuns* (20 *tuns*)	1,389,600 days
A4	0 *tuns* (360 days)	from 4 Ahau
B4	0 *uinals* (20 days)	8 Cumku,
A5	0 *kins* (days or suns)	= *c.* AD 692

B5   8 Ahau (Sacred Round sign XX)

A6   8 Uo (second week)

A   B

1
2
3
4
5

Right

Stela 'D', Copan

A1   Maya Era glyph

B1	9 *baktuns*	}
A2	15 *katuns*	1,405,800 days
B2	5 *tuns*	from 4 Ahau
A3	0 *uinals*	8 Cumku
B3	0 *kins*	= *c.* AD 736

A4   10 Ahau (XX)

B4   4th of Nine Figures
       (night count)

A5   8 Ch'en (ninth week)

If this calendrical devotion is evident in the first example here, from the city of Tila near Palenque, it is even more so in the second, from Copan near the eastern frontier of the Maya. The normal 'bar and dot' numbers and the signs for quantities of days on the Tila stela are quite transmuted in the Copan stela, the better to celebrate the achievement of the calendar itself. For what appears to be a double column of exquisite cameos on the Copan stela can be clearly *read*, as a Maya Era inscription. The quantities of days are shown as fauna: loads or weights borne by their numerical co-efficients, who are human beings (their value is given by details of their persons: cheek dots and beard = 9; fleshless lower jaw = 10; '*tun*' head-dress = 5 etc., see Table 2b). The Number and Sign of the day arrived at – 10 XX – are shown as characters too (A4), as is the member of the Nine Figures (4th, B4) who carries the night, represented here by a rolled up jaguar skin whose spots are shown as stars. As enriched forms, the glyphs used here express the underlying concepts of the Maya calendar and what may be called their philosophy of time: the inescapable duty of man, regardless of status, is to support the entities of time and, using the native tumpline or other means, to bear them as a burden essential to existence.

IV.8 *Hieroglyphic text for Katun 9 Ahau (AD 1539)*

Deteriorated as it is, the Paris screenfold is unique in showing how the Maya calendar survived in post-Classic times. This page is from a series of thirteen pages which are dedicated to the period of 13 *katuns* (about $256\frac{1}{4}$ years), known as the 'Katun Round'. With the economic 'collapse' of the cities of the Classic period, after which no more 'Maya Era' stelae were erected, the Maya of Yucatan grouped themselves into a federation of towns, between which power rotated according to the *katuns* of the 'Katun Round'. (This dating system simply named each *katun* after its terminal day sign which, since the 7,200 days of the *katun* are divisible by 20, was always Ahau (XX in the Twenty Signs), the sequence of numerical co-efficients being: 11, 9, 7, 5, 3, 1, 12, 10, 8, 6, 4, 2, 13 Ahau). As the Spanish missionary Avedaño reported in 1697: 'These ages [*katuns*] are thirteen in number; each age has its separate idol and its priest, with a separate prophecy of its events. These thirteen ages correspond to the thirteen parts into which this kingdom of Yucatan is divided.'

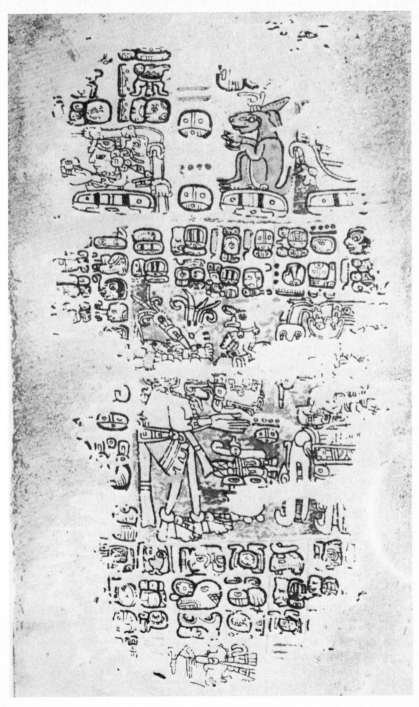

Paris screenfold

This description helps us to understand the basic structure of the pages in the Paris Katun Round series, even if the glyphs themselves are largely illegible. Leaving out the upper third of the page (which deals with sequences of 20 *tuns*), we detect three blocks of paragraphs: to the left, above, and below the main picture, which is of a ceremonial offering to a seated figure (right), and in which the *katun* ending date is given: '9 Ahau', 1323. This paragraph division matches Avedaño's description and corresponds also with that of the later alphabetic transcriptions of hieroglyphic Katun Round texts in the Chilam Balam books: first, the place and the ruler of the *katun*; then its general qualities, and last, its specific events. By means of the Katun Round texts, the Maya left an account, which is only now being deciphered, of what might be called their 'speculative history': an elaborate interweaving of forecast with the historical facts of their daily lives.

IV.9 *Alphabetic text for Katun 13 Ahau (AD 1539)*

The backbone of the Community Books from Chumayel and other Yucatecan towns, written in the Roman alphabet in the post-Columbian period, may properly be said to be the texts of the Katun Round, which carry on the tradition of hieroglyphic *katun* texts like those in the Paris screenfold. The Katun 13 Ahau of 1283 came not long after the Itza invasion of northern Yucatan while that of 1539 marked the Spanish invasion; a whole cycle on again this date was associated with the resistance which led to the Caste War begun in 1847, when the Maya drove foreigners out of much of their territory.

Unluckily, the Katun texts which have survived remain partly impenetrable to us. We are confronted by the names of historical and deity figures about whom little is known (Ixma Chucbeni; Yaxaal) and by a highly sophisticated Maya rhetoric in which historical experience is collated with forecasts for the future. Yet we may discern a division in this text into three paragraphs, as in the hieroglyphic example. This first deals with the town in which the *katun* commemorated by a stela is 'set up' (here, Kinchil Coba), with its ruler and its president or 'face' (Itzamna), and with the elaborate interweaving of the *katun's* influence backwards and forwards in time, from 2 Ahau before it to 11 and even 9 Ahau after it. The second paragraph treats of its 'food' or general qualities.

The third recounts its political 'charge', in terms of the relationships between official governors: the supreme authority or real man (Halach Uinic), his local agents (Batab), the priests (Ah Kin) and the military (Nacom), as well as his advisers the prophets or planners (Ah Bobat) and the scholars (Ah Naat). In this third paragraph there are allusions to particular events and personages. Though their significance is lost to us we can readily appreciate the highly wrought rhetoric of the text, which – like the 'Mankind's ideal course' passage (*II.2*) in the Chumayel – aims to keep alive the calendrical core of the Maya tradition.

Katun 2 Ahau ends so that Katun 13 Ahau may be set up. Katun 13 Ahau ends in the sixth *tun* of Katun 9 Ahau: it will keep company with 11 Ahau in the Katun Round. This is its word. Kinchil Coba is the seat of Katun 13 Ahau; and Mayapan. Itzamna, Itzam tzab is its face during its reign.

The ramon nut will be its food. For five *tuns* nuts and fruits will fall from the ramon tree. Three *tuns* will be locust *tuns*, ten generations of them. Bread and water will be unobtainable. The fan shall be displayed, the bouquet shall be displayed, held by Yaxaal Chac in the heavens; Ixma Chucbeni shall arrive to eat sun and moon.

The charge of the katun is doubly heavy. The Batab, impotent and lost, the Ah Kin, impotent and lost, because of Ixma Chucbeni. Perdition of the Halach Uinic, of the Ah Bobat and the Ah Naat; drunkenness of the Ah Bobat and the Ah Kin, because of Ix Dziban Yol Nicte. Derangement through lewdness and adultery begins with the Batab, who are corrupt at the start of the reign of Ah Bacocol, who wants devotion and reverence only for himself; the Halach Uinic are scorned in the communities, in the bush and rocky places, by the offspring of the lewd and the perverse, those who despise their elders and forget their maker, the sons of Ah Bacocol. The bread of this katun is not whole because its people are also under Ah Bolon Yocte, those of the two-day mat, the two-day throne, the motherless and the fatherless, the offspring of mad and lewd schemers. The face of the sun and of the moon will be eaten and Balam, the Jaguar, will speak and Ceh, the Deer, will speak, and suffer the stick with groans and make payment to the world by their sudden deaths and their pointless deaths. The charge of sudden and violent deaths will not be over when the great hunger has ceased. This is what the charge of Katun 13 Ahau brings.

Chilam Balam Books

V Cosmogony and the birth of man

How the universe was formed and where we come from are questions which have not received final answers, though theories that fail to conform with what is currently accepted as 'scientific' knowledge tend to be dismissed as mythical. Most American accounts of the creation were composed, like the biblical Genesis, from the particular point of view of a tribe or locality. This is true, for example, of such sixteenth-century texts as the so-called 'Bible of America', the *Popol vuh* or Book of Counsel of the Quiche Maya, neighbours of the Cakchiquel in highland Guatemala; the Aztec Legend of the Suns; and the fourteenth-century epic of Quetzal-coatl in the Vienna screenfold of the Mixtecs. Yet, again like the Bible, these and other fundamental texts also draw on a larger body of beliefs about man and his place in the universe. Characteristic of these beliefs in the New World are the need above all for temporal definitions, the notion of successive creations or 'world ages', and a philosophical emphasis on the 'conception' and birth of man.

World and time

Nowhere in American cosmologies do we find the world considered independently of time. In other words, notions of static space and matter, as posited in the Ptolemaic co-ordinates of sky and earth, and as discussed philosophically from Euclid to Newton and Kant, find no place in New World descriptions of cosmic reality. While temporal accounts of the world exist in abundance, no systematic plans or charts of it are known from pre-Columbian times. Moreover, the contemporary world does not exist somehow detached from the remote and scarcely imaginable 'beginning of time', but as one of a *series* of creations, whose beginnings and endings are the matter of prime concern.

The belief in a succession of world ages, traces of which survive in the Old World in Hesiod's *Works and Days*, Ovid's *Metamorphoses* and the Bible itself, is a norm in pre-Columbian America. The details of what these ages were like and how they ended vary or are incomplete in this or that part of the continent; but we may detect a common sequence of events. The Quechua, the Maya, the Toltecs and the peoples of the Southwest have or had in common a cosmogony of four world ages, the present being the most recent (and sometimes separated off as a fifth). About the first two ages there is striking agreement, down to points of detail. They ended respectively in a flood and in prolonged solar eclipse, both catastrophes being directly or indirectly the result of malfunction in the sky or upper regions. The two (or three) subsequent ages are theatres for struggles between forces more terrestrial in nature; for example, the 'hail of fire' in which the third age ends often emerges from a volcano into which a god has transformed himself. Also, these struggles prepare the way for the creation of contemporary man.

The literatures of Mesoamerica, in native and in European script, reveal the huge importance attached to this version of world history. In the Toltec tradition, major rituals were designed to ward off the catastrophes of the past, which were named and identified in the calendar. The Maya went further, using their calendar for astronomical research and positing resonances between the rhythms of celestial and terrestrial life millions of days forwards and backwards from the start of their Era. The celestial bodies with whom they were most concerned, Venus and the sun, have exact counterparts in Toltec ritual, in the figures of Quetzalcoatl and Royal Lord.

Quetzalcoatl, the 'Precious Twin', resists summary description, because of the variety of roles he plays as a god and because of his connection with the earthly ruler of the Toltec capital Tula. But all accounts agree on his celestial identity as Venus; and one exquisite version of his last days at Tula (*V.2*, below) tells how the heart of the earthly Quetzalcoatl was transformed into that planet, the brightest body by far in the sky after sun and moon. Unique as the Evening and the Morning star, Venus appears on both the western and the eastern horizons, and disappears while moving from one to the other and back again, at inferior and superior conjunction, taking about 584 days for the synodic cycle as a whole. On 'journeying' from west to east over eight days at inferior conjunction, the planet was believed to pass through the underworld (*mictlan* or Dead Land in Nahua), where it, or he, faced humiliation and suffering. After this, he rises in the east, just before sunrise, heliacally. This capacity to reappear as herald of the sun (which the full moon does not have) distinguished him as a victor over death, with a resilience over time (the 'ewige Wiederkunft') through which catastrophe could be averted. Personified as Quetzalcoatl, with his Wind mask, Venus held the sky separate from the water, against the forces of Tlaloc who obliterated the horizon, the line between day and night, and tended towards the primeval unity of sky and sea (the *teoatl* or cosmic ocean). The Vienna screenfold shows him actually lifting the sky out of the sea, in answer to the Flood in which the first world age ended. In South America a similar role to Quetzalcoatl's is played by Bochica, who drained Cundinamarca and made it fit for the Chibcha to inhabit; also, petroglyphic inscriptions record the Flood by marking the height from which the waters sank.

Since he suffered in the underworld, Venus avenges himself on re-emerging in the east: with the shafts of his heliacal light he wounds the 'sources of water' as well as victims among mankind. As the victim turned aggressor, he combines the qualities of the Toltec Year-Bearers of the eastern horizon: Rabbit (VIII) the planet-wanderer, and Reed (XIII) the deadly arrow of his rays. In the Maya Twenty Signs, the equivalent of the Toltec Rabbit is in fact Venus (VIII, 'lamat'); and in the Walam Olum and the Midewiwin tradition generally it is the Great Rabbit or Hare (Michabo,

Above
Fig. 9. Manabozho/Nanabush in: (*left*) Ojibwa Mide chant: (*right*) the Walam Olum.

Right
Fig. 10. Venus as Rabbit: Maya sign VIII, Lamat (after Dresden screenfold); and emerging from earth (after Borgia screenfold).

150

Manabozho) who combats the Flood which ended the first world age and who pierces with arrows the victims of shamanist spells.

The resilience of Venus during his passage through the underworld made him exemplary for the shaman's trance journey, for the numbering and timing of ritual (Nine Nights, eight days – see p. 88), and for the calendar proper of the Toltec and the Maya, as the basis of the night count. The Toltec and the Maya also matched the whole synodic cycle of Venus with the solar year so that, in accord with the shaman's distinction between 'courses' of time, immediate or entranced, the *days* which it takes the planet to emerge in the east could be correlated, via number (8), with the *years* it takes it to get back into step with the sun ($8 \times 365 = 5 \times 584 = 2,920$ days). The Maya went on to compile tables to allow for the minutest deviations from this equation which build up over centuries.

In addition to this, the movement of Venus, and of the sun, were correlated with those of the moon, notably by the Maya, in order to predict the phenomenon with which the second world age ended: eclipse. Whenever the sun was 'afflicted' by darkness and faltered in its course of light, the memory of that catastrophe was awakened, most readily among the tropical peoples, for whom total eclipse is a more frequent experience. The very stars, it was feared, would again monstrously emerge from the darkened day-sky to descend and devour mankind, to tear at their flesh with the relentless teeth and claws of jaguars. While the Toltecs and others 'cured' this affliction mainly by shamanistic means (cf. *III.8*), the Maya, with their superior calendar, devoted their finest astronomy to working out the nodes at which eclipses could occur. Again, the object was to ensure the continuity of the world in time, without which its space and matter, and the 'firmament' itself, counted for nothing.

Birth of man

In the scheme of world ages, the creation of contemporary man usually involves his being distinguished from the inferior or redundant races which preceded him. Assuming a direct interest in his birth and welfare, creator heroes like the Feather Snake Quetzalcoatl meditate at length, either alone or in the company of fellow gods, in order not to repeat the mistakes of the past. Their efforts may involve struggles with rival Luciferan and other counter-heroes, the details of which vary considerably from culture to culture. In any case, whether part of a world-age scheme or not, the birth of contemporary man is presented as a climactic event, the triumph of the 'engenderers and shapers' among the gods, and of man's own capacity to fix his image in time.

In order to confirm a claim to territory and other rights, the first men of this creation are often born within the locality lived in by the authors of the account in question, and sometimes they emerge literally from a hole in the ground (the 'mundus' of the Etruscans and the Romans). Or they may bear the names of the 'founders of the tribe', as the ultimate guarantors of lineage and genealogical history. Differing in this way, their nature and constitution may also keenly reflect local cultural priorities. The mentions of modern man's superiority over apes and other near-humans (in the genesis of the Aztec, the Maya, the Quechua, and even the distant Iroquois), or of the hunter-warriors of the fourth world age as his immediate predecessors (Quiche-Maya, Quechua), or of the substance from which he is formed, have different connotations in each case. The inscriptions at Palenque, the *Popol vuh*, and the Navajo Emergence Way, alike follow the widespread doctrine that modern man is a rooted creature, dedicated to a maize economy because created from that plant. However, within this tradition the Aztecs, for example, consciously require that man's flesh have as an ingredient the penitential blood first drawn by Quetzalcoatl, a symbol of man's need himself to perform blood sacrifice in order to sustain the flow of time and his own place in it.

Similarities with the biblical Genesis

Taken in isolation, many of the creation stories written down in America after contact with the Old World appear to reflect the teaching of Christian missionaries. To take some examples: the lines about man's creation from mud or clay in the Book of Chumayel (*V.14*) seem to follow the verses of Genesis which relate God's creation of Adam; but then we see the notion occurring again in the *Popol vuh* (*V.6*), and even among the Iroquois, where moreover woman is made simultaneously with man and not from a 'spare rib' (*V.12*). The close association between an evil snake and human mortality encountered in the Walam Olum closely resembles the Fall of Man in the Garden of Eden; however, this motif is found in the very heart of Mesoamerican ritual in V (Snake) and VI (Death) of the Twenty Signs, whose sequence is paralleled in other instances in the Algonkin text (cf. *V.11*). As for the Flood of the Guarani, it looks like Noah's: yet, as we have seen, it should sooner be placed in the American scheme of successive world ages.

Again, the references to the differentiation of languages in David Cusick's history of the League of the Iroquois (1825; cf. *V.12*) will bring to mind the Tower of Babel; yet we find exactly the same references in the *Popol vuh*. Before attributing such similarities to the *influence* of the Bible we should carefully compare American texts with each other, and with their pre-Columbian models. Comparisons of this kind normally make it seem more reasonable to view the Bible as the expression of beliefs common to humanity which developed in their own way in the New World. This point has not been lost on the American authors themselves who deal with cosmogony, having some knowledge of the Bible. The Huarochiri Narrative (*V.8*), for example, ingeniously integrates biblical teaching into the prior scheme of world ages: the Flood is *expressly* compared to Noah's, just as the Eclipse is said 'probably' to be the darkness at noon which marked Christ's death. In this respect, the most outstanding example is the genesis story told in the Book of Chumayel, in which the Bible is tested step for step against an understanding of origins inherited from the Maya Classic period. This particular narrative or poem about cosmos and man embodies what can only be called a philosophy of origins and of time.

V.1 *The present and past ages of the world*

Known as the 'Sun Stone' or the 'Calendar Stone' of the Aztecs, this famous low-relief carving, over 13 feet in diameter, once served as an altar for the blood sacrifices performed by the priests of Tenochtitlan. The designs on its surface recall that such sacrifices were meant to sustain the sun on his daily course. At the centre, in 'heaven's heart' surrounded by an unbroken ring of the Twenty Signs, we see the face of Royal Lord, the sun; to either side he clutches human hearts in his claw-like hands. Around the periphery are wound two snakes from whose segmented bodies blood-like flames gush into the sky, with its eight alternating solar emblems. That this is a flow of temporal energy is confirmed by the identity of the faces which emerge from the snakes' maws (bottom): Xiuhtecuhtli, Year- or Fire-Lord (left) and, again, Royal Lord (right), the 1st and 3rd of the Nine Figures. Their tongues are sacrificial Flint knives. Sustained by blood, the sun is better able to prolong the present world age. The calendar name of this age, in the Aztec tradition, is given in the sign around the central face of the Sun: 4 Movement (XVII), or earthquake, this being the

153

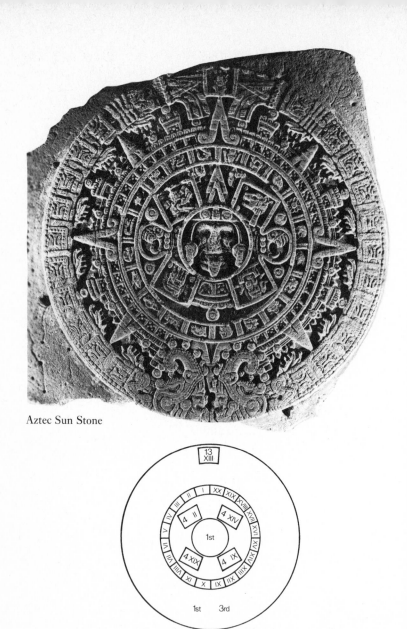

Aztec Sun Stone

catastrophe to which it is doomed. The sign Movement incorporates the dates of the four previous ages which are recorded in the year boxes which ingeniously make up its limbs, and show five ages in four. On the right, reading up, come: 4 Water (IX), the age of the Flood, when men metamorphosed into fish; and 4 Jaguar (XIV), which ended in Eclipse and when jaguars ate mankind. Then on the left, also reading up, come 4 Rain (XIX) with its Hail of Fire; and 4 Wind (II), when men turned into apes during a Hurricane. These fates, recorded in part beside the calendar dates, are recounted more fully in the Legend of the Suns (part of the sixteenth-century Nahua manuscript known as the History of the Kingdoms), in which Quetzalcoatl plays a major role in creating the men of this age (cf. *V.3*). At the top of the disk, in the year box between the tails of the snakes, there is a further date, 13 Reed (XIII). This was acknowledged as the year on which Quetzalcoatl created modern man, many Calendar Rounds ago. It is also probably the year in which the stone was carved, 1479, in the reign of the emperor Axayacatl, at the height of Aztec imperial expansion.

V.2 *Quetzalcoatl burns himself and becomes Venus*

In the saga of the earthly Quetzalcoatl, this hero is driven from power in Tula by the warlike Tezcatlipoca (cf. p. 134). Foreseeing his death, he abandons his subjects and all he has given them – the whole wealth of the place. The endings of the story vary considerably, however. He is said: to have journeyed eastwards overland to Xicalanco; to have sailed over the sea on a raft of interwoven snakes; or to have burned himself and become the planet Venus. This last version is found in Nahua, in the History of the Kingdoms of Colhuacan and Mexico, which opens with a version of the cosmogonal 'Legend of the Suns'. After his defeat and humiliation at the hands of Tezcatlipoca, he again becomes a power through the act of self-immolation at the place of the 'Black and the Red'. The riches he gave to Tula ('jade, turquoise, gold, silver, red- and whiteshell, plumes of quetzal, cotinga, roseate spoonbill, oropendola, trogon and blue heron') reappear around him in the sky, embers that are scintillating bird plumage. His heart burns to incandescence and becomes the planet Venus. This version, quoted here, relies most on Toltec ritual and cosmogony. Of course the authors of the text were quite aware that Venus existed before Tula did: rather the apotheosis of the earthly Quetzalcoatl endows him with the qualities of cosmic resilience proper to the planet in its long synodic cycle through west and east. For after entering the sky and then descending in the west, he disappears for four plus four days, on his way down to and up from the Dead Land, where he suffers trials and humiliation. This experience qualifies him not just as the rival of Tlaloc and his Flood but as man's creator, from whom he exacts payment for his pains. According to the calendar sign of the day of his heliacal rising in the east, he wounds with his shafts of light, Rain and Water, the old and young, the mighty and children.

Then he said to his heralds:
'Before we go, on every side conceal and bury what we have made here, joy and wealth, the whole of our possession.' And his heralds did so. They hid everything there, in the place where Quetzalcoatl bathed, which was called Atecpan, Water Palace, Amochco, Tin Place. And Quetzalcoatl left. He stood up, summoned his heralds and wept over them.

They then set off searching for the place of the Black and the Red, the place of Incineration. And they travelled and wandered far, nowhere pleased them.

When they reached the place they were searching for, now again there he wept and suffered. In this year 1 Reed (so it is told, so it is said), when he had reached the ocean shore, the edge of the sky-water, he stood up, wept, took his attire, and put on his plumes, his precious mask. When he was dressed, of his own accord he burnt himself, he gave himself to the fire. So that where Quetzalcoatl burnt himself is called the place of Incineration.

And it is said that when he burned, his ashes rose up and every kind of precious bird appeared and could be seen rising up to the sky: roseate spoonbill, cotinga, trogon, blue heron, yellow-headed parrot, macaw, white-fronted parrot, and all other precious birds. And after he had become ash the quetzal bird's heart rose up; it could be seen and was known to enter the sky. The old men would say he had become Venus; and it is told that when the star appeared Quetzalcoatl died. From now on he was called the Lord of the Dawn.

Only for four days he did not appear, so it is told, and dwelt in Dead Land. And for another four days he sharpened himself. After eight days the great star appeared called Quetzalcoatl on his ruler's throne. And they knew, on his rising, which people, according to Sign, he penetrates, shoots into and loathes.

History of the Kingdoms, §§ 141–54

156

V.3 *Quetzalcoatl brings bones from Dead Land and makes man*

In the Toltec and the Aztec tradition, Quetzalcoatl struggled with the Dead Land Lord, during his journey through the underworld, to obtain the substance with which men of this world age were created: bones, said to be his father's. Among the gods of Sky and Earth, Quetzalcoatl is the one ready to move down and back, like Venus, self-sacrificially. Here, identified by a set of epithets or aspects of himself, he discusses the creation of man with the pair of goddesses Star Skirt and Milky Way, a feminine 'mesh' through which he moves as a planet. As for the 'story' itself (also from the History of the Kingdoms), it has certain oral qualities: the rather heavy ironies in the exchanges between Quetzalcoatl and his *nahual* or companion spirit may be found in many a Mexican folk-tale. And the 'labour' of holding on to 'precious bones', at one's peril, is a motif that recurs in the oral traditions of the Araucanians and in folk sources as far removed as *Märchen* of the brothers Grimm. At the same time this version refers to images used in the hieratic screenfolds, notably the watery 'jade circle' vulnerable to the Wind music of his conch (cf. *V.4*), Venus's equivalent of the solar or Royal Lord's trumpet. And the Dead Land Lord is the 5th of the Nine Figures just as the Quails who try to prevent Quetzalcoatl's emerging from Dead Land, Mictlan, are number 4 of the Thirteen Birds. When Quetzalcoatl does emerge, the bones are ground up by Quilatzli, the 'Snake Woman' Earth figure, who earlier is said to have given birth to Quetzalcoatl over the four days of his emergence from the underworld. The preparation of man's substance strongly recalls the grinding up of the maize in the Maya creation story in the *Popol vuh*, where Quilatzli's role is played by the grandmother Oxomoco (cf. *V.6*); and elsewhere in the Toltec tradition perfect man is said to be made of maize. However, while for the Maya maize and water were 'enough' to make man, as they took care to emphasize, the Aztecs here require bone-meal enhanced by penitential blood, only later to be fortified by maize (white, black yellow and red) from the 'Food Mountain'. The creation story in the Maya Book of the Cakchiquel stands midway between these two versions: there, men of the present age need penitential blood but are made of maize, not bone-meal. The riddles in the Books of Chumayel and Tusik (used in civil service examinations under the *katun* system of government in Yucatan) show us further that the bones sought and carried up by Quetzalcoatl were also thought of as vegetal, like maize. In those riddles the buried parental bones are said to be manioc roots; Quetzalcoatl's red penitential blood is thus also the fire-heat needed to rid that vegetable of its volatile poison and make it fit for man's flesh.

> And thereupon the gods conferred and said:
> 'Who now shall be alive?
> Heaven is founded, earth is founded,
> who now shall be alive, oh gods?'
> They were sorrowful:
> Star Skirt and Milky Way,
> and (with them) the Bridger, the Emerger,
> the Earth-firmer, the Tiller;
> Quetzalcoatl whom we serve.

And then Quetzalcoatl goes to Mictlan, the Dead Land.
He approached the Lord and Lady of Mictlan and said:
'What I have come for is the precious bones which you possess;
I have come to fetch them.'
And he was asked:
'What do you want to do with them, Quetzalcoatl?'
And he answered:
'What worries the gods is who shall live on earth.'
And the Lord of Mictlan then said:
'All right. Blow this conch and carry the bones four times round my jade circle'.
But the conch is totally blocked up.
Quetzalcoatl summons the worms, they hollow it out.
The large and the small bees force their way through.
He blows it; the sound reaches the Lord of Mictlan.

And the Lord of Mictlan next said to him:
'All right, take them.'
But to his vassals, the Micteca, he said:
'Tell him, oh gods, he should leave them here.'
But Quetzalcoatl answered:
'No; I'm taking them with me.'
And then his nahual said to him:
'Just tell them: "I've left them here." '
And so he said, he shouted to them:
'I have left them here.'
But then he really went back up, clutching the precious bones,
male bones on one side, female on the other.

He took them and wrapped them up, and took them with him.
And the Lord of Mictlan again spoke to his vassals:
'Oh gods, is Quetzalcoatl really taking the bones? Dig him a pit.'
They dug him one; he stumbled and fell in.
And Quails menaced him and he fainted.
He dropped the precious bones and the Quails tore and pecked at
   them.
And then Quetzalcoatl came to and weeps and says to his nahual:
'Oh my nahual, what now?'
And the reply came:
'What now? Things went badly; let it be.'

And then he gathered the bits, took them and wrapped them in a
   bundle
which he took to Tamoanchan.
When he had brought it there it was ground up by the
woman named Quilaztli, that is, Cihuacohuatl.
Then she placed the meal in a jade bowl and Quetzalcoatl dropped
   blood on it by piercing his member.
Then all the gods named here did penance like
the Bridger, the Tiller
the Emerger, the Earth-firmer,
the Plunger, the Shooter:
Quetzalcoatl.
And they said:
'The servants of the gods are born'. For indeed they did penance
   for us.
Then they said:
'What shall they eat? The gods must find food'.
And the ant fetched
the maize kernels from the heart of the Food Mountain.

History of the Kingdoms, §§ 1417–1440

V.4 *Quetzalcoatl appears as Venus and lifts up the sky*

In this passage from the Vienna screenfold (reading right to left),
Quetzalcoatl is first seen (top) sitting naked above the sky-band in
heaven's heart, where he ascended after his self-incineration.
Guarded by two elders, he is surrounded by the attire proper to him
as a god (for which a Toltec definition is 'the well-dressed one'):
round hat, Wind-mask, old-man chin piece, plume head-dress with

eyes, feather-fringed shirt and other objects like weapons and his conch. Above him are the four palaces he is said to have built in Tula, of turquoise beams, redshell, whiteshell and precious feathers. When he emerges later in the same year, 6 Rabbit (VIII), on the down-tufted rope or umbilicus hanging in the (western) sky, he is in full regalia; identified as '9-Wind', he has a moon-bearer to the left and a sun-bearer to the right. At the base of the column he holds the spears and spear-thrower characteristic of him as Venus, particularly at the moment of his heliacal rising in the east. The general appearance of this planet was similarly described elsewhere in North America; in his vision, Black Elk reported: 'two men were

Vienna screenfold, pp. 48–47

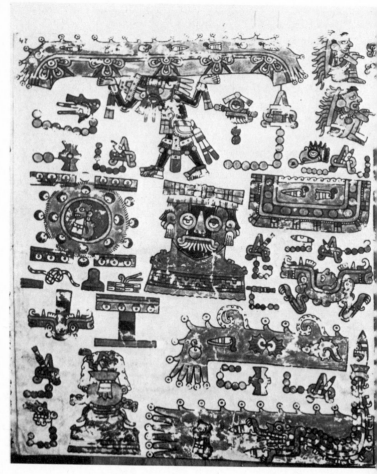

coming from the east, head first like arrows flying, and between them rose the day-break star'.

Formally, this celestial birth of Quetzalcoatl is inserted into the boustrophedon narrative as a special event. The Quetzalcoatl of the sky is thus neatly conjoined with the earthly one who, two pages previously, was shown being born from a Flint on the date 9 Wind in the year 10 House (III). The figures in the next column who welcome him as Venus include Oxomoco and her husband (cf. *IV.2*), and a jade and a gold Xolotl (cf. *III.12*). He then goes on to perform the epic feat of lifting up the sky, so that the water runs off, on the date 2 Rain in the year 10 House. Below him is his opponent

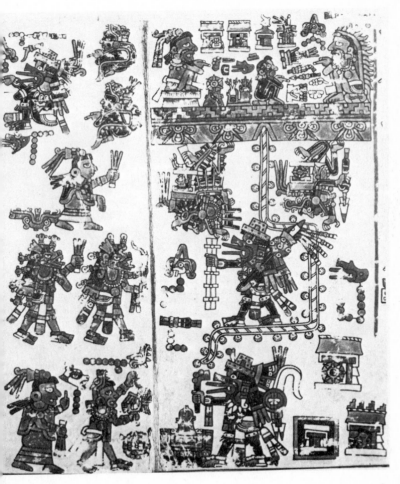

Tlaloc, the deity responsible for the Flood shown at the bottom of the page (the water-monster armed with Flints also appears in the Flood depicted in the Walam Olum). The episodes referred to here form part of the long prelude to the first Fire-Drilling ritual in the first chapter of the Vienna, which also deals with Quetzalcoatl's prowess as the creator of the Mixtecs who adopted Toltec religion.

V.5 *Quetzalcoatl supervises the birth of the Mixtecs from Apoala*

According to the Vienna screenfold, having raised up the sky (in the year 10 House), Quetzalcoatl, the first 'Fire-Driller' (cf. *III.12* and *V.4*) turned his attention to inaugurating the Mixtec tribe, the

Vienna screenfold, pp. 38–37

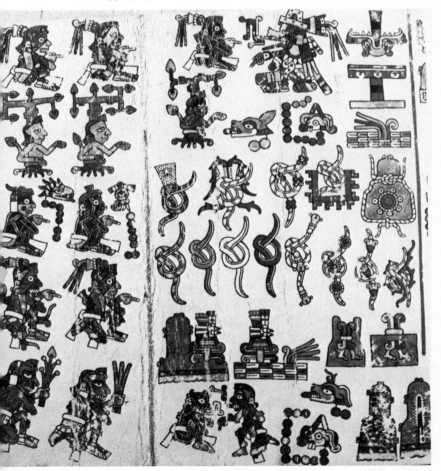

authors of that ritual document. Facing him here, on the day 2 Deer in the year 13 Rabbit, are the sons of earlier creations (right centre), who in part resemble those mentioned in the *Popol vuh* (*V.6*) and in Algonkin texts. Having heard Quetzalcoatl's orders, two of them, 7-Rain and 7-Eagle, assist with the birth of the Mixtec nobility, who emerge from the 'cleft' in Apoala, both a tree-plant and a woman. To the right she bears three 'male' arrows, and to the left circular snake-earth markings. Topographically, the place-sign derived from this image, which appears in most of the Mixtec screenfolds, refers to Apoala (a place in Mixteca Alta, west of Oaxaca). The list of the first founding fathers of the tribe beginning in the left-hand column goes on for several pages and includes political rulers mentioned in the Nuttall and elsewhere. The aristocratic figures reappear by turn in later chapters, as officiators at the Fire-drilling ceremonies to which the Vienna as a whole is dedicated.

V.6 *The four ages of the world and the making of men from maize*

The fullest known American account of the four ages of the world and the birth of man survives in the *Popol vuh* or Book of Counsel of the Quiche Maya, neighbours of the Cakchiquel in highland Guatemala. Though written (in the Roman alphabet) in the interests of a particular clan of the Quiche – a fact which becomes obvious in the closing sections – it is grand enough to deserve the title 'Bible of America'. Before the moment when modern men (the forefathers of the Quiche) were 'invented', we learn at length about the 'four creations' and the 'four humiliations' of the world, i.e. its ages and their endings. The clay men of the first age were too sloppy and 'dissolved in the water'; those of the second were too stiff and perished when 'the face of the earth was darkened'. Before the men of this world age could be made, the forces of the underworld, Xibalba in Quiche, had to be conquered. Setting off by the 'black road' of the west, the magic Twins go to Xibalba to redeem (like Quetzalcoatl: the 'Precious Twin') the buried bones of their father who, travelling the same road from the west, had perished there, 'halfway' to the east. Intuiting as if genetically the traps laid for travellers by the Lords of Xibalba, the magically conceived Twins win their way through to the east; burning themselves (again like Quetzalcoatl) to prove their 'essence', they 'walk into the sky' to serve as Venus-heralds of sun and moon at east and west. Only then does the time come for Gucumatz (Quetzalcoatl in Quiche, rendered as 'Quetzal Serpent' here) to create modern man, from maize, in company with fellow 'shapers and formers'. After immense meditation, white and yellow maize ears are brought out from 'Cleft', a feminine inner-earthly store of such American fruits as mameys, anonas and nances. The kneading of man is done by the Twins' grandmother Xmucane (Oxomoco in Nahua).

Culturally, the *Popol vuh* fuses the indigenous Maya tradition with that brought in by the Nahua-speakers who drove on south from highland Mexico through Mixtec territory to Guatemala long before the Spaniards arrived. Besides presenting the names and epithets of Toltec deities, the text says of itself that it was transcribed from an original in Toltec script (*u tz'ibal Tulan*). Yet it makes no reference to the Toltec calendar, so prominent in the Aztec 'Legend of the Suns' and the Vienna screenfold of the Mixtecs. At the same time, despite firm adherence to the Maya doctrine that man was made from maize and that this world age and its economy are better than previous ones, it does not invoke the Classic Maya calendar either. As for Mesoamerican *ritual*, Toltec and Maya, it is unsurpassed as cosmic exegesis.

And this is the beginning when man was invented,
 And when that which would go into man's
  body was sought.
Then spoke the Bearer,
 And Engenderer,
Who were Former
 And Shaper.
Majesty
 And Quetzal Serpent by name,
'The dawn has already appeared;
 The creation has already been made,
And there is clearly a nourisher appearing,
 A supporter,
Born of light,
 Engendered of light.
Man has already appeared,
 The population of the surface of the earth,' they said.
It was all assembled and came
 And went, their wisdom,

In the darkness,
    In the night time,
As they originated things,
    And dissolved things.
They thought;
    And they meditated there
And thus came their wisdom directly, bright
    And clear.
They found
    And they maintained
What came to be
    Man's body.

In Cleft,
    In Bitter Water by name,
There came then yellow corn ears
    And white corn ears.

And they rejoiced then
    Over the discovery
Of the marvellous mountain,
    Filled
With quantities
    And quantities
Of yellow corn ears,
    And white corn ears,
And also loads of cacao
    And chocolate,
Numberless mameys,
    Custard apples,
Anonas,
    Nances,
Soursops
    And honey.
It was full of the sweetest foods,
    In the town
At Cleft,
    And at Bitter Water by name.
There was food there
    From the fruit of everything:
Small vegetables,
    Big vegetables,

Small plants
    And big plants.
The road was pointed out
    By the animals.
And then the yellow corn was ground
    And the white corn,
And nine bushels
    Were made by Xmucane.
The food came
    With water to create strength,
And it became man's grease
    And turned into his fat
When acted upon by Bearer
    And Engenderer,
Majesty
    And Quetzal Serpent, as they are called.
And so then they put into words the creation,
    The shaping
Of our first mother
    And father.
Only yellow corn
    And white corn were their bodies.
Only food were the legs
    And arms of man.
Those who were our first fathers
    Were the four original men.
Only food at the outset
    Were their bodies.

Popol vuh, lines 4709–38, 4747–50, 4771–4822

V.7 *The dire effects of Venus at heliacal rising*

Unlike the *Popol vuh*, cosmogonical texts found in the Maya hieroglyphic screenfolds and in the Chilam Balam books of Yucatan rely heavily on the Classic Maya calendar. Indeed, creation here is inextricable from calendrics and astronomy. In the Dresden screenfold, shown here, the cosmic hero Venus is described above all in numerical terms. His very name in Yucatec – '*chac ek*', 'big star' – also means red-black: referring to east and west, this pair of colours was added to the white and yellow of maize to make up a basic set of hieroglyphs (cf. p. 189); in addition they have a precise function in Maya mathematics, as we see below. True, as in the Toltec tradition, Venus still appears as a dramatic figure, especially in the illustrations which accompany this hieroglyphic text, exacting payment for his trials in the underworld by spearing victims with his heliacal light. Yet his synodic course is measured with an accuracy which has its own reward and justification; the astronomy here is unrivalled in America for the exactness with which it describes the 'reign of the good stars' and hence the proper 'course of mankind' (to quote the Book of Chumayel: cf. *II.2*). The following notes are intended only as an elementary guide to the technically complex Venus chapter in the Dresden. The first page introduces the Venus table as a whole; the second is the first of the five pages of the table itself, which cover the 2,920 days which it takes for Venus to get back 'in step' with the sun (five synodic periods or eight years).

p. 1 [24], left side
a–b: general statement of the effects of Venus's heliacal risings, on water sources and on different groups of mankind, equivalent to those in the History of the Kingdoms (cf. *V.3*); c: mathematical introduction, in which the table as a whole is positioned in the Maya Era at 9.9.16.0.0. (AD 7th century), several centuries before it was copied in the Dresden. Note the base date of the Maya Era in the corner lower left: 4 Ahau 8 Cumku.

p. 1 [24], right side
the actual calendar dates, all Ahau (XX), used in the table, with corrections to allow for the 5 days which Venus loses on an average of 584 days over 65 synodic periods (104 × 365-day years), plus multiples of 104 years.

p. 2 [46], left side
a: the signs Cib (XVI), Death (VI), Cib (XVI) and Maize (IV), with

thirteen sets of co-efficients, part of the exhaustive list of signs on the five pages of the table, giving all possible dates on which the four stations of Venus occur, starting with east; b–c: the four stations of the planet – 236 days in the east, 90 at superior conjunction (*xaman*), 250 in the west, and 8 at inferior conjunction (*nohol*); numbers in red, lowermost in c. The four stations are named in the hieroglyphs, second line from the bottom (compare the head *xaman*, or zenith, with the 9th of the Maya Nine Figures; the closed hand for west or sunset is generally used in Indian sign language). The sign Venus (VIII) appears – third line up – with the affix 'red'. Other data include the first four of the twenty presiding deities in the table, a running total of days (236, 326, 576, 584; in black lowermost in b), and calendar dates involving the weeks of the Classic calendar relevant to solar eclipse prediction (itself the subject of a yet more complex chapter in this screenfold).

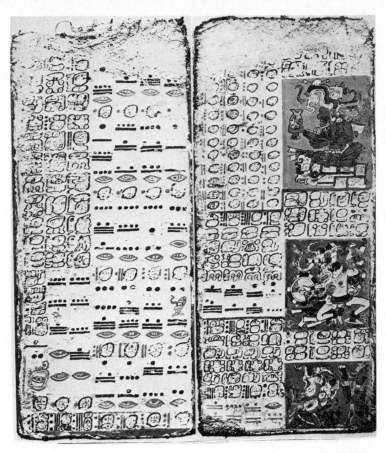

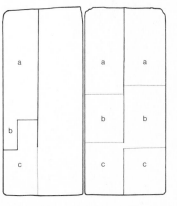

Dresden screenfold, pp. 24, 46

p. 2 [46], right side
a: a lordly onlooker or president,
sitting on a throne with celestial
markings and holding a vase (of post-
Classic design); hieroglyphic caption
largely effaced;
b: Venus at heliacal rising, with his
shield and raised spear-thrower; his
especial victims in this 'year' are 'the
sowers of second maize crops';
c: Venus's victim, a portrait version
of the 4th of the Nine Figures, lies on
his back with a spear stuck in his
bowels.

V.8 *Solar eclipse and domesticity in the second world age*

Brief as it is, this chapter of the Huarochiri Narrative says much about Quechua belief in the ages of the world. In the pattern found throughout the Americas, it is the end of the second of these ages which is marked by the sun's death, or eclipse. In several versions the people who lived during this age and who are called *'uari'* (original, or uncouth) in Guaman Poma's work are set upon not just by the jaguars from the sky but by their domestic utensils and animals as well. The reason for this fate is given in the *Popol vuh* where the people of the second world age meet exactly the same end, except that, reflecting differences in economy, the domestic animals that turn on their masters are not herds of South American llamas but the hunter's Dog and the planter's Turkey of Mesoamerica (see above p. 112). The domestic revolt is explained as revenge for the 'heartless' exploitation (the term also used in the Book of Chumayel) which they have suffered as useful objects. In the succession of catastrophes which end the world ages in the American tradition, Eclipse comes after Flood, both preceding such terrestrial disasters as the 'hail of fire'. This is the order found in the Huarochiri Narrative, which also makes explicit parallels with the Bible: the Flood is said to have been Noah's while Eclipse is associated with the 'darkness at noon' which marked Christ's death. For his part, in his account of the world ages Guaman Poma pays less attention to their catastrophic endings than to the habits of the men who lived during them: *uari viracocha* (original 'white', equated with Adam and Eve), *uari* (original), *purun* (rustic – cf. p. 45 above) and *auca* (warrior). In his drawings the first two ages are distinguished from succeeding ones in being directly subject to celestial forces, emblemized by the sun (to right and left), and by the fact that men then had yet to learn to weave (note the distaff and the clothing in picture 3). The incipient domesticity of the second age is nonetheless clearly signalled by the appearance in the landscape on a 'pucullo', a small house or fixed abode.

> How the sun died.
>
> Long ago the sun is said to have died.
> For five days after its death it was night.
> The stones began to jostle each other;
> the mortars, large and small, began to eat people,
> the pestles too.

The mountain llamas attacked people.
As Christians we account for this today
by saying that it was the eclipse at Jesus Christ's
death. And possibly it was.

Huarochiri Narrative, chapter 4

Guaman Poma, *Nueva corónica*, pp. 48, 53, 57, 63

V.9 *The cave-mouths at 'Dawn-Inn', whence the Inca emerged*

In Guaman Poma's chronicle, the Inca, who were the last race to appear, earn their pre-eminence thanks not just to conquest but also to their social philosophy. After such near-humans as the Anti have been banished to the forests (like the Apes in the Maya tradition), the Inca dynasty is established, along with a more advanced agriculture. Having descended from the sky on an umbilical rope, the first emperor Manco Capac and his *coya* or queen Mama Ocllo, and the aristocratic pairs who accompanied them, emerge from three cave mouths (*tampo tocco*) at a place called Paccari Tampo, Dawn Inn, on the mountain Huanacauri, eighteen miles south-east of Cuzco. Their emergence marked man's entry into the civilized world, and the start of the ten clans or *ayllus* of the state, ruled over of course by them and their descendants. The original pair and their son were identified with the sun (*inti*), moon and Venus, a mark of their divine right to rule. Though anxious not

Guaman Poma, *Nueva corónica*, p. 264

to endorse Inca 'idolatry', Guaman Poma records the essentials of this doctrine. With sun, moon and Venus above them, the three here pay homage to their own origins, in his drawing, at the three-tiered altar of the Paccari Tampo shrine, or *huaca*, in Cuzco. The Sapa Inca has placed his crown on the altar step below the three caves, and he and his son wear royal triple-patterned belts, like that of the Inca Tupac Amaru (cf. *I.11*).

V.10 *How the first world of the Guarani was engendered*

Among the Guarani and other South American peoples inhabiting the vast lowland forests east of the Andes, the world ages are most sharply distinguished as the ante- and post-diluvian, those before and after the Flood. This passage from the Guarani genesis deals with the creation of the first world 'Yvy Tenonde', a time and place of pristine reality (in the Platonic sense), except for the men who inhabited it. The father Ñamandu is reported thinking this first world into existence, without the support of literacy, calendrics or even complex numeracy. Rather he relies on the power of speech alone: creation is the 'Origin of Human Speech' or 'Ayvu Rapyta' as the Guarani genesis chants are called. In the first of the Ayvu Rapyta chants Ñamandu finds a firm place for his feet; in the next, quoted here, he thinks the material world into existence. Out of the darkness he engenders through a process of thought association: speech, love and the chant itself, to arrive at the *logos* or word-soul (*n'eng* in Guarani), the core of existence. Creation is a gradual searching, a fostering, and a developing or unfolding, just as the discourse is cumulative, with its verbs of anticipation (*ra*), consolidation (*ma xy*), and warranty (*ma vy*): things are always forethought before they are brought into being. (This incidentally explains why the biblical Genesis appeared to the Guarani priests to place too violent an emphasis on the single word 'fiat' – cf. p. 62.) As parents for the first race of men Ñamandu invents companions of his spirit, three fellow-creators who matched with their women begin human genealogy, a line or thread like that of speech itself. These three are Karai, the eastern Fire god; Jakaira, god of rising mist and medicine; and Tupa, god of rain and hail (sometimes identified with the Christian God – see p. 49). It is Jakaira who later brings about the next world age after the Flood, consoling its inhabitants, in their imperfection, with tobacco and pipe, and the knowledge of plants, and illuminating them from the east with his soundless lightning.

The true father Ñamandu, the First One,
    from a minimum of his spirit,
    from the knowledge in his spirit,
    having his engendering knowledge,
made the flames, the mists arise.

Having stood,
    from the knowledge in his spirit,
    having his engendering knowledge,
he himself conceived the origin of future speech;
    from the knowledge in his spirit,
    having his engendering knowledge,
our father fostered the origin of speech, made it of his spirit;
    when the earth was not
    in the heart of the eldest darkness
    when knowledge was not,
the true father Ñamandu, the First One,
    fostered the origin of future speech, made it of his spirit.

Having himself conceived the origin of future speech,
    from the knowledge in his spirit,
    having his engendering knowledge,
he himself conceived the origin of future love;
    when the earth was not,
    in the heart of the eldest darkness,
    when knowledge was not,
    having his engendering knowledge,
he himself conceived the origin of future love.

Having fostered the origin of future speech,
having fostered a minimum of love,
    from the knowledge in his spirit,
    having his engendering knowledge,
he fostered the origin of a minimal chant;
    when the earth was not,
    in the heart of the eldest darkness,
    when the knowledge was not,
he himself fostered a minimal chant.

Having himself fostered the origin of future speech,
having himself fostered a minimum of love,
having himself fostered a minimal chant,
    he prospected who
        should share the origin of speech,
        should share the minimum of love,
        should share the thread of the chant;
having prospected,
    from the knowledge in his spirit,
    having his engendering knowledge,
he fostered the future companions of his spirit.

Having prospected,
    from the knowledge in his spirit,
    having his engendering knowledge,
he fostered the big-hearted Ñamandu
he fostered them equally with the brilliance of his knowledge,
    when the earth was not,
    in the heart of the eldest darkness;
he fostered the big-hearted Ñamandu
    as the true fathers of many future sons,
    as the true fathers of the logos of many future sons,
he fostered the big-hearted Ñamandu

In addition,
    from the knowledge in his spirit,
    having his engendering knowledge,
with the true father of the future Karai
with the true father of the future Jakaira
with the true father of the future Tupa
he shared the knowledge of his spirit;
    as the true fathers of many future sons,
        of the logos of many future sons,
he shared with them the knowledge of his spirit.

In addition,
the true father Ñamandu,
to reciprocate his heart,
shared the knowledge of his spirit
with the future true mother Ñamandu;

the true father Karai
    shared the knowledge of his spirit
    to reciprocate his heart
with the future mother Karai.

The true father Jakaira, likewise,
    to reciprocate his heart,
    shared the knowledge of his spirit
with the future mother Jakaira.

The true father Tupa, likewise,
    to reciprocate his heart,
    shared the knowledge of his spirit
with the future mother Tupa.

They having shared in the knowledge of the spirit of the First One
          in the origin of future speech,
          in the origin of love,
          in the thread of the chant,
they joined together in the origin of his engendering knowledge.

    So we call them too
        the excellent true fathers of the logos,
        the excellent true mothers of the logos.

Ayvu Rapyta, chant 2

V.11 *Genesis, according to the Walam Olum*

In the cosmogony of the Algonkin and other heirs to the Mound Builders of the Ohio and Upper Mississippi (Sioux, Iroquoian), creation is chiefly the task of the 'great spirit' called Manito in Algonkin. In the opening stanzas of the Walam Olum (which was composed by Mide shamans in conscious response to biblical teaching), Manito shapes water, land, wind and sky (symbol 4, read anticlockwise from the left), the creatures of the world (13), and the first race of men (18). In this first world 'before the Flood' (24)

Manito acts as a triad of himself (9) and is rivalled by a snake-like evil principle (14, 21). In the following stanzas (not quoted here), this evil monster brings the 'rushing water' of the Flood, combated by the hero 'Great Rabbit', and harmful beasts like those who attacked mankind during the Eclipse of the second world age. Set in the traditional Midewiwin form of four plus four symbols or houses (note the house upended in 15 and properly aligned in 16), these stanzas concord with the ritual cosmogony of Mesoamerica. The Ground supporting Manito (1) is shown to be a Turtle (17 and 24), an 'earth-beast' like I of the Twenty Signs. The Wind which clears off the water (7 – note the two downward strokes) is like the Wind (II), Quetzalcoatl's mask, and is similarly associated with the proper movement of the celestial bodies (6). The shape of the 'first mother' (11) recalls the sign House (III; *calli* in Nahua also means chopsticks, suggested here by the enclosing legs). The plant of 'first abundance' (19) is equivalent to sign IV and even has the timeless half-night, half-day disk above it which accompanies the maize plant in the Toltec screenfolds (see p. 211). Finally, the snake in symbol 21 and the skull in 23 clearly correspond to the pair of signs Snake (V) and Death (VI).

Immediate and there, all water above ground,
land and water in a thick mist, the Great Manito was.
Immediate and forever, unseen and everywhere, the Great Manito
    was,
and shaped water, land, wind, sky:

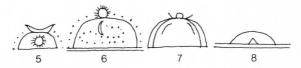

He shaped sun, moon, stars
these he made to move well.
Strong wind blew the water off;
clean, the islands found their place.

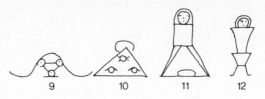

9   10   11   12

The Great Manito, Manito of Manitos, spoke again
Manito to all beings and grandfather of Men;
He gave the first mother,
mother of beings:

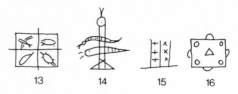

13   14   15   16

He gave fish, turtle, beast, bird;
An evil Manito shaped monsters.
He shaped the flies, he shaped the gnats.
All beings were then friendly.

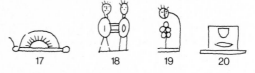

17   18   19   20

Truly the Manitos were active and kindly,
They fetched the very first men and women.
They fetched the first abundance, the first food;
All were glad, all easy, all happy.

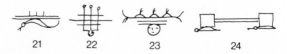

21   22   23   24

Only under cover there was evil, the magician snake.
He brought negativity, discord, grief;
brought storm, sickness, death.
All this happened before the Flood, on the first earth.

Walam Olum, part 1

V.12 *The struggle between the Good Mind and the Bad Mind of the Iroquois*

As an introduction to his history of the League of the Iroquois (1825), David Cusick wrote a native cosmogony, translating Iroquoian accounts into his own idiosyncratic English. With the emergence of the giant Turtle known as the 'Great Island', two heroic 'Manito' figures or Minds, Good and Bad, rival each other as creators of worlds and men, the Good Mind working against the chaos of the Flood and harmful beasts. The struggle between them is resolved by the defeat of the Bad Mind in a whirlwind. A further hint of the scheme of world ages comes in the reference to apes as near-humans of a past age. Since this species was quite unknown in the northern territory of the Iroquois, this motif must derive from what Cusick himself calls 'the southern parts of the Island', towards Mexico. The inhabitants of those parts are acknowledged as superior in moral philosophy, having been made by the Good and Bad Minds in collaboration.

When he [Enigorio, the Good Mind] had made the universe he was in doubt respecting some being to possess the Great Island; and he formed two images of the dust of the ground in his own likeness, male and female, and by his breathing into their nostrils he gave them the living souls, and named them Ea-gwe-howe, i.e., a real people; and he gave the Great Island, all the animals of game for their maintenance; and he appointed thunder to water the earth by frequent rains, agreeable to the nature of the system; after this the Island became fruitful, and vegetation afforded the animals subsistence. The bad mind [Enigonhahetgea], while his brother was making the universe, went throughout the Island and made numerous high mountains and falls of water, and great steeps, and also creates various reptiles which would be injurious to mankind; but the good mind restored the Island to its former condition. The bad mind proceeded further in his motives, and he made two images of clay in the form of mankind, but while he was giving them existence they became apes; and when he had not the power to create mankind he was envious against his brother. Again he made two [images] of clay; the good mind discovered his brother's contrivances, and aided in giving them living souls,* (It is said these had the most knowledge of good and evil.) The good mind now accomplishes the works of creation, notwithstanding the imaginations of the bad mind were continually evil; and he attempted to enclose all the animals of game in the earth, so as to deprive them from mankind; but the good mind released them from confinement, (the animals were dispersed, and traces of them were made on the rocks near the cave where it was closed.)

* [original footnote:] It appears by the fictitious accounts that the said beings become civilized people, and made their residence in the southern parts of the Island; but afterwards they were destroyed by the barbarous nations, and their fortifications were ruined unto this day.

David Cusick, *Sketches . . . of the Six Nations*, pp. 3–4

V.13 *Forms of life in Sky and Earth*

The two figures in this Navajo sandpainting emblemize the reciprocity between Sky and Earth which runs through Southwestern accounts of the four world ages. Each with their own body frames, head and mouth to the east, and with complex internal designs, they are really two sandpaintings in one. To the left, the 'upper' side as in the Toltec convention, is Sky. In a line from his eastern mouth to his invisible heart we see the three brightest moving bodies he possesses, Venus, moon and sun, who travel through the mesh of 'fixed' stars. These are identical with the goddesses who discuss the creation of man with Venus in the form of Quetzalcoatl (cf. *V.3*): Milky Way, the zigzag north-sound band, and Star Skirt, with her slowly revolving constellations. To the right, Earth has at her heart the dark lake from which four plants grow, here principal figures: maize (top), erect, from which the Speaker and Hogan gods, sons of Earth and themselves maize creatures, created man; tobacco (left) which consoles him; squash (below); and bean (right). Their mouths linked at east by enlivening pollen, Sky and Earth reconcile the two basic forms of existence – celestial movement through time, and rooted vegetal growth – which recur throughout American cosmogonies. In the phrase of blessing intoned during the Navajo Night Way they are invoked in a pun between walking far in time (*saa nagai*) and thriving as a plant (*sa'aa nagai*) on the path of or according to the ideal (*bike hozhon, bigke hozhon*). As for the door guardians, Big Fly (left) has the same relation to day as Bat (right) has to night.

This design is closely related to the four sandpaintings of the Emergence Way. There (fig. 11) man's birth into the successive

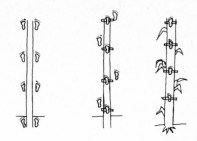

world ages is marked in detail by 'horizons' of the four maize colours (black, blue, yellow, white) at which he must 'get in step'; his path overall finally becomes synonymous with the maize plant, seen here growing upright in Earth.

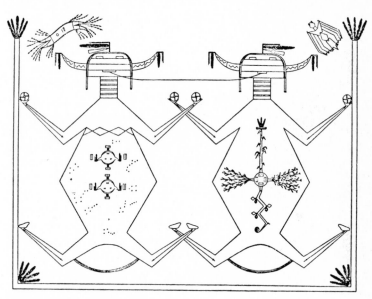

Sky and Earth sandpainting

V.14 *The journey of the* uinal *and the time-count of the world*

In contemplating the origin of the world and of time itself, the Maya of Yucatan composed this 'song' about the journey of the *uinal*; it concludes the section of the Book of Chumayel dedicated to the ages of the world, in which there are echoes of the Venus chapter in the Dresden screenfold. A cognate of *uinic*, man, the *uinal* is the entity who both embodies the Twenty Signs of ritual and exists as the quantity of 20 days in Maya calendrics, the unit of the second order in place-value notation (cf. lines 46–7). As related here, its (or his) journey from emergence to plentitude draws deeply on Maya philosophy and matches it with Old World cosmology. Napuctun (line 1) is the name of a Maya sage and scholar like Chilam Balam himself, while 'Merchise' is Melchisedek, the first character in the Bible said expressly to be a philosopher. At the same time the *uinal*'s journey from the nether darkness up the 'steps in the sky' to true life in heaven's heart is recognizable as a shaman's account of the journey of the soul (cf. Pontiac, *II.4*, and the Sioux liturgy, *VIII.12*), and indeed corresponds to the Mide symbol of a man walking up a celestial half-arch from the east (fig. 12).

The very first proof of the *uinal*'s existence is movement (line 3), inherent and axiomatic, prior to matter, structure and even thought. Once mobile, he is defined by kinship, being held vertically and laterally as in a 'mesh' of women (like Star Skirt's Constellations), themselves in motion (lines 5–7). The women anticipate his separate existence yet his birth, consummated in line 16, is not from a *mater*-ial womb but from a place that could as well be external as internal, the outer as much as the inner cosmos. At first he is no more than the steps on the road, foreseen and then seen by the women. But his tracks reveal that he is indeed a man, a two-footed *homo erectus*. And it is by means of his steps that the reality embodied in him may be counted and enumerated. This count is prepared for when his steps are first measured, that is, when their intervals and rhythms (*ppiz*) are consciously registered (lines 8–10). Order of a specifically Maya kind is then instituted (*tzolan zihci*, line 12) and the way is ready for the enumeration of the world through the signs and numbers carried within the *uinal*.

'Named' and categorical creation starts with an actual demonstration of the power of the mind, in the multiple pun in line 11, in the phrase '*xoc lah cab oc lae lahca oc*'. *Xoc* means count, *lah cab* means whole world and *lahca* the number 12; *Oc* is foot or footprint and is the name of X in the Twenty Signs and, therefore, among the Maya, a day name. These puns engage us in the internal logic of the *uinal*, which overcomes those 'paralogistic' problems (as Kant called them) of explaining the 'beginning of time'. For, from *lahca(b) Oc* we move immediately to 13 Oc, as the other foot comes forward. In the Sacred Round terminology now unequivocally invoked, such a step is impossible: no two consecutive numbers may ever have the same Sign. But by virtue of being unthinkable it aptly corresponds to that moment of stasis shown to be undefinable in the Eleatic paradoxes, when the one foot is exactly even with the other moving past it (cf. the Navajo design, fig. 11). This is the moment of the eastern horizon, the space-time edge of the day unit. It is the start position of right with left, of even with odd (12, 13), not *ex nihilo* (0 to 1; note that the Maya head glyph for 13 contains the *uinal* sign). This initial parity is characteristic of Mesoamerican and Southwestern dualism as a whole, exemplified here in the dual Earth-Sky, mistress-god figure of lines 9–10, and in the two decimal subsets of the Twenty Signs, between which we now are poised. Elaborated with a numerical precision peculiar to the Maya, this moment starts the sequence which enumerates the world day by day.

Fig. 12. Mide vision symbol:
the walk from east to zenith.

Having 'made' the eastern horizon (line 11), like the sun and Venus the *uinal* walks on up into the sky, on the 'tooth' (*Eb*) steps of the stairway replicated in the east-west pyramids of Mesoamerica. As he goes up, so the events of creation are enumerated sign by sign, twenty in all. These day-events allude to the world ages (6 Water), past races of men (13 Night), the struggles with the underworld (3 Death), as well as to the Bible. Moreover, they involve puns, like those made in Maya hieroglyphs, and pose impossible difficulties for the translator. For example, 6 Water (*muluc*), the last day of this first *uinal*, with its watery associations, plays on the verb *mucchahal*, to drown. Since as hieroglyphs they both mean 'to count', *muluc* also neatly complements the *xoc* which introduced 12 and 13 Oc at the start of the sequence. Other day events are discussed in the notes.

Once the *uinal* reaches heaven's heart, its constituent Twenty Signs join hands, making a ring like that on the Aztec Sun Stone (*V.1*). As these are a proven source and a principle of creation with their own 'sufficient reason', their spokesman Ahau asks why the word of the Christians, if universally true, was not revealed to them and why they, the Maya or American party, were not allowed even to put their case or declare themselves (lines 50–51).

It was set out this way by the first sage Melchisedek, the first
> *Bay tzolci yax ah miatz Merchise yax ah*

prophet, Napuctun, sacerdote, the first priest.
> *bovat Napuctun sacerdote yax ah kin*

This is the song of how the *uinal* was realized, before the world was.
> *Lay kay uchci u zihil uinal ti ma to ahac cab cuchie*

He started up from his inherent motion alone.
> *ca hoppi u ximbal tuba tu hunal*

His mother's mother and her mother, his mother's sister and his sister-in-law, they all said:
> *Ca yalah u chich ca yalah u dzenaa ca yalah u mim ca yalah u muu*

'How shall we say, how shall we see, that man is on the road?'
> *bal bin c'alab ca bin c'ilab uinic ti be*

These are the words they spoke as they moved along, where there was no man.
> *cu thanob tamuk u ximbalob cuchie minan uinic cuchi*

When they arrived in the east they began to say:
> *catun kuchiob te ti likine ca hoppi yalicob*

'Who has been here? These are footprints. Get the rhythm of his step.'
> *mac ti mani uay lae he yocob lae ppiz ta uoci*

So said the Lady of the world,
> *ci bin u than u colel cab*

And our Father, Dios, measured his step.
> *cabin u ppizah yoc ca yumil ti D[io]s citbil*

This is why the count by footstep of the whole world, xoc lah cab oc, was called lahca oc 12 Oc.
> *lay u chun yalci xoc lah cab oc lae lahca Oc*

This was the order born through 13 Oc,
> *lay tzolan zihci tumen oxlahun Oc*

When the one foot joined its counter-print to make the moment of the eastern horizon.
> *uchci u nup tanba yoc likciob te ti likine*

Then he spoke its name when the day had no name,
> *ca yalah u kaba ti minan u kaba kin cuchie*

as he moved along with his mother's mother and her mother, his mother's sister and his sister-in-law.
> *ximbalnahci y u chiich y u dzenaa y u mim y u muu*

The *uinal* born, the day so named, the sky and earth,
   zi uinal zihci kin u kaba zihci caan y luum
the stairway of water, earth, stone and wood, the things of sea and
      earth realized.
eb haa luum tunich y che zihci u bal kabnab y luum

1 Ape, the day he rose to be a day-ity and made the sky and earth.
   Hun Chuen u hokzici uba tu kuil u mentci caan y luum
2 Eb he made the first stairway. It ebbed from heaven's heart,
   Ca Eb u mentci yax eb.   Emci likul tan yol caan
   the heart of water, before there was earth, stone and wood.
   tan yol haa, minan luum y tunich y che
3 Reed, the day for making everything, all there is,
   Ox Ben u mentci tulacal bal, hibahun bal
the things of the air, of the sea, of the earth.
   u bal caanob y u bal kaknab y u bal luum
4 Jaguar, he fixed the tilt of the sky and earth.
   Can Ix uchci u nixpahal caan y luum
5 Men, he made everything.
   Ho Men uchci u meyah tulacal
6 Cib, he made the number-one candle,
   Uac Cib uchci u mentci yax cib
and there was light in the absence of sun and moon.
   uchci u zazilhal ti minan kin y u
7 Caban, honey was conceived when we had not a caban.
   Uuc Caban yax zihci cab ti minan toon cuchi
8 Flint, his hands and feet were set, he sorted minutiae on the
      ground.
   Uaxac Etznab etzlahci u kab y yoc ca u chichaah yokol luum
9 Rain, the first deliberation of hell.
   Bolon Cauac yax tumtabci metnal
10 Ahau, evil men were assigned to hell out of respect for Dios
   *Lahun Ahau uchci u binob u lobil uinicob ti metnal tumen Ds
      Citbil*
that they need not be noticed.
   ma chicanac cuchie
11 Imix, he construed stone and wood;
   Buluc Imix uchci u patic tuni y che
he did this within the face of the day.
   lay u mentah ichil kin
12 Wind, occurred the first breath;
   Lahcabil Ik uchci u zihzic ik

it was named Ik because there was no death in it.

Lay u chun u kabatic Ik tumen minan cimil ichil lae

13 Night, he poured water on the ground.

Oxlahun Akbal uchci u c̄haic haa, ca yakzah luum

This he worked into man.

Ca u patah ca uinic-hi

1 Maize, he canned the first anger because of the evil he had
   created.

Hunnil Kan u yax mentci u leppel yol tumenel u lobil zihzah

2 Snake, he uncovered the evil he saw within the town.

Ca Chicchan uchci u chictahal u lobil hibal yilah ichil u uich cahe

3 Death, he invented death –

Ox Cimil u tuzci cimil

as it happened the father Ds. invented the first death.

uchci u tuzci yax cimil ca yumil ti Ds

—

5 Lamat, he invented the seven great seas.

Ho Lamat lay u tuzci uuclam chac haal kaknab

6 Water, came the deluge and the submersion of everything

Uac Muluc uchci u mucchahal kopob tulacal

before the dawning. Then the father Ds invented the word

ti mato ahac cabe. Lay uchci yocol u tuz thanil ca yumil ti Ds

when there was no word in heaven, when there was neither stone
   nor wood.

tulacal ti minan tun than ti caan ti minan tunich y che cuchi

Then the 20 deities came to consider themselves in summation and
   said:

Catun binob u tum tubaob ca yalah tun bayla

'Thirteen units + seven units = one.'

Oxlahun tuc: uuc tuc, hun

So said the *uinal* when the word came in, when there had been no
   word.

Lay yalah ca hok u than ti minan than ti

And this led to the question by the day Ahau, ruler,

Ca katab u chun tumen yax Ahau kin

Why was the meaning of the word not opened to them

ma ix hepahac u nucul than tiob

so that they could declare themselves?

uchebal u thanic ubaobe

Then they went to heaven's heart and joined hands.

Ca binob tan yol caan ca u machaah u kab tuba tanbaobe

Book of Chumayel, pp. 60–2

186

VI Hunting and planting

WHEN the earth's first fruits fail or are not enough, man has to provide for himself, to win from the earth what otherwise had been a spontaneous gift. In this enterprise, hunting and planting emerge as socially essential tasks which are both akin and antithetical. Indeed, in the absence of a developed pastoral-lacteal tradition in pre-Columbian America, except to some degree among the Inca, the antithesis between hunter and planter, mobile chaser the one, the other earth-bound and sedentary, takes on a special clarity. It is evident in the two symbols given to Black Elk in his vision: the arrow, and the bowl of still, sky-reflecting water; in the Reed-arrow (XIII) and the Water (IX) of the Mesoamerican Twenty Signs (which as a set is quite uncomplicated by the concern with cattle-wealth that inaugurates our alphabet, 'a' being an ox-head and 'c' a camel); in the rituals of antagonism between such Venus-figures as Quetzalcoatl hurling his arrows at the sources of water from the east, and the thunder-rain gods, static at heaven's heart, like Tlaloc; and in the *Popol vuh*'s contrapuntal account of the magic Twins' discovery that their true calling was to be blowpipe hunters and not field workers.

Yet, just because the antithesis is so sharp, so is the logic by which it is resolved. The water-killer Venus, for example, may act as the antidote to too much rain; he firms the earth so that it can be properly tilled and is thus also a culture-bringer (cf. p. 132). And as providers the hunter and the planter each have their *domestic* companion, Dog and Turkey being explicitly recognized as such in the Mesoamerican sets of Twenty Signs and Thirteen Birds. Moreover, they design the shafts and heads of essential tools, club and planting stick, spear and plough, whose phallic equivalence is continuously noted. In the 'target' body itself yet more radical parallels may be discovered: in the outer skin which through imitative magic disguises the hunter, and clothes gods like Xipe (cf. p. 106) as a sign of the earth's rejuvenescence; in the inner flesh, a seminal store like the horned hunchback sheep of the Southwest, the animal and the vegetal being in this respect quite interchangeable, as indeed man himself is with maize; and in the life-blood of the heart, the hunter's most intimate trophy and, in the Nahua phrase, the planter's most 'precious water'.

Hunting

The equipment of the pre-Columbian hunter included club, mace, spear, sword, blow-gun, poison dart, sling, hatchet, rope, net, lasso – all used variously in trapping, stalking and open chase. An important addition to these basic arsenals was the spear-thrower. In Mesoamerica the use of this device (related in principle to the Eskimo harpoon-launcher) spread from Teotihuacan to the Maya, and it is depicted at Tikal at about AD 500. At about the same time it appears on the pottery of the coastal empires of Peru which preceded the Inca, and was known to the Mound Builders of Ohio. Along with the spear-thrower came the bow and arrow. As developed by peoples north of Mexico, it was brought south by the Nahua-speaking Chichimec and played a big role in Mesoamerica in the centuries immediately prior to the Spanish conquest. Because of its range and accuracy, this weapon was frequently related to the very notion of restless ambition and military expansion, and to what the Aztecs called the 'acquisitions of the hunt'.

The hunter's prey varied according to habitat, the buffalo of the Plains being the biggest game. More widespread, deer hunting is represented on early pottery (Chimu) from pre-Inca Peru; and in the Twenty Signs of Mesoamerica it is the pair Deer and Rabbit (VII and VIII) who represent prey, the victim buck and doe. Conventionally the smallest and most defenceless prey, Rabbit himself becomes the hunter through the logic of compensation, which corresponds to the victim Venus's identification with the Rabbit. A Sioux tradition relates how the Rabbit as hunter, rising early in the east, always found himself preceded by the footstep of the sun, until one day trapping the sun, he walked first up into the sky to make his kill (i.e. rose heliacally; cf. p. 168).

Fishing – by netting and spearing – was also regarded as a form of hunting; totem poles from the Pacific Northwest make the analogy quite clear. Chimu pottery, from thousands of miles further down the same coast and from a much earlier date, also deals with this activity and shows the use of reed boats and elaborate tackle. The importance of the fisherman's transport, such as the canoe, is brought out in early Classic Maya texts, in the Walam Olum, and in

Navajo lore concerning the magic 'logs'. In all these cases, however, fishing is shown as a special enterprise, somehow between hunting and agriculture, and perhaps prior to both (a dictum many anthropologists would agree with). While predatory, fishing is related also to agriculture, through the fact that it may be a sedentary activity, and through rain-making (as in the Laud screenfold; cf. *III.6*) and fertilization of the soil. The Algonkin selected and named a particular type of fish as manure for their maize hills (*munnawhatteaug*, 'fertilizers'); and, as we have seen, with the Maya a fish held in the hand like a sacrificial victim's heart designates the Maize God (4th of the Nine Figures). Also, the Maya rain gods – the Chacs – act as both fishermen and planters.

Planting

Agriculture proper lends itself well to archaeological description because the remains of cultivated plants can be plotted and dated with fair accuracy. Indeed, this is one of the main factors in the arguments of those who speak of a 'nuclear' America, an area in northern South America from which 'culture' in all its aspects spread out over the continent. A striking feature of one of America's oldest stone carvings, a monolith from Chavin, a city in the Andes which flourished *c*. 1000–300 BC, is that it clearly shows four agriculturally developed plants as properties of the original alligator-like Earth beast: gourd, chili pepper, manioc and peanuts (among the Tupi Guarani, manioc became the staple food referred to in their curses). Potatoes and other crops were also grown from an early date in South America, and were developed into literally hundreds of varieties by the Inca. Along with Southeast Asia, pre-Columbian America has in fact been one of the world's major suppliers of cultivated plant varieties (cultigens), many of them known by their native names: hickory, pecan, squash, persimmon, cocoa, tomato, avocado, chili, maize, papaw, banana, cassava/yucca/manioc, cashew, coca, lima beans, cherimoya, quinoa, oca, mate, and of course tobacco.

Of all these, maize – American corn – has a special place. It is celebrated on Chimu pottery with its characteristic tassels and 'tiered' stem, while in Mesoamerica and the Southwest it was considered human in its attributes if not identical with man, the creature made from white and yellow maize. For millennia, maize kernels have been cultivated not just in this pair of colours, but in the complementary 'astronomical' pair red and black, the colours arising from the absence or presence of carotin (white/yellow), the presence of anthokyam (blue-red), or of both (black). These four colours were prized in Mesoamerica, as the screenfolds show, by the Iroquois and the Algonkin to the north, and in the Caribbean, for ritual purposes and to mark the planter's identity. The fields at the Pawnee town of Arikara were separated according to these colours. Furthermore they supplied the basic set of colours recorded as Maya hieroglyphs (Table 5), and possibly the colours of the *quipu* as well, white and yellow being more statistical (denoting population and food resources) and red and black being more calendrical and concerned with the acquisitions of war (cf. Table 4). Traditionally, maize was also linked with the bean plant, the two plants being synonymous with food in Nahua. Among the Algonkin the bean was normally grown together with maize, whose stem served as a support.

Agriculture in all its aspects is a recurrent theme in Classic Maya art, and in the contemporaneous murals of the great city of Teotihuacan. These show the abode of Tlaloc, Tlalocan, as a place of serene abundance, a model for the historical wealth of Tula. Further, as elsewhere, the process of sowing, cultivation and harvest, related to the power of the imagination itself, is stated to be no less enhancing than the hunter's acquisitiveness.

Over the continent as a whole, traditional sources of food supply varied enormously, according to climate and terrain, and ranged historically from nomadic gathering to the highly diversified practices of the Inca state. Yet planting and hunting emerge as dominant forms of providence, reciprocal activities of first importance in community life. They come to exemplify two complementary modes of existence: that of rooted growth (by thirteen stages in Mesoamerica), vertical and vegetal, fed by rain from heaven's heart; and that of the armed walker who relies on all twenty digits and who moves in time between the western and eastern horizons, rising like Venus by footsteps into the sky.

VI.1 *An Eskimo list of game*

Having the clarity characteristic of Eskimo pictography, this piece of nineteenth-century incised ivory is a hunter's tally. It comes from Alaska where agriculture has only recently become practicable. It

shows the hunter himself, with bow or harpoon, in a threatening stance, near the hut or lodge used in the summer hunting season. Between him and the hut a shaman-like figure leans on an upright supporting the ridge pole, on which skins and meat are dried. Animals caught face to the right, and (reading from left to right) are: 5 martens, a weasel, a land-otter, a wolf, 2 deer and 3 beaver. Interspersed with these are animals desired but not caught; they face left and (reading from right to left) are: porcupine, seal, walrus, fox and bear.

VI.2 *Deer and buffalo encircled*

Traditionally, the inhabitants of the Plains, the western 'land of buffalo' as the Walam Olum calls it, were both hunters and planters; only with the advent of Europeans did hunting dominate, especially among the Algonkin (Cheyenne, Arapaho) and the Sioux. In the design on this buffalo hide, taken from the Mandan Sioux early in the nineteenth century, the gestures and attitudes of hunter and hunted evoke the speed and drama of the chase as it was transformed by the use of horses, and of long-barrelled rifles like the one held by the horseman in the middle. Yet within the swirling, apparently random picture older notions of hunting have their place. While the hatted figure (top) suggests a European gun-supplier, the figures and symbols constraining the power of the game on the other three sides belong to a previous economy. The hunter and shaman figures to the right (elongated as in sandpaint-ings) are matched on the left by a horned figure who resembles the hunch-back seed-bearers of the Navajo and who has with him the domestic companion of the planter, the Turkey (three plus an egg), and a Dragon Fly, another 'guardian' symbol. Below, the two so-called 'shield-figures', common as a petroglyph all over northern America, represent the disk of Venus walking into the sky with his spear; in Midewiwin hunting texts, this symbol stands for the fourth line of the stanza: 'I rise / at the join of earth and sky, / I walk through the sky / as the morning star'. Their spears, then, are part of a cosmic scheme involving both hunter and planter, like the lasso held by the horseman next to them, which recalls the 'finding rope' to which emblems of abundance are attached in sandpaintings

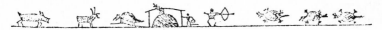

Sioux buffalo-skin robe

(cf. *III.4*). As for the buffalo, the principal prey, they provided food in many forms (pemmican or berry cakes for instance), clothing and footwear, tipi covering, and the surface on which designs like this one were painted. In the 1880s these buffalo were massacred by machine-guns mounted on trains, provoking the famous Ghost Dance in which Wowoka promised the return of the animals and of a 'whole' life (prior to the US 'admitting to the Union' the vast territories of North and South Dakota, Montana, Idaho, Washington, Wyoming, Utah, Oklahoma and the states of the Southwest). Buffalo shoulder had a eucharistic function, for which the sign is an albino buffalo head; and they were considered powerful agents in rain-making, for which purpose they are shown aligned in sets of four, as in the 'Four Buffalo' sandpainting and like the four smaller buffalo in the lower register of this design, males to the right and females to the left of the larger male, who is dropping dung.

VI.3 *The rise of the hunters, described in the Walam Olum*

Having dealt with cosmogony in Part 1 of the Walam Olum, the Lenape go on, in Part 2, to record their own history as a nation and as 'men' (the meaning of their name in Algonkin). They first appear as a northern house or group, living after the Flood on the Turtle (41), the 'Great Island' of North America in Algonkin and Iroquois lore. This single abode opens in time and space into the two lands of deer and buffalo, indicated by the horns to east and west of the 'prosperity' sign (43); these correspond historically to Algonkin settlement of the Woodlands and the Plains. A further binary division occurs culturally between the planters (who later acquire superior maize from 'the south') and the hunters, shown with their respective implements (44). At this point they balance each other as alternatives. But then the hunters' power to shoot out in four directions (45) causes restlessness in the group as a whole, and the decision is made to find better things to the east in 'Snake Island' (48; possibly one of the Great Lakes peninsulas). On the way two of the hunter leaders, named after predators on land, Bald Eagle and White Wolf, turn to fishing in the lakes (51). With their canoes they win another wealth like the light of summer itself (52). When, later the lake freezes, the tribe crosses it as three clans (compare 50) and, once across, the hunters elect the first of the Lenape sachems. This second part of the Walam Olum differs from the first in being set in historical time (the format now consists not of double stanzas but of chapters of four or five sequential stanzas). And it is literally the hunters' energy and movement which carry the story line along, up to the moment when chronology proper begins, with the election of sachems and the record of their reigns (cf. *I.13*).

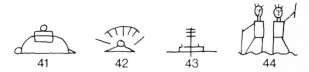

41   42   43   44

After the Flood the Lenape lived close together in their houses in
    Turtle Land;
Where they live it freezes, it snows, it's windy and it's cold.
Coming out of the northern winter, with milder weather, they had
    many deer and buffalo and became strong and rich in mind;
the planters separated [from the hunters].

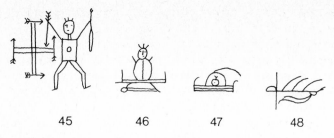

45 46 47 48

The braver, the more allied, the cleaner were the hunters, who
 showed themselves to north, to east, to south, to west,
in the old land, the northern land, Turtle Land, the hunting land
 of the Lenape.
All the hearths of that land were unsettled and everyone said to
 their snake priest: 'Let's leave';
eastwards to Snake Land they went, moving off, lamenting.

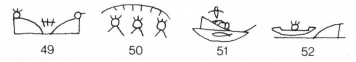

49 50 51 52

In several bands, quivering, their land desolate, they went torn and
 broken, towards Snake Island;
their own men, unmolested, they left the north and the snow in
 separate parties.
The fathers Bald Eagle and White Wolf stayed by Fish Lake and
 Mussel Lake;
Floating in their canoes, our fathers were rich, they were in the
 light among the islands.

Walam Olum, part 2

VI.4 *The sun's gift of four precious arrows*

Used in the Shooting Way, this Navajo sandpainting celebrates the
acquisition, function and essence of the arrow, the hunter's weapon
and, in medicine, the cause of shooting pains, in order to fit it into a
larger harmonious scheme. It depicts the four arrows given by the
sun to his offspring the Twins when they travelled Venus-like from
the west to his palace in the east. They are made of the four precious
materials proper to the sun's palace and to objects in it, including
for example the sun's trumpet (compare the Toltec Royal Lord's

trumpet, p. 106). Whiteshell and Turquoise, Redstone and Abalone, these materials emblemize the four world ages commemorated by calendar signs in the Aztec Sun Stone. In this painting they appear as round hills around the fifth central hill (an actual pile of sand) in reciprocal pairs, like the arrows above them: Whiteshell with Turquoise inner at east with its negative image at west; Abalone with Redstone inner to the left with its opposite to the right. Having received the arrows, the Twins first use them when, journeying to the zenith with the sun, they kill the sources of water, Rain Boy and his companions, whom the sun later restores to life. Here, the interests of the planter, dependent on water, are represented by the four plants in the painting, starting as usual with maize, upper right. The roots of the plants are protected from the hunter's arrows by the four hills, understood and named as the boundaries of Navajo territory, just as the hills are protected in their turn by the arrows, with the Flint-skirted 'Arrow People' standing

Arrow People sandpainting

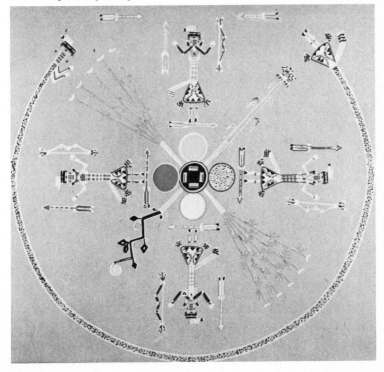

on them, holding further arrows, and bows of ash and other woods, in their hands. Outermost, the expansive thrust of the Arrow People is curbed by the encircling, *hogan*-shaped 'mirage' frame, and at the eastern door by two guardian arrows.

VI.5 *The Chichimec shooting song*

Nahua-speakers from the mountain deserts of northern Mexico, where they located the legendary tribal birthplace Chicomoztoc, 'Seven Caves', the Chichimecs were famed as archers. Two centuries before the arrival of Cortés they invaded and rejuvenated the Toltec empire. In this song, uttered by the 8th of the Thirteen Birds in favour of the 3rd, Hawk, they celebrate the founding of the 'house' and 'mat' of their power in their deserts of cactus and thorny agave, and their capacity to expand it by shooting out with their bows, in four directions each with its own colour, as in the Navajo Shooting Way. However, unlike the Navajo they describe their targets as self-sufficient, the 'real thing', choosing carefully from the set of Twenty Signs to name them: Eagle and Jaguar (XV and XIV), fellow-predators whom they emulate as 'pure' hunters; Snake and Rabbit (V and VIII), mementos of their hard rations in the desert where, like wild dogs (*chichimec*), they ate reptiles and the smallest mammals. This second pair of signs may also denote emulation: with the sexual rival and with the victim-hunter Venus, respectively. As the ruler of Cuauhtitlan, Hawk, with his predatory habits, was explicitly contrasted with his contemporary at Tula, Quetzalcoatl, who is the cultural harbinger among the Thirteen Birds.

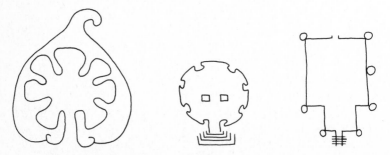

Fig. 13 (*Left*) The 'Seven Caves', Chicomoztoc (after Annals of Cuauhtinchan); (*centre*) plan of the Painted Chambers, or caves, used for second burials, at Tierradentro, Colombia; (*right*) the Seven Hills in the third sandpainting of the Navajo Emergence Way.

When the Chichimec empire began, a certain woman named Obsidian Butterfly called them and said:

You shall set up Hawk as your ruler.
Go to Nequameyocan, where of the Wild Agave is.
Found the Cactus House, the Wild Agave House
and there spread out the Cactus mat, the Wild Agave mat.
Then go towards the east and shoot your arrows,
and towards Mictlan, the inner earth, and shoot again,
and towards Huitzlampa, the Thorn Place, and shoot again,
and towards the Place of Fields, the Place of Flowers and shoot
    again.
When you have shot you will have struck the real thing,
the green and the yellow, the white and the red,
Eagle and Jaguar, Snake and Rabbit.

History of the Kingdoms, §§ 43–4

VI.6 *The Aztecs define themselves as hunters in the year 1 Flint (1168)*

The Aztecs left several accounts of their ancestral migrations, of how they left their nothern homeland Aztlan and, under the guidance of Huitzilopochtli, journeyed to Tula and the Valley of Mexico to found Tenochtitlan, the capital of their future empire. The most valuable of these accounts is the Boturini screenfold of Tenochtitlan, the opening pages of which are shown here. Made of native paper and folded like the Mixtec screenfolds, this work combines a calendrical narrative (Year-Bearer Annals from 1168 to 1355) with the more open form of a route map. (The only sure sign that it is post- and not pre-Columbian is the style of the foliage on the tree, p. 3.)

In the year 1 Flint (XVIII), probably AD 1168, the ancestors of the Aztecs paddle away from Aztlan; this unlocated origin is named by the signs Water (*a–tl*) and Reed (*acatl*). On the other shore they meet Huitzilopochtli, in the attire of the hummingbird, first of the Thirteen Birds. He speaks to them from a cave, telling them to conquer the eight 'Houses' listed (p. 2), from the bottom up: Huexotzinco, Chalco, Xochimilco, Colhua, Malinalco, Tlahuica, Tepaneca and Matlazinca. Adopted by the four Aztec leaders, Huitzilopochtli is carried in a medicine bundle on the shoulders of the first of them, and then (p. 3) placed in a sanctuary on a pyramid where a ceremonial meal is held. At this point the body of eight

Boturini screenfold, pp. 1–4

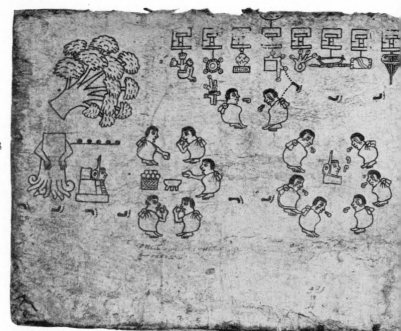

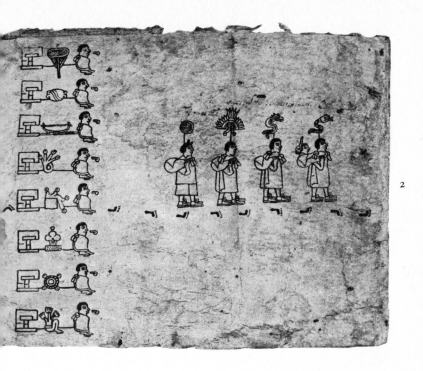

2

4

Houses which the Aztecs are to conquer splits into two. With great weeping the first four Houses are ordered by an Aztec to turn off to the east (note the trail of footprints), while the other four are left to carry on; they are thus destined respectively for the eastern and western positions which they actually occupied in relation to each other, though long before the Aztecs arrived on the scene. When the Aztecs did eventually incorporate these places into their empire they recognized a main administrative division between them, with the Colhua towns to the east and the Tepanec towns to the west. Here (p. 3), this division is explained, retrospectively, in just those terms with which this chapter is concerned, for the eastern Colhua towns correspond to the planter as the western Tepanec ones do to the hunter. The planter towns are (p. 3, from the left): Huexotzinco, with three leafy willow buds evocative of that green tree and of the syllable '*xo-*', to flourish; Chalco, a jade (*chalchiuitl*), a synonym for water; Xochimilco, a flowering field; and Colhua, which includes the sign Water (IX). By contrast the next four names, have hunting and trapping symbols: Malinalco, cord(?); Tlahuica, a bow; Tepanec, a stone (*te-tl*); and Matlazinca, a net (*matla*). It is the hunting ethos of this latter group for which the Aztec leaders show an implicit preference. On the same road and carrying bags for game, they shoot an Eagle (p. 4) and sacrifice three human victims mercilessly stretched back over cactus plants.

VI.7 *The booty promised to the Aztecs by Huitzilopochtli*

The Aztec migration depicted in the Boturini screenfold (*VI.6*) was described in several later Nahua texts, the most notable being a fragmentary history by an Aztec who adopted the Spanish name Cristobal de Castillo. Castillo's averred purpose as a national historian was to show his people the wickedness of their past. In practice, the extraordinarily powerful rhetoric of his Nahua, among the purest extant, often seems to work against him. This is certainly true of the passage in which Huitzilopochtli, speaking from his cave, persuades the Aztecs to work with him. With undeniable logic he urges them not to become agriculturalists themselves, but to hunt, enslave and exploit others, caring principally to be excellent men of war and rulers ennobled by the Toltec insignia listed in the Aztec 'Priests' Speech' (*II.1*). All that was necessary for existence, from staple food to the requirements of the civilized sophisticate, was to be acquired rather than produced, the reward of a vast economic and diplomatic system protected by force, in all its essential metaphors: Eagle and Jaguar, Fire and Water, arrow and shield. The acquisitions of the hunter-warrior 'on the road' are listed in the sequence of the Aztec tribute lists: the woven clothing of authority (*tilmatli*); the lavish warrior costumes of featherwork; agricultural produce and 'whatever else' they wanted.

And so Huitzilopochtli answered: 'That's good, oh my slave. I will truly lay out before you the orders of my will and I shall give you control, with all its precisions. Sustain your hearts on this, follow my form well. In the end I will take you on – I shall certainly not abandon you through neglect and I shall surely call to you when the time comes to move, when we take to the road. Don't feel uneasy, because I will be with you – I'll not get stuck here. I shall truly console your heart and it is precisely at this point that I instruct you. This is the first quality with which you will enhance yourself:

   Eagle & Jaguar; Fire & Water; Arrow & Shield

This will be your indispensable food, this you will live by, so that you proceed striking terror. The payment for your breast and heart will be your conquests, your overrunning and destroying the common people, the dwellers in all the places you reach, and when you take captives you will cut open their chests with a Flint on the sacrificial stone and you will offer their hearts to the brilliant Movement in the sky. And as soon as the heart, rich with blood, is thrust out, you will offer it in the direction of Huitztlampa, the Thorn Place, as a sacrificial object, and the blood too, and the bloodiness. And when you have done this I shall be there. Towards Tlaloc also, and then to all my friends, those gods known to you. And you shall eat the flesh unsalted. You may add to it only a little cooked maize, so that it may be eaten.

   And the second thing: For those who are special warriors, the brave, the valiant, the impetuous, their name will be The Capturers as I order it and they are the ones who will be without fear for themselves. They will acquire the quilted mantle; the loin-cloth; the painted mantle. Quetzal feathers shall be their insignia; you will go to the source of the feathers and the jade and they shall be given to you and the people will fit you out with them. You will go to those populations who have not known combat, who are unpractised in war and unskilled, those who have settled together on the land, those who have dwelt a long time in one place and where things are flourishing and organized, places in flower, where want has been banished and where everything can be had for the taking by those who work at war.

You will be limited by nothing; nothing will escape you. They will bend to your every wish, whatever your greeds are you will be satisfied, you will take women where and when you please, nothing will escape you, you will receive gifts of everything – the best food, the greatest ease, fragrance, the Flower, tobacco, song, everything, whatever it is.'

C. de Castillo, *Historia . . .*, chapter 2

VI.8 *The shooting of the Carib snake*

In the Arawak tradition the action of this story follows genesis, which for its part resembles other American creation stories with its reference to the world ages and to the umbilical rope which once served as the connection for mankind between heaven's heart and earth below (this rope is one of the commoner petroglyphs of northern South America). Part of a whole cycle concerning the tasks and taboos related to menstruation, the fable seeks to explain the characteristic enmity between Arawak and Carib as a tragedy that lies within kinship and is in part the result of the sheer technology of the hunter. The story recalls Eve's disobedience in the Garden of Eden, but closer connections may be made with the American symbols Snake and Death, especially as they appear in the Shooting song of the Chichimecs, for example. Told recently in Guyana, the story is nearly identical with one told over a thousand miles away, in Colombia, by none other than a Carib tribe; there, the Carib role is played by a ferocious creature called 'Spaniard' – a response to the armed invasion of the sixteenth century.

Right
Fig. 14. Umbilical 'ropes from the sky': (a) Toltec;
(b) Guyanese ideograph or *timehri*.

Below
Fig. 15. Ideographs (*timehri*) of northern South America: (a) man; (b) snake; (c) ape; (d) frog. After Koch-Grünberg.

Among both the Arawak and the Carib, the totuma fruit gathered by the girl in the story is traditionally incised with designs denoting ritual and esoteric knowledge, which are common throughout northern South America and which are sometimes replaced by alphabetic letters. These designs, known as 'timehri' in Guyana, underly the structure of this story, which falls neatly into halves, female and male, about gathering and hunting, the four stanzas of each half being balanced through opposition or affinity; note for example the girl's questions, first about menstrual blood, then about her brothers' hunting weapons.

When she came to menstruate, the first girl was instructed by her parents not to sit on the ground. She asked why and was told: 'You're a woman now'; she asked why again and was told: 'It must be so'.

She sat on the ground and a snake, banded in white and black, entered her.

She went to gather the calabash called totuma; once by the tree she doubled forward so that the base of the basket on her back rested against the trunk. The snake slipped out up the tree and gathered the totumas for her with great speed.

Her early return with a full basket surprised her three elder brothers. The next time she went off they spied on her and learnt her secret.

The three brothers set about making the first bow and arrow. The girl asks: 'Why are you making those things, brothers?'. 'To hunt, sister'. 'You never needed them before: why now?'. 'Why do you need to ask, sister?'.

When she goes totuma-gathering the brothers 'fell' the snake from the tree with an arrow. She kneels over its body and weeps.

The youngest brother says: 'We must shoot her too'. The middle one says: 'Yes, or there'll be *war*'. The eldest one says: 'Only if you kill me too; she's our sister'.

The girl's belly swells; she goes off, makes a round hole in the ground and gives birth to snake-worms which metamorphose into men. These are the Caribs and they ask for their father. Their mother says: 'Your uncles killed him'.

Cuthbert Simon: 'The origin of the Caribs'

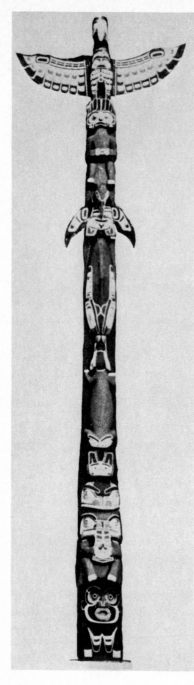

1 Thunderbird or Eagle (curved beak and 'horns'), ruler of the elements, with a human face on his breast.

2 Chief Galgungassa, ancestor of the owner of the pole who, with the help of Raven, made his home, Rivers Inlet, into rich salmon country.

3 Raven (straight beak), maker of salmon and crest of Chief Galgungassa's clan, who lured the salmon in from the sea.

4 Salmon, staple food of the maritime peoples of the Northwest; first caught by Galgungassa, who fastened his teeming nets to a tethering pole like this one, called Nhe-is-bik in Kwakiutl.

5 Wolf, a sign of the landsman's cunning of the Rivers Inlet people who catch huge quantities of salmon each year as they swim upstream to spawn.

6 Whale, lord of the sea, the source of the salmon; whale-hunting is also prevalent in Northwestern iconography.

7 Bear, who bites on a copper or ceremonial shield denoting the wealth and high rank of the chief.

8 Tsonoqua, female spirit of forest and wind who stole children away for food, just as the Rivers Inlet people lure the salmon inland for their food.

Willie Seaweed, 'Nhe-is-bik Salmon Pole'

VI.9 *How salmon are lured inland*

The peoples of the Pacific Northwest are sedentary, yet non-agricultural. Their traditional economy (strongly defended in U.S. law courts today) owes much to the protection from the ocean given by the off-shore islands, and to the superb timber supplies for boat-building. Their main source of food is mainly depicted by analogy with hunting on land and in the forest. Beside Raven, Wolf is invoked as a sympathetic spirit, and both sponsor the catching of salmon when these fish swim upstream to spawn. Typical of the cedar carving and painting practised in the region is this sixty-foot pole which was made by the Kwakiutl, Willie Seaweed, in 1892 for Wahkus, descendant of Chief Galgungassa of Rivers Inlet, British Columbia. The eight characters read from top to bottom (see opposite).

VI.10 *A Classic Maya fishing scene*

Now partly effaced, this exquisite seventh-century scene is incised on a bone found at Tikal and shows the great delicacy of Classic Maya art. The three fishermen are Chacs, the long-nosed Maya rain-makers: the reciprocity between rainfall and aquatic creatures in Mesoamerican ritual was made quite clear in the page of the Laud screenfold dedicated to Tlaloc (*III.6*). Their catch is varied: the Chac in the seething lake water has one type of fish in his hand and another in the basket on his back. The Chac sitting in the canoe holds his fish in the manner of the 'caught fish' glyph which stands for the Maize God (4th of the Nine Figures). The six-glyph caption, reading left to right, concerns the canoeing prowess (1st glyph) of the ruler (*batab*, 2nd glyph) named 'Moon' (4th and 5th glyphs), who died at Tikal (6th glyph) in his fourth *katun* in AD 671, and in whose tomb other such incised bones were placed.

Incised bone, Tikal

VI.11 *A table concerning rain and crops*

In the Maya screenfolds of the post-Classic period (AD 1000–1500), agriculture is a major topic. Many of the chapters of the Dresden screenfold are devoted to prognoses, on the basis of Sacred Round dates, of such activities as planting, in which priests dressed as Chacs, the long-nosed rain gods, take part. Here, they themselves act as planters, walking in the rain (second from left), treading the field (third from left, denoted by the glyphs for food, and soil – XVII in the Twenty Signs), and scattering seed while holding a hand-plough in one hand (fifth from left). The Signs and Numbers of the Sacred Round dates are given respectively in the left-hand column (Rain XIX, Night III, Deer VII, Ape XI and Eagle XV)

Dresden screenfold, pp. 38b–39b

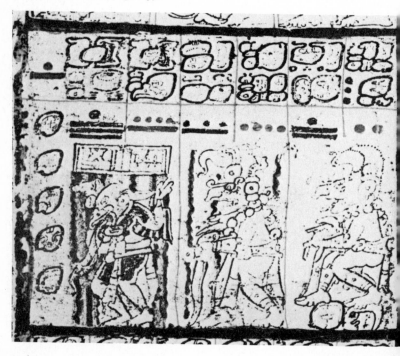

and beneath the hieroglyphic captions (9 over the first picture, of 'vulture rain', is separated in the sets of Thirteen Numbers by 16, beside to the left, from the opening co-efficient 6, given above the column of Signs). The hieroglyphic captions explain the illustrations and give information conveyed by position, gesture, and actual colour in the Toltec screenfolds. For example, the captions for the three Chac illustrations mentioned above read (A1, B1, A2, B2): 'The planter / is the white chac; / a good yield / in the field'; – 'There walks / in the field / the yellow chac; / very [three dots] good news'; '[undeciphered] / the red chac / through the field; / abundance of maize'. The motif of rain poured from a jar like that in the fourth illustration along is found in the Toltec screenfolds, in sandpainting and in Inca ritual (see pp. 102, 120).

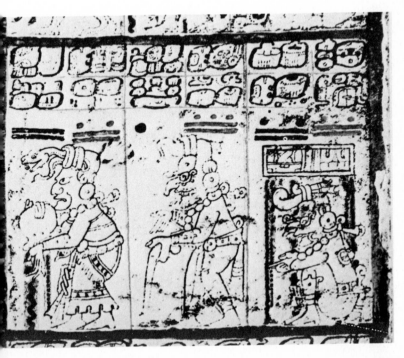

VI.12 *Maize planting and crop prediction by the Twenty Signs*

In this table, from the Fejérváry screenfold, maize planting is related to the four signs (right to left): Movement (XVII), Wind (II), Deer (VII) and Teeth (XII), all of which have the co-efficient 4. In the middle of each section sits the maize plant itself, shown in human form, in three of its four conventional colours – yellow (twice), white and red (black being the fourth). Details of weather and soil condition are also given. Guarded from behind by four of the Nine Figures, the plants have in front of them offerings made on their behalf, in the field itself: copal incense, hand-ploughs, and birds. One of the ploughs is broken (4 II) and the other is wrapped round with a loin-cloth (4 VII). In this and other screenfolds, an

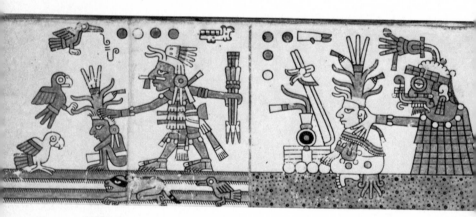

Fejérváry screenfold, pp. 34–33

(4)		(3)	
	4 XII	4 VII	
11th			
	1st		9th
13th	RED (Unrooted)	YELLOW	
MIXED		FRIABLE	

explicit analogy is made between the plough, which digs into the earth to release its treasure, and the penis. Breaking the plough means performing the penitential act of Quetzalcoatl in creating man (cf. *V.3*). The prediction of one good crop (4 VII) out of four is a Toltec norm: it occurs with the combination of the hunter's prey, Deer (VII), with the watery Tlaloc (9th in the Nine Figures).

VI.13 *Crop prediction by years*

Like the planting table in the Fejérváry, this page from the Borgia deals with weather and maize-yield. But it is based not just on the Twenty Signs but on the four Year-Bearers of the Toltec calendar, set out in boxes under four symmetrically arranged sections. In

	(2)		(1)
Cloudy day	Clear night	4	rain
4 II			
	3rd		6th
	WHITE		YELLOW
	MIXED		FLOODED XVII

Borgia screenfold, p. 27

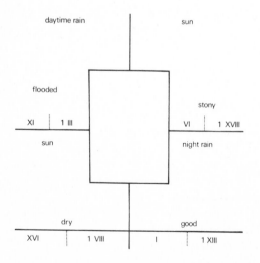

each section, and in the central fifth section, there is a strutting Tlaloc; head back, holding axe and snake lightning, he pours water from his hands and crotch. His head-adornments correspond in each section to the Signs given in the boxes in addition to the Year-Bearers, and each has its colour: Ground (I) and black, Death (VI) and yellow, Ape (XI) and blue, Vulture (XVI) and red. The types of weather and fates of the harvest are vividly shown. Starting with the year 1 Reed (XIII; lower right), the maize planted in the Ground or Earth-beast itself flourishes under night rain (note the stars inset in the clouds). Above, the maize of 1 Flint (XVIII) is devoured voraciously by Disney-esque insects as it grows in stony ground under blazing sun. In 1 House (III) the floods brought by the day rains drown the maize plants, who hold up their arms as if for help. Last, in 1 Rabbit (VIII; the famine year brought by Venus), the maize, in parched earth, is eaten by rodents, again under a blazing sun. The central picture is 'timeless', having not a calendar sign but a disk that is half-sun, half-night (the symbol found also in the Walam Olum; cf. *V.11*). Here the fifth, striped Tlaloc stands above a jade bowl, shield and arrows turned vertically down within the rain streaming from his right hand. This imposing page design in the Borgia differs from the table in the Fejérváry screenfold (cf. *VI.11*) in that the maize plants here are less human in form while their 'guardians', all Tlalocs, are less protective than overbearing, even in the good year 1 Reed (XIII).

VI.14 *Bounty and abundance at Tula*

According to the Franciscan Sahagún's informants among the Aztecs, whose reports are collected in the Florentine Codex, quoted here, one of the many excellences attributed to Tula was the complete absence of hunger and want. As in Tlalocan, the biggest and best crops were available there, including gigantic maize ears. There are many parallels in other cultures to this vision of abundance; the Golden Age described in Virgil's Fourth Eclogue provided three types of naturally coloured wool, for example. The chromatic range of the cotton grown in Tula is notably larger, and it is worth noting that the tribute paid to Moctezuma included naturally coloured cotton, along with other products also listed here (cf. *VII.10*). This description of utter abundance has bravura and a wry humour, especially in the final flourish, which implies a certain disbelief that such an economy could be self-regulating.

the toltecs were certainly rich
food was not scarce enough to sell
their vegetables were large
melons for example mostly too fat to get your arms round
maize ears millstone size
and they actually *climbed*
    their amaranth plants
cotton came ready dyed
in colours like crimson saffron pink violet leaf-green azure
    verdigris orange umbra grey rose-red and coyote yellow
it all just grew that way

they had all kinds of valuable birds
blue cotingas quetzals turpials red-spoonbills
which could talk and sang in tune
jade and gold were low-priced popular possessions
they had chocolate too, fine cocoa flowers everywhere

the toltecs did not in fact lack anything
no one was poor or had a shabby house
and the smaller maize ears they used as fuel
to heat their steam baths with

Florentine Codex, Book 3, chapter 3

VI.15 *The famine of the year 1 Rabbit (1454) and its consequences for the Aztecs*

The terrible consequences which the famine of 1454 had for the Aztecs are described with detachment here by the historian Chimalpahin in his Nahua annals. Coming from Chalco, he viewed them as hunter-upstarts, unpractised in agriculture. It is noteworthy that the aqueduct and irrigation system were installed in this same year with the help of the Texcocans from across the lake. Like the Chalcans, the Texcocans formed part of the eastern Colhua division of the empire, which in the Aztecs' own eyes was the one expert in agriculture, being so described in the Boturini screenfold. That the Aztecs, even after their rise to grandeur and power in the Valley of Mexico, were prepared to sell themselves in order to save at least some of their number points to a grim capacity for survival. Their customers were the Totonacs from Cuextlan, the Gulf Coast area named after the Huaxtec Maya (relatives of the Totonacs). In the Toltec calendar 1454 was a 'Rabbit' year, that is one especially subject to the dire effects on 'the sources of water' of Venus's arrows of light.

The year 1 Rabbit, 1454. In this year of disaster there was widespread death and thirst. And then there arrived, to stuff themselves in Chalco, frightful packs of boars, poisonous snakes, and vultures as well. And the hunger was so great that the imperial Mexicans sold themselves, and others hid themselves away in the forest, where they lived as wood people. In that region there was nothing to eat for all of four years, so that two separate parties of the Mexicans sold themselves into slavery. It was mainly to buy slaves that the Totonacs came to Mexico with maize, and it was from Cuextlan that they brought it. Before that the Mexicans had not used maize to make loaves. They crawled into holes and died anywhere. The vultures then ate them, and no one buried them. It was every man for himself.

It was also in this year the Texcocans came to build the aqueduct at Chapultepec. It was commissioned by Nezahualcoyotl, the ruler of Colhuacan, so that water would come to Mexico-Tenochtitlan and serve his uncle, the great ruler Moctezuma I, Ilhuicaminatzin ('guardian of the sky').

Chimalpahin, *Relaciones*, f. 168v.

VI.16 *Inca agriculture*

Under the Inca, the state assumed responsibility for food supply. In the dearth of wild prey and of fish in the Andean area, agriculture was highly developed as the major source of food and was officially monitored and controlled at all stages and levels through the calendar and the *quipu*. Even requests to Viracocha for favourable weather followed the reasonable supposition that since he has 'made and established' the Inca population through his representative the Sapa Inca, then he should also feed them. The time around the winter solstice was important for co-ordination generally. An exhaustive census, of people and resources, was conducted and working land distributed according to need. In Guaman Poma's 'revised' calendar (cf. p. 73 above) July, shown here, is called *chacra conacuay quilla* ('land allotment month'), though the drawing concerns the other main activity of the period: bringing in food (*aimoray*) to the communal stores and silos. Sacks of maize (*sara*) and potatoes (*papa*) are carried by workers (the woman using the tumpline), and by llamas, pastoral animals which served the planter both as prime sacrificial objects and as beasts of burden. Benefiting from the plenty are the domestic pair, Dog and Turkey, the latter being identified with the cock and hen brought by the Spaniards. Turkeys, first domesticated in Mexico, were imported from there in pre-Columbian times.

Oh Viracocha, ancient Viracocha,
skilled creator,
who makes and establishes,
'on the earth below
may they eat
may they drink'
you say;
for those you have established
those you have made
may food be plentiful.

'Potatoes, maize,
all kinds of food
may there be'
you say, who command and
   increase;
so then they shall not suffer,
and not suffering, do your will;
may there be no frost, no hail,
keep them in peace.

               Zithuwa ritual

Guaman Poma, *Nueva corónica*, p. 1050

VII Conquest

CONQUEST is the prize of the hunter who learns to 'work at war', to use Castillo's Nahua phrase. The warrior intent on a human target shares the hunter's mobile energy and uses much the same weaponry. The Maya sign Ahau (XX), Lord or victor, equivalent to the pre-eminent Flower of the Toltecs, has the rounded mouth of the blow-pipe hunter. Yet he is more closely defined as a professional, by insignia and uniform. The two chief military orders of the Toltecs, for example, wore the dress of the arch predators in their animal kingdom, Jaguar and Eagle (XIV and XV in the Twenty Signs). Also, his material and political rewards are far more varied: *access* to hunting or planting land, for example, or to water (the prize taken by the Aztecs at Chapultepec), or to mines, of copper, gold, silver, tin and, again as Castillo put it, the 'source of the jade'. Indeed, the warrior's trophies may include manufactured goods, like those that flowed into the markets of Mesoamerica: all kinds of furniture and clothing, paper, featherwork, specialist tools, paints; and intellectual products like screenfolds and songs. To the warrior were due: 'the best food, the greatest ease, fragrance, Flower, tobacco, song, everything, whatever it is'. That song should have been one of the American rights of conquest is confirmed in Peru by Guaman Poma; and in Mexico by the *Cantares mexicanos* manuscript of Nahua poetry (cf. *IX.6* and *7*), in which songs are set out according to their provenance, as in a tribute list. The Book of the Cakchiquel also expressly notes that in the Toltec tradition a conqueror took not just the material goods of a locality, but also its songs, should he deem them worthy of consideration. Beyond this again, the conqueror could clearly expect to control the means of manufacture and put his subject populations to work for him, to build cities, and to wage further wars. Without the systems built up over millennia on this basis, the Spaniards could not have administered their New World conquests as they did.

Records of conquest

Conquest is a rich source of iconography. Not just weapons and armour but whole vocabularies of insignia may be identified in conquest records by characteristic shapes, along with designs for fortress, palisade and such manœuvres as spy, ambush, surround and besiege. Throughout the continent, capitulation is conventionally shown as a seized forelock, defeat as a stripped body, and death as a closed eye. The names of places conquered are struck by an arrow, or toppled. Graphic accounts of martial exploits are to be found on household items, like the pottery of the Chimu in Peru, and on clothing, like the battle shirts and the more elaborate buffalo robes of the Sioux. These last were also hung up for display, as indeed were screenfold annals like the Selden which adorned the walls of the royal houses and palaces of the Mixtecs. Such historical accounts were made part of the actual architecture of Maya houses as carved stone lintels and panels. And most prominent and permanent of all, the large columns (stelae), which dignify the plazas of many ancient Mesoamerican cities, stood – and stand – as monuments to military success.

The purpose of all this recording activity could be just self-glorification, to cow the defeated and inspire one's own party. But most often there is another reason for it: to validate the conquest as the *status quo*. To this end conquest was depicted as a ritual fact, unanswerable in its spatial and numerical logic. Once 'arrived at' along the exploratory trail of footprints or along the chevron warpath, the victory is fixed 'forever' in the synchronic patterns of ritual. Just this quality distinguishes plans and maps of subject territory, those of the Toltecs also involving calendrical logic. To this end, too, devices on shields and other equipment invoked the conqueror's gods as invincible. In the Toltec tradition these included: Tlaloc, whose storms brought strife between the elemental opposites of fire and Water; Quetzalcoatl, the Fire-Kindler and herald of the sun whose arrows avenged humiliation and ignominy; and Tezcatlipoca, the warrior proper, owner of all known arms and insignia, whose might protected the city and trade, whose single foot made the Ground tremble. Also, borne high on the ornate litters used by the Chibcha, the Inca and the Chimu in the south and by the Mound Builders in the north, conquering royalty would aspire to the image of the mightiest life-force, the sun.

At the same time, within this kind of collective validation, comes the secular emphasis on individual pedigree for its own sake. In economically complex societies the deeds of patrilinear conquerors may be presented chiefly as a warranty for their descendants, against usurpers and sibling rivals. While adorning the walls of royal houses, screenfolds like the Selden also established the genealogical claims of its occupants; and the same is true of the dynastic inscriptions carved on Maya houses. As late as the eighteenth century, in response to pressure from the Spanish Crown, Land Books were produced in the Valley of Mexico, which depict the first (pre-Columbian) conqueror of a locality with his descendants growing like a tree from his navel. This remarkable patrilinear-umbilical concept, as a means to claiming title to power and property, appears also in the Inca empire, where the first sun king and his family claimed to have emerged from Cuzco, itself the navel. It appears too on the tomb of Pacal, the ancestral ruler of Palenque.

Fig. 16. (a) Pacal on his sarcophagus lid, Palenque, AD 736; (b) ancestral ruler, Tepotzotlan, AD 1740.

Paternal lineage and miraculous conception

A remarkable fact about the validating hero myths of certain American empires is that, while relying fully on this paternal-umbilical logic, they introduce into it an apparently contradictory motif: miraculous conception. While pure genealogy serves as a plausible warranty for inherited conqueror's rights, it may also become imaginatively restrictive and embarrassing in any 'higher' or large-scale enterprise. The Aztec and the Inca versions of the motif of miraculous conception or parthenogenesis are given in this chapter. The first exults in the 'scandalous' power enjoyed by Huitzilopochtli, the Aztec sun- and war-lord, precisely because of his illegitimacy (*VII.9*). By origin, Huitzilopochtli was the poor tribal mascot we saw in the Boturini screenfold (*VI.6*). Themselves regarded as *parvenus*, as late arrivals, in the Valley of Mexico, the Aztecs made their unprepossessing origins into the source of their strength, rejoicing in the very absence of a venerable father. In complete contrast to this, though still through the motif of miraculous conception, the Inca did everything to venerate the father principle. The son of the solar Viracocha was ingeniously shown to *need* his father, who for his part was pleased to own the responsibility for him (*VII.13*). This 'policy' conforms with the pronounced paternalism of the Inca state, towards present and prospective subjects.

For their part, the Maya offer yet another interpretation of parthenogenesis, in the *Popol vuh* story (cf. *V.6*) of the miraculously conceived Twins who – Venus-like – avenge their father in the Underworld. The emphasis here is less on self-assertion or on paternalism than on sibling rivalry. For, engendered like Viracocha's son from a fruit in a tree (in this case their father's severed head), the Twins win acceptance only through proving themselves abler than their elder half-brothers (despite her family loyalty, the grandmother Xmucane cannot help laughing at the antics the elder brothers are made to perform by the Twins and thus disowns them). Notable in this Maya account is the role of wit as validation, linked with the system of elder and younger fraternities. This system was possibly developed to co-ordinate the military interests of the federal Maya cities in the Classic period. As part of the Maya calendrical system of government it flourished in Yucatan long after the centralized 'solar' systems of the Aztec and the Inca had fallen into the control of conquerors from beyond the New World.

VII.1 *Exploits of Cheyenne warriors*

This battle scene, painted in the early nineteenth century on cow buffalo hide, celebrates a victory of the Cheyenne, the Plains Algonkin tribe, over a gun-carrying enemy (see bottom right) who are probably Pawnee. The feather head-dresses and round tasselled shields denote membership of Cheyenne warrior societies. One of the victors (upper left), a medicine man, holds a ritual gourd rattle and wears a tooth amulet. The elongated figures, very close to those of Southwestern sandpainting, are drawn in the old Plains style. While the enemy lie in disarray or cower as their forelocks are seized, the victors form strong fourfold ranks across the field. Below their four differently coloured horses (yellow, green, blue and red) appear two fourfold groups of foot-warriors. Those to the left include a woman, who like her three male companions, commands a trail to the conquered and the dead.

Cheyenne buffalo-skin robe

VII.2 *Four defeated towns in a ritual plan*

This single-page Mixtec manuscript commemorates the defeat of four towns, by arranging them symmetrically above and below a central circle (now largely effaced). The victors stand in pairs on the chevron warpaths leading to and from them. Twinned at east (top) and west (bottom), the defeated towns have their sanctuaries toppled from their pyramids, struck by an arrow and burning, while

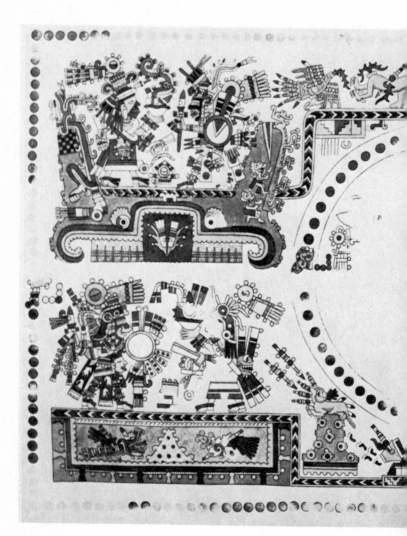

in one case (upper left) their vanquished Eagle and Jaguar defenders stand headless by. The design closely resembles the scene from the Lienzo of Tlaxcala discussed above (*I.2*) and has the same roots in Toltec ritual. Here, in addition, the Sacred Round is invoked. The triumphant pairs beside the defeated towns and in the centre are each named in two series, male and female, by signs and numbers 52 places apart (hence the five lines of fifty one dots): 5 Lizard (IV) with 1 Deer (VII), upper right; 5 Vulture (XVI) with 1

Aubin manuscript, no. 20

Rain (XIX), upper left; 5 Reed (XIII) with 1 Ape (XI), centre; 5 Flower (XX) with 1 House (III), lower right; and 5 Tooth (XII) with 1 Eagle (XV), lower left. The calendar proper is also invoked. For the decorations along the ceremonial areas on which these pairs stand (in the same sequence: Sun and Sky; Mountain and Cave; Earth-maw; Underwater sand island; and Skull sanctuary with 'fish' hearts) correspond to those on the architectural structures listed in the 2nd, 5th, 6th, 7th and 8th Fire-Drilling chapters in the Vienna screenfold (also a Mixtec document; cf. *III.12*).

The males of the triumphant pairs are magnificently attired as warriors, with arrows and shield, flaring head-dress, loin-cloth and decorated spear; the females hold bowls with cult objects and one (upper right) is menstruating strongly as a token of being 'well-fed'. Between them there is an intricate counterpoint of decorative motifs: hearts, hands, gold chains, skulls and skull and crossbones. The two upper pairs (male to the right, head-dress swept backward) complement the lower two (male to the left, head-dress swept forward).

VII.3 *A canoe-launched night attack by the Mixtec forces of 8-Deer, AD 1046*

Canoe-launched attacks appear to have been a speciality of the Mixtec hero 8-Deer, to whose life the reverse of the Nuttall screenfold is dedicated. As was customary, his conquests were principally aimed at taking prisoners alive, for sacrificial purposes. But they also served to extend political power, and historical records like the Nuttall confirmed territorial rights through patrilinear descent: 8-Deer appears as a dynastic father in several of the Mixtec screenfolds – the Bodley, the Selden and others. This conquest, depicted in the Nuttall, which took place on 12 Deer (in the year 8 Rabbit; AD 1046), is a night operation, as the stars in the sky-band show. The campaigner 9-Water leads the attack on the island town named by the 'Loin-cloth' laid along its wall; he has support from 11-Death and 10-Snake, who share a canoe. All three go armed with spear and spear-thrower. They receive matching support from the water creatures below, feather Snake, bird-fish and mollusc, who put to flight the alligator which represents the Ground on which the conquered town, struck by an arrow, stands. The sign Ground conventionally serves as a base for buildings, and water creatures act as assistants in ceremonies depicted in the Laud and other ritual screenfolds. In the boustrophedon calendrical narrative of Part 2 of the Nuttall, this scene is exceptional in occupying a whole page. The detailed reciprocity between its two registers lends it a ritual aspect, as do the regularly defined water area, modelled on the sanctuary pool and the House-like structure which bears the sky-band.

Nuttall screenfold, p. 75

VII.4 *The lineage and the map of Teozacoalco, 1580*

This map was drawn up in 1580 to accompany the *Relación Geográfica* of Teozacoalco, the Mixtec town west of Oaxaca. It was one of a number of regional surveys conducted at the time, and it graphically depicts the intrusion of one ruling dynasty, that of Tilantongo, shown in the left-hand column, into Teozacoalco. The three columns of figures, reading from bottom to top, record the ancestors of the ruler living in 1580, whose son – Francisco de Mendoza – is shown at the top of the column in the map (the only figure without a name sign). Although on European paper and dating from over fifty years after the arrival of the Spanish, the map

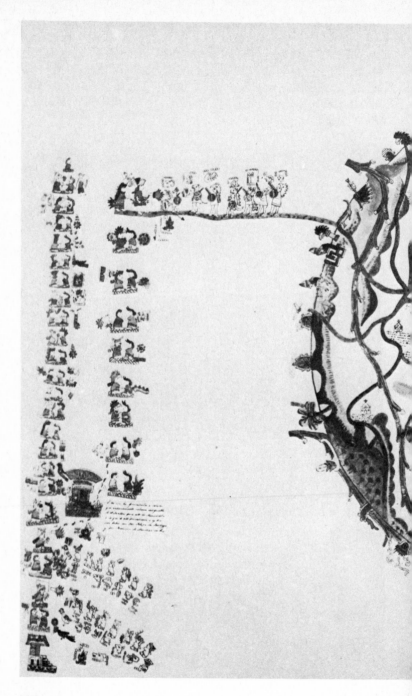

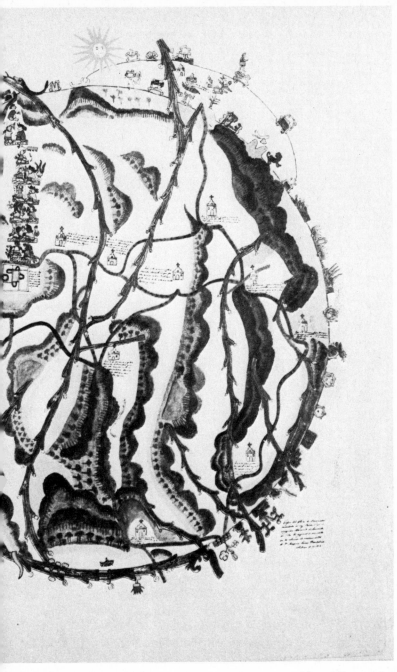

Map of Teozacoalco

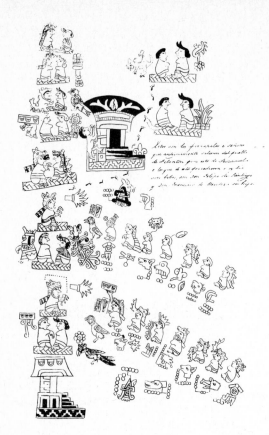

is clearly based on original documents and is drawn in a native hand
(the accompanying *Relación* was itself prepared from the testimony
of the oldest inhabitants of the town). Like screenfolds such as the
Nuttall, it sets out historical and geographical information
according to calendrical and ritual norms. East here is at the top;
the circle defines the juridical boundary of Teozacoalco, and the
semicircular appendage at the top indicates a town formerly under
the domination of Teozacoalco. Although the thirteen *estancias* of
the district, and the town itself, are shown in the form of Spanish
churches, the names of the towns bordering the map are given in
Toltec writing. The place sign for Teozacoalco (which has a
separate bell-tower and a plaza in the map) figures prominently
between the two columns to the left (see detail). Footprints indicate
movement in both time and space. The first column has the date 12
Flint (AD 972) as a starting point; the second year date on the

manuscript is 10 House (Cave; AD 1269), which marks the start of the third dynasty. Here the 'path' enters the map; along it stand seven heavily armed warriors. The famous ruler 8-Deer 'Jaguar Claw' (1011–63), whose history and conquests are related on the reverse of the Nuttall, is the left-hand figure in the third pair from the bottom (see detail). His eldest son, indicated by the row of footsteps leading from 8 Deer to the second pair of the second column, married into the Teozacoalco dynasty probably to seal and ratify a conquest.

VII.5 *Cuauhtinchan and its boundaries (1176–83)*

The Annals of Cuauhtinchan comprise both a series of drawings mostly devoid of calendar dates, of which this is one, and an accompanying Nahua text, which is calendrical in nature. They tell

Annals of Cuauhtinchan, pl. 24–5

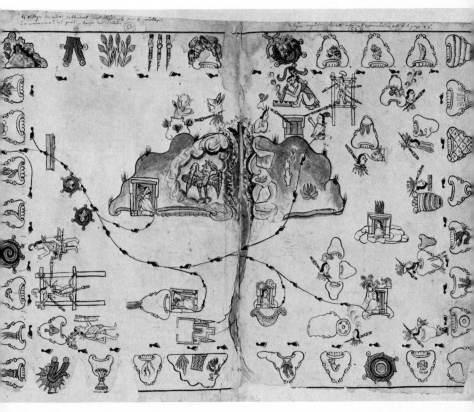

of the remote Toltec-Chichimec origins of the rulers of Cuauhtin-chan, a town which still exists, southeast of Cholula in the modern state of Puebla. After emerging from 'Seven Caves' (cf. *VI.5*) and visiting Tula, the ancestors of these rulers moved gradually south and east conquering as they went. This drawing shows the important moment of their arrival at Cuauhtinchan, which dominates the page as a complex 'hill' or place sign, in which its various epithets are infixed: Maguey Hill, Growing-Maize Hill, both to the right of the river gorge; Eagle House (Cuauhtinchan), Jaguar House, Cave in the Red Cliff (to the left). On approaching their final goal, the wanderers ceremonially walk the boundaries of its territory, a total of 33 places round the edge of the page. In addition, a series of local conquests is shown, each by means of an arrow through the neck of a local ruler, two of whom are shot on the scaffold frame (also known to Indians north of Mesoamerica). A local woman, Hill-Flower, is given to one of the Toltec Chichimec invaders, who marries her; above them a Fire-Drilling takes place. Calendrical details of all these events are provided in the accompanying Nahua text, this drawing corresponding to the years from 8 Reed to 3 Flint (1176–83). In the undated drawings everything is 'read' according to a route of footprints. The conquering trail here comes to its end. It loses its impetus and forms a ritual, two-dimensional map, with Cuauhtinchan at the centre. Like the *Popol vuh*, the Annals of Cuauhtinchan were prepared around 1550 as legal evidence. In this case the evidence had been previously cited in a dispute with the neighbouring town of Tepeycac, in which Moctezuma II acted as arbitrator. The drawings stem from native sources and do not refer to the European conquest.

VII.6 *An early record of conquest from Oaxaca,* 300 BC

The earliest inscriptions found in the Valley of Oaxaca have been dated by the radiocarbon method to the mid-first millennium BC. Though iconographically reminiscent of the Olmec culture to the east and south, they have a style of their own and are sometimes ascribed to the Zapotecs who still live in the area. This inscription is typical of those at Monte Alban, Oaxaca, prior to the start of the Classic period. The central column has been read as a record of conquest. The date is given in two parts, with the year 6 Turquoise(?) at the top and 11 House(?) at the bottom. The spreading glyph in the middle is a toponym with a grasping hand above it and an inverted glyph denoting ruler below. In parallel inscriptions, this inverted glyph is clearly a human head; as we have seen, the principle of inversion itself, to negate or oppose, is found elsewhere in American writing (cf. p. 51). The vertical reading sequence strongly resembles that of the Olmec and Maya; but it is spatially irregular and wholly lacks the exact arithmetical positioning determined by the Maya Era calendar. Moreover, in being an annual year-based record it is closer to Toltec conventions, with which Zapotec writing largely fused with the rise of Tula as an imperial centre in the first millennium AD.

'Slab J', Monte Alban

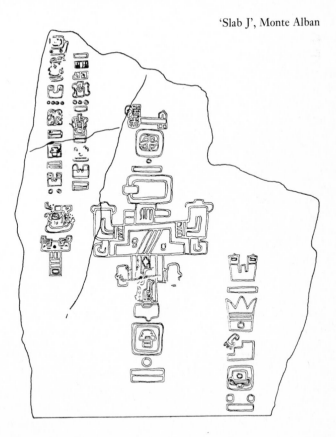

VII.7 *A commemorative lintel from Yaxchilan, AD 755*

In the Maya city of Yaxchilan, on the Usumacinta river, a series of lintels commemorates the military exploits of the Jaguar dynasty which ruled there in the eighth century AD. The conquest recorded on this lintel is between pairs, according to the fraternal Maya model found in the *Popol vuh*. Bird Jaguar, on the right, captures one enemy, whose name, 'Jewelled Death', is engraved on his thigh. His companion makes the other capture, grabbing his enemy by the hair. Both the victors wear elaborate head-dresses and loin-cloths, and Bird Jaguar carries a decorated spear. The hieroglyphic text records the event. The block upper left has the date 7 Ground 14 Zec (10 May 755), the glyph for 'capture' and the name Jewelled Death. On the right, the second glyph is the name Bird Jaguar and below it is the emblem Yaxchilan.

Lintel 8, Yaxchilan

VII.8 The wars of the Aztec emperors and the apotheosis of Huitzilopochtli

Chimalpahin, the aristocratic historian from Chalco, left a highly perceptive account of the Aztec rise to power in the Valley of Mexico. In brief digression under the year 1440 in his Annals, he subtly draws attention to the self-made 'upstart' character of the Aztecs in their conquests of the towns of their Colhua and Tepanec neighbours to east and west (Azcapotzalco, see line 5, was the Tepanec capital). He also tells how Tlacaeleltzin, nephew of the emperor Itzcohuatzin ('Obsidian Snake'), enhanced the image of the tribal warrior-god, Huitzilopochtli, for political ends. In a later entry (1509), Chimalpahin reveals how Aztec diplomats came to use the mere *idea* of the fatherless Huitzilopochtli as a weapon in psychological warfare. Presented as one who is '*tetzahuitl*', that is, frightening because 'scandalous', Huitzilopochtli helps to strengthen Aztec imperial control of the Colhua town of Chalco, Chimalpahin's own birthplace.

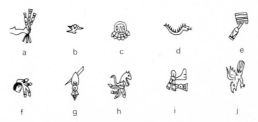

Fig. 17. Aztec emperors' name glyphs: (a) Acamapichtli (1376–95); (b) Huitzihuitl (1395–1414); (c) Chimalpopoca (1414–28); (d) Itzcoatl (1428–40); (e) Moctezuma I (1440–69); (f) Axayacatl (1469–83); (g) Tizoc (1483–6); (h) Ahuizotl (1486–1502); (i) Moctezuma II (1502–20); (j) Cuauhtemoc (1520–4).

13 Flint (1440). This was the year Itzcohuatzin died, the ruler of Tenochtitlan, who had governed for 14 years. He was the bastard son of Acamapichtli, who had been the first ruler of Tenochtitlan. And they say the woman who was his mother came to Azcapotzalco as a seller of herbs. Even though her son was not legitimate, he became the great Itzcohuatzin. By then, his father Acamapichtli had been dead for 45 years.

Itzcohuatzin waged war mainly with the help of his nephew, Tlacaeleltzin. They fought and subjected Azcapotzalco, Coyoacan, Xochimilco, and Cuitlahuacan. Tlacaeleltzin was an enterprising campaigner; and although he did not seek civil power in Tenochtitlan, he acquired the insignia of a great man, he increased his estate and enjoyed a rich life.

Next there reigned five other great rulers in Mexico Tenochtitlan: the great Moctezuma Ilhuicamina; Axayacatl; Tizoc; Ahuitzotl, and Moctezuma, the last of the line, in whose reign the Spaniards appeared. These were the great rulers who made themselves feared on every side. But the one who won the highest and the most renown was the captain and war-maker Tlacaeleltzin, as will be seen in these annals. It was he who was able to change the devil Huitzilopochtli into the god of the Mexicans, by the power of his persuasion.

4 House (1509). In this year there was a rebellion in Chalco. When they arrived from Tenochtitlan, Moctezuma's envoys spoke as follows to the rebels: 'We are sent here by your lord Tetzahuitl Huitzilopochtli whose breath is in the rushes and in the reeds and who has let this be known: "Say to Necuametl and his uncle Itzcahua that I will certainly take over this little bit more for Mexico Tenochtitlan; war is certainly said somehow to be dying out now, altogether." '

Chimalpahin, *Relaciones*, pp. 116–7

VII.9 *Huitzilopochtli's prodigious birth*

On attaining imperial power, the Aztecs radically refurbished the image of Huitzilopochtli, a tribal patron of unprepossessing, possibly plebeian, ancestry. He was associated with Tezcatlipoca and, more important, given solar attributes as the son of Coatlicue, Snake Skirt, a Mesoamerican Earth Mother. She was said to have conceived him miraculously while sweeping, being impregnated by a ball of fluff or down. Her family felt dishonoured by the unexplained fat belly and swore to kill her. In the choreography of the mass ritual dramas of the Aztecs, the scripts of which are typified by the Twenty Sacred Hymns, this story was acted out in and around the main pyramid of Tenochtitlan, Coatepec, Snake Hill. Coatlicue's brothers approach her by stages defined by its architecture (Sacred Sand enclosure, platforms etc.), while Huitzilopochtli comforts his mother from within her womb. When her attackers close in he leaps out of her, fully armed, and slays them to a man. Celebrated in the hymn quoted here, this feat has a solar dimension (sunrise 'killing' the stars) and epitomizes the power to strike instantaneously and definitively. As we noted earlier, it is contempt for Huitzilopochtli's illegitimacy, never explicitly denied, and for his uncertain authorship and fatherhood which provoke this terrible energy of his, the one 'born on his shield'.

> Hymn of the one born on his shield and the motherhood of the earth

> The great war lord has burst from Earth's swollen belly born on his shield.

> The great war lord has burst from Earth's swollen belly born on his shield.

> Astride the Snake Hill he triumphs,
> between the pyramids,
> with his face-paint on and his shield teueuelli.
> No one is so potent as he
> And the Earth quivers.

> Who else can assume his face-paint and his shield?

> 'Chimalpanecatl icuic'; Twenty Sacred Hymns, 5

VII.10 *Records of tribute received by the Aztec capital, 1502–20*

The victorious Aztec emperors had tribute due to them carefully recorded on documents like the Tribute Roll of Moctezuma, a copy of which is quoted here. Like the historical 'map' in the Annals of Cuauhtinchan (cf. *VII.5*), the Tribute Roll lists the towns and villages of a province or tributary district in an outer band, round the edge of the page; within this the tribute is listed, in conventional order. This page tallies fourteen towns centred from east and west on Tepecuacuilco ('painted-mask hill'), a town 85 miles south of Tenochtitlan near the river Balsas, on the old road to Acapulco (they may still be seen on a modern map of the State of Guerrero). The place-names and the tribute items regularly due from the province are given in Toltec writing, with Spanish glosses. The tribute is listed like the ritual prerequisites shown in the Vienna screenfold (cf. *III.12*, with conventional signs for number (see Table 4), for measure (basket, bowl, hod) and where necessary for special qualities of size, colour and texture. From the various provinces subject to him Moctezuma received live birds; skins; round stones; conch shells; sheets of paper; lengths of rough, smooth and round wood; blocks of salt and bars of gold; bunches of feathers; bundles of firewood and cane shafts; hods of lime, cocoa beans, cotton, chili peppers; bushels of cereals 10 ft high finished inside with mortar; bowls of cocoa powder and of gold-dust; pans of paint and of turquoise fragments; jars of liquidambar, honey and syrup; baskets of pinole and copal; bags of cochineal and down; clothing; bowls and plates and other crockery; wickerwork seats and chairs; cigar-holders; masks; bells; diadems, and a whole range of other materials and products. The commonest containers, hod, bowl and jar, could of themselves denote a measure of the item they most often contained: lime, cocoa and honey.

Tribute varied from province to province according to the natural resources and artisan traditions of each. But overall it fell into the four main categories mentioned by Castillo (cf. *VI.7*) and in the Aztec Priests' Speech (cf. *II.1*); they are all represented on this page. Reading from top left, we have first the category mantle (*tilmatli*). This is the woven blanket-cape with knotted ends, worn

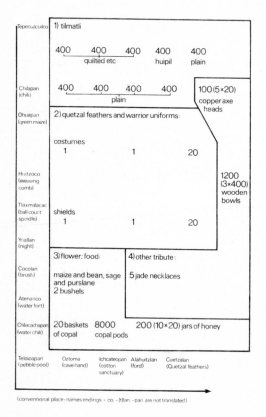

(conventional place-names endings - co. - (t)lan, -pan are not translated)

Mendoza Codex, p. 39

by the ruling class, which was of various thickness (shown by fingers) and could be quilted, striped, ornate or plain; the third mantle here has a Tlaloc-mask device. The mantle design also served as a glyph for clothing in general: the fourth mantle has a *huipil*-blouse drawn in it (loin-cloths were also itemized in this way). In the second category are the luxurious feather and gold

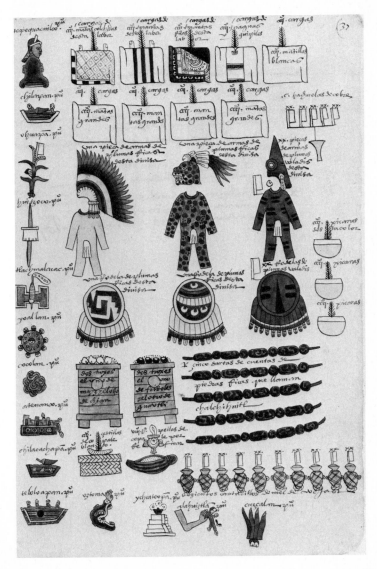

Eagle and Jaguar outfits of the warriors; of the Eagle type, fashioned with small feathers, 20 are required. The shields denote rank. Third comes the Flower of plant life and its derivatives: bushels of white maize and black beans (each with its flour/flower), purslane and sage (*chia* and *guauhtli*), all being staple foods; 400 baskets of refined, and 8,000 buds of unrefined copal; 200 jars of honey. Items in the miscellaneous fourth category are read back up the page to the right: 5 jade necklaces, 1,200 wooden bowls, and 100 axe-heads made from copper (*teputzli*) mined in the region.

VII.11 *The Chimu overcome their opponents*

The decoration on a vase from the northern coast of Peru is the source of this vivid celebration of conquest. It was found not far from Chan Chan, the Chimu capital. Chimu art is highly illustrative of life in that area, which was incorporated into the Inca empire in 1464.

The Chimu warriors, to the left in each pair on the lower row and to the right above, are clearly distinguishable from their opponents who, skirtless, wear baggy loin-cloths and bear star-shaped maces. Two of the enemy carry square boards with a shrunken-head design on them, which motif suggests a connection with the head-shrinker Jivaro beyond the Andes. As for the Chimu, their ear-plugs, and above all the fret design on their tunics, are reminiscent of Mexico, where such frets mean defensive armour or wall (cf. *I.2*, for example). The placing of the naked enemy-victim on a cactus also echoes the Aztec practice shown in the Boturini (cf. *VI.6*). Note also the seized forelocks; and, in the uppermost register, the eye

Chimu vase decoration

closed in death, in the naked body left by the triumphant Chimu who marches off to the left with his haul of captured weapons.

From the Chimu (and from the Mochica before them), the Inca learned some of their military techniques; also, the Chimu had standard-width roads, a system of runners (*chasquis*), and were arithmetically adept. The total of the Chimu warriors credited with this conquest equals the *quipu* number, ten.

VII.12 *Guaman Poma's 'Mappamundi of the Indies', 1613*

To illustrate his account of Spanish conquests in South America, Guaman Poma drew this 'mappamundi of the Indies'. In fact the territory it covers does not far exceed that conquered or explored by the Inca, on whose political system Guaman Poma based his ideas of 'good government'. At the centre is not the Spanish but the Inca capital, not Lima but Cuzco, the 'navel' sacred to Viracocha high in the mountain range through which the Inca pushed their imperial roads, as far as Potosi with its silver mines and the Araucanians of Chile on the one hand and, on the other, as far as Huamanga, Quito and Colombia ('Nobo reino'). Cuzco is also placed at the headwaters of the tributaries of the Marañon and Amazon (upper left) and the Pilcomayo (upper right) which however do not penetrate the enclosing arc of forest, a *terra ignota* for the Inca, full of monstrous and dangerous beasts and backed by quite imaginary mountains. Beyond them again is the 'northern sea', a primeval sky-ocean of both fish and stars. By contrast, the Pacific coastline, lowermost, is well documented. Surveyed here by Spanish galleons, it was previously charted by the high-prowed ships of the Inca navy (modern versions of which are still to be seen on this coast and on Lake Titicaca). Ports listed range from Mapuche in Chile (right) to Panama in Chibcha territory (left), with the principal ports of Peru, Arica, Pisco and Collao (Lima), in between. Running east and west, the roads, rivers and coastline are, above all, routes along which towns are shown in a sequence more than an actual position (Potosi is on the 'wrong' side of the road to Chile, for example). Moreover, they are made to conform to the near-symmetrical shape of the mappamundi as a whole, which bears only limited resemblance to actual geography. For, like the empires of Mesoamerica, the Inca Tahuantinsuyu was originally conceived in east-west terms, Cuzco being at the junction of the Collasuyu (east), and the Chinchasuyu

237

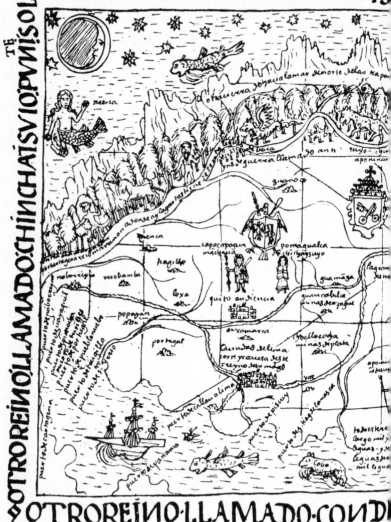

Guaman Poma, *Nueva corónica*, pp. 983–4

EINO·DELAS·INS
ACIA·EL·DERECHO·DELAR·MAR·DE·NORTE

OTRO·REINO·LLAMADO·COLLAS·VIOS·ALE·SO

HACIA·LA·MAR·DE·SVR·LLAL·

239

(west); above was the Antisuyu, inhabited by the near-human Anti of an earlier world age, and below, the more advanced coastal civilizations of the Condesuyu. This pattern was established by the emperor Pachacuti ('Earth-shaker') between 1438 and 1463, when he pressed the empire to Tiahuanaco, the 'edge of the world' in the east, and to the pass of Junin in the west. The result was that the subsequent conquests of Chile in the one direction and of the Chimu and of Quito in the other were considered as extensions of the Collasuyu and the Chinchasuyu respectively, though in true geography they lie more to south and north than to east and west. So despite its frame, which puts north at the top in the style of Renaissance European maps seen by Guaman Poma, this mappamundi is truest to ideals inherited from the Tahuantinsuyu.

VII.13 *Viracocha's child crawls to him in recognition*

In the Quechua Huarochiri Narrative, we hear a version of parthenogenesis which is closely related to the origins of the Inca state. In the early heroic days of the gods, it is said, Viracocha both founded the towns of the state and established himself as superior to other gods who represented only local interests. At first less prepossessing than they, he nonetheless ousts them 'in his wisdom' and reveals himself as nothing less than a solar father, 'enlightening the earth', like his later representative the Sapa Inca. (It was Inca policy to encourage those living at the borders to be adopted into the empire of their own accord rather than be conquered militarily.) Yet we may detect a certain scepticism in this tale, which preserves a resiliently provincial view of the metropolitan power of the Inca. The setting, Anchicocha, is a town near Huarochiri. Later on in the narrative Viracocha is shown to be slightly disreputable and even a little silly, especially beside the local deity Pariacaca (cf. *I.10*), whose descendants subsequently undertake the 'real' conquest of the region. The joke at Viracocha's expense here is that, successful as he is in being recognized by his baby son, the mother really cannot stand the sight of him, as pauper or as king.

> In the ancient past, this god Cuniraya Viracocha walked and travelled as a man, making himself look like a pauper, with his mantle and shirt torn. Those who didn't know him called after him: 'Flea-ridden wretch!'. Now this man founded all the towns here. By his word alone

he created fields and terraces with their solid retaining walls. He taught irrigation and opened the canals by dropping the bloom of the pupunha. And thereafter he travelled around, doing this and that, and conquered other, local, gods in his wisdom.

At this time lived a woman, also a god, called Cavillaca. This Cavillaca was still a virgin, though very beautiful, so that her fellow gods were always thinking how to bed her. She said yes to none of them.

One day this woman whom no man had ever touched sat down by herself to weave at the foot of a lucuma tree. In his wisdom, Coniraya Viracocha perched on this tree as a bird. Then he put his seed into a ripe lucuma fruit and let it fall near the woman. She ate it avidly. In this fashion she became pregnant, without actually knowing a man. In the ninth month she gave birth; she breast-fed the child for a year, asking herself: 'Whose son is this?'

When the child was a year old and could crawl, she summoned her fellow gods, to discover who the father was. On receiving the summons, the other gods were much pleased. They all put on their best clothes and arrived thinking: 'Maybe I'll be the lucky one'. The gathering was held in Anchicocha, where the woman lived. After all the gods had sat down in a row, the woman said: 'See, good men and lords, look at this child. Who among you engendered him in me? You, or you . . .?', and she asked each of them, and no one said: 'I did.'

Now since Coniraya Viracocha had sat himself right at the end of the row and looked really wretched, she didn't ask him in her disgust, thinking: 'How could the child be the son of this beggar?', for the rest were finely dressed.

As no one said: 'He's my son', she said to the boy: 'Go and find your father yourself', and she warned the gods: 'If one of you is his father, he'll try to climb up on to you.' The boy began crawling along and ignored everyone until he came right to the other end of the row where his father sat. At this point he chuckled and crawled up into his father's lap.

However, when the mother saw this she exclaimed angrily: 'Have I borne so wretched a son!', and picking the child up went off towards the sea. Reckoning she would love him for it, Coniraya Viracocha put his golden suit on and, while the local gods trembled, pursued her. He stood up and cried: 'Sister Cavillaca, come back please; look at me, I'm quite handsome now.'

At which he illuminated the earth.

Huarochiri Narrative, chapter 2

VIII Healer

In the native American tradition, diseases and their cures are inseparable from the larger scheme of things. 'Medicine' is a ritual matter, most intricately so in the case of the Navajo 'Ways', for example (cf. *III.4*). As in Europe up till the eighteenth century health or 'wholeness' was believed to depend on elements and forces which affected far more than the individual body. That is why the listing of specific complaints, such as 'burning chest' or 'head-ache' amounts of itself to a comprehensive moral and philosophical statement in a text like the Maya 'Ideal course of mankind' (cf. *II.2*). In some cases the causes of diseases themselves may have a clear cosmic significance and role, harmful winds, for example; or the moon whose variable waxings and wanings and baleful influence are guarded against in Midewiwin scrolls, in Maya screenfolds and in Inca medical texts.

At the same time, like the warrior, the healer is a professional, who has skills and codes proper to him. He has a specialist knowledge of plants and herbs, of the allo- and homeopathic chemistry of the gall stone (the original 'calculus'), of surgery or 'handwork'; and he knows how to shrink or restore the inner head or soul. Pachacuti's Inca laws punished faulty medical knowledge, and the Aztecs assessed the performance of individual healers, appreciating the 'good physician and diagnostician' as one who has 'examinations, experience and prudence'. The factor of 'experience' stands out most clearly in everything relative to the healer as the psychopomp, the shaman bearer of the soul.

In most medical texts the healer acts as the guide of his patient's soul, counteracting soul-loss and retrieving errant souls. He 'hits' his foe, the disease, as with a hunter's arrow, and summons the spirits of brave warriors as supports for the soul in his charge and as protection against the malevolent dead. An expert in plants, he draws on the inner forces of the earth, its elements, drugs and herbs, adopting an emphatic personal role and deploying them less as material or botanical objects than as characters, often women. With hypnotic rhetoric he recounts entire life journeys, like those of Gilgamesh, Aeneas or Quetzalcoatl, whose therapy consists in activating the confidence to survive the tests along the spiritual path. Indeed, the shaman does not recognize an illness as 'terminal'. Like Christ the physician, he reserves his strongest medicine for the most hazardous path of all, that through death, which he will have travelled himself at least once. The migration of the soul through the underworld past the eastern horizon to the 'heart of the sky' is one of the constants on his cosmic medicine.

Shamanistic chants and narratives composed to heal the soul in sickness and in death are known in a large number of American languages. They form, too, an important element of the continent's written literature, in scripts familiar from previous chapters and in others introduced here for the first time.

VIII.1 *Hieroglyphic chants to cure seizure due to the moon*

The Dresden screenfold of the Maya contains several chapters devoted to the treatment of disease. They are all based on the Sacred Round, which provided days and intervals for diagnosis and cure much as the Zodiac did in medieval European medicine. The table quoted here, for the cure of seizures, is regulated by four of the Twenty Signs: Water (IX), Jaguar (XIV), Rain (XIX) and Maize (IV), each separated from the next by 65 days ($4 \times 65 = 260$). Each period of 65 days falls into six subdivisions, 8, 13, 13, 13, 8 and 10 days apart, according to norms now obscure to us.

The hieroglyphic texts for the last three of these subdivisions are set in vertical columns without an illustration; but the first three show the Moon goddess Ixchel. On her shoulders she carries a burden (*koch*) of various birds, lunar creatures which affect health and fortune. In the first glyph of each of the six hieroglyphic texts these birds are named and closely resemble those in the set of Thirteen Birds: screech owl, quetzal, macaw, vulture, zopilote and turkey. The particular afflictions connected with them include seizures or spasms (*tancaz*), a category to itself, and eruptions or pox (*kak*), like scabies and eczema. The shamanistic chants recorded alphabetically in the Yucatec manuscript known as The Ritual of the Bacabs (cf. *VIII.3*) were possibly related to tables like

Dresden screenfold, pp. 16c–17c

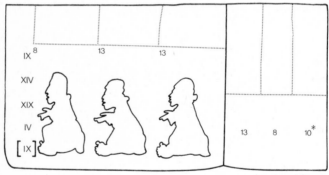

*corrected from 12

this one. The link between the macaw and seizures recurs in the Chilam Balam books, in an illustration in the Book of Kaua (*VIII.2*).

VIII.2 *The seizure known as 'spider-snake macaw'*

The macaw here is recognizably the same disease-bringing bird as the one who sits on the moon goddess Ixchel's shoulders in the Dresden screenfold (*VIII.1*). The 'spider-snake' (*am-can*) which further identifies this particular seizure is entwined under its feet. In the caption, written here in the Roman alphabet and not hieroglyphs, the disease is said to 'fall' on 12 June ('tu lahcapis Junio') on the entry of the sign Cancer, rather than on a Sacred Round date. It is also described as a breath, draught or Wind (*ik*) which may afflict a patient, and is assigned the colours purple (*tzitz*) and green (*yax*), characteristic of shamanistic diagnosis. The page forms a link with pre-Columbian Maya medicine but beyond these details it is hard to interpret.

Book of Kaua, p. 4

VIII.3 *A Maya chant to cure fever and 'fire'* *(skin eruptions)*

Fever is one of the sicknesses which upset 'Mankind's ideal course', according to the Maya. 'Fire' ailments, like seizures, form a category of disease dealt with in their screenfolds, as well as in the collection of oral chants known in English as The Ritual of the Bacabs, quoted here. To cure his patient, the shaman persuades him of his power over the disease, sometimes (not here) invoking the aid of brave tutelary figures known as 'bacabs'. Among his equipment he carries cloths in the four colours of the basic hieroglyphic colour set, and the emblematic fan also used, for example, in the peyote cult of northern Mexico. He personally receives the heat afflicting the patient's skin, hypnotically insisting on the coolness of his own body. In a climate where snow is unknown he invokes coloured hail (*bat*) and white aquatic plants. *Zizbaten*, 'cool hail', is a general term in Maya for anything cold; and thus coloured it is said by the Navajo to have been given by the sun as a remedy for evil and disease. The Maya name of the water-lily, 'palm of the hand', is associated with the healer's own cool hand.

This is to cool burning fever and to cool fire, the ailment fire.

My foot's coolness, my hand's coolness,
    as I cooled this fire.
Fivefold my white hail, my black hail, yellow hail,
    as I cool the fire.
Thirteenfold my red cloth, my white cloth, black cloth,
yellow cloth,
    when I answered the strength of this fire.
A black fan my emblem,
    as I answered the strength of this fire.
With me comes the white water-maize,
    and I answered the strength of this fire.
With me comes the white water-lily,
    and I have answered the strength of this fire.
Just now I settled my foot's coolness, my hand's coolness.
    Amen.

Ritual of the Bacabs, p. 63

VIII.4 *Herbs used in Aztec cures*

The original illustrations of this Aztec herbal are exquisite; several use elements of Toltec writing. They accompany an explanatory text (in thirteen chapters) by the Aztec physician Martín de la Cruz, translated into Latin by his colleague Juan Badianus of Xochimilco.

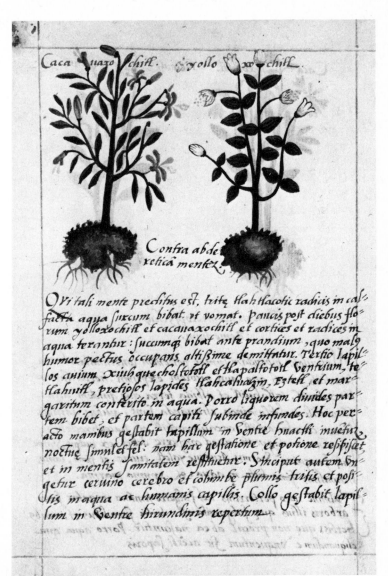

Both scholars were members of the Franciscan Sahagún's college at Tlatelolco. The herbal, entitled *Libellus de Medicinalibus Indorum Herbis*, was presented to the son of Antonio de Mendoza, viceroy of Mexico, in 1552. On this page we see the flower of the cocoa bean (*cacaua xochitl*; left) which, as an item of ancient Mesoamerican commerce, is traditionally rendered. Beside it, the half-opened bud of the 'heart flower' (*yollo xochitl* = *Magnolia glauca*) strongly resembles sacrificial hearts depicted in the ritual screenfolds. Both plants are depicted growing in sandy soil, with conventionally exposed roots.

Against stupidity of mind

Let one who is possessed of such a mind drink the crushed roots of the *tlatlacotic* in hot water, that he may vomit. A few days later let the roots and flowers of the *yollo-xochitl* and *cacaua-xochitl* be crushed in water, and let him drink the liquor before eating, wherewith the evil humour in the chest will be largely driven out. Third: let the small stones in the stomachs of the birds *xiuhquechol-tototl* and *tlapa-tototl*, the *tetlahuitl*, the precious stones *tlacal-huatzin*, *eztetl* and pearl be ground together in water; after this divide the liquor into three parts, one of which he drinks and the second is at once poured on his head. Having done this, let him carry in his hands the stone found in the stomach of the *huactli*, or hawk, together with its gall-bladder; with this and the drink he will come to himself and his sanity of mind be restored. Let his head also be anointed with the brain of a raven and a dove's feathers crushed and put in water with human hairs. On his neck let him carry the stone found in a swallow's stomach.

Martín de la Cruz, *Libellus de Medicinalibus Indorum Herbis*, p. 53v.

VIII.5 *Encouragement given to a herb to fight a disease*

In this Aztec healing formula, the medicine is addressed by the shaman-doctor as 'green woman', which here is peyote. Swallowed by the patient as an antidote, it is said to descend to the Seven Caves (*chicomoztoc*), signifying both the stomach and the womb of tribal history (cf. *VI.5*). For the shaman, directing and exhorting the medicine is a means of establishing his own power. Against the anonymous 'him' who threatens the patient, described as the medicine's 'creature', the shaman asserts his own identity as the one in control.

> Hey, come along, green woman;
> scare, scare the green fever, the blackish fever,
> the red fever, the yellow fever:
> I have already sent you to the Seven Caves.
> Not tomorrow nor the day after,
> but right now you will make him leave.
> What god, what prodigy,
> thinks to destroy your creature?
> The lord of magic is me and me alone.

Aztec healing formula

VIII.6 *Human anatomy and the Twenty Signs*

Two separate traditions, Toltec and European, are fused in this figure, taken from the Aztec Ríos Codex. As icons of Toltec ritual, the 'anatomies' of Tezcatlipoca, Tlaloc and other figures appear in the screenfolds together with the Twenty Signs in a variety of arrangements, there being no fixed spatial connection between any one sign and any one part of the body. In European astrology, by contrast, the 12 signs of the Zodiac, and the 7 celestial bodies (sun, moon and five planets), each affected specific organs and limbs, from Aries at the head and face to Pisces at the foot. European astrological figures circulated in New Spain in almanacs known as 'reportorios', and the interest of this page lies in the way it fuses the two traditions. According to the European model, the Twenty Signs are now firmly attached, for blood-letting, to specific organs and limbs. The connection here between the genitals and Snake (V) even recalls the European assignment of Scorpio to that area. Other 'parallels' are not exploited, however, Leo and Jaguar (XIV), Aquarius and Water (IX), for example. More striking, in this frontal figure, is that members of a pair (hands, feet, etc.) *each* have a sign, a dualism evident generally in Mesoamerican frontal figures. Moreover, the sequence is not 'straightened out' to follow the simple order of the Zodiac. It retains all the complexity of pre-Columbian logic, in which diseases were treated according to the sign on which they began, in time.

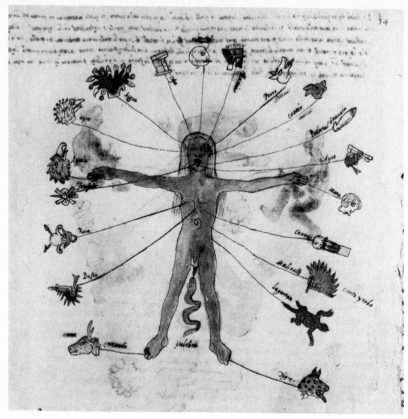

Ríos Codex, p. 53r.

VIII.7 *The occupant of a Spanish hospital (1565)*

To the first of the two hands to write on this page are due the picture of the hospital and the statement, in Nahua and in Toltec writing, of the quantity of building material supplied for its construction: 350 hods of lime. The second writer specifies, in Spanish, that the hospital in question was 'for Indians', that the material was ordered by the viceroy Luis de Velasco, and that the suppliers were not paid. A further note 'pagado', upper left, reveals that they eventually were. Architecturally, the hospital resembles a House or sanctuary but does not make a cheerful impression. The man in it is said to be *cocoxqui*, that is, sick and withered; he is old and groaning (note the signs around and before his mouth) and, above all, alone, as if about to pass unaccompanied through the western House of darkness on the journey beyond death.

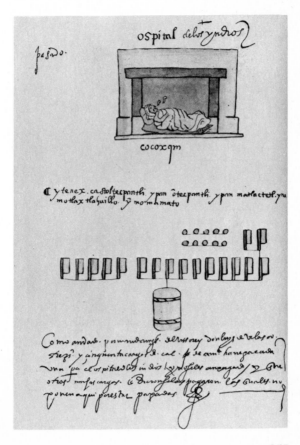

Osuna Codex,
p. 38

VIII.8 *The Iroquois antidote to the disease of public grief*

When one of the chiefs of the Iroquois Great League died, he was replaced at an elaborate ceremony for which chiefs from all the member Nations gathered. The mourning tribe welcomed the others as companions able to console and requicken them. The dangers of disintegration and anarchy are not underestimated; on the contrary, they are insisted upon. The horror of death is fully contemplated in the remains of the deceased chief; and the demonic Great Destroyer is said to be ever-watchful, the 'faceless' Atarapaho conquered by Hiawatha when he founded the League in the sixteenth century. Death threatens anarchy, expressed as actual physical illness in the bodies of the survivors, which drains their soul and life force. This concept echoes that in the 'Mankind's ideal course' passage in the Book of Chumayel (cf. *II.2*); and also like the Maya, the Iroquois constituted themselves federally, as Elder and Younger brothers, the one moiety acting as consoler to the other. The cure for this illness is then also collective, the Ritual of Condolence as it is known, agreed upon by the federal chiefs who founded the League. The main liturgy consists of a series of articles, each read from a string of 'attesting wampum', of which this article, called 'Within his breast', is the fourth.

Is not what has befallen thee then so dreadful that it must not be neglected? For, at the present time, there are wrenchings without ceasing within thy breast, and also within thy mind. Now truly, the disorder now among the organs within thy breast is such that nothing can be clearly discerned. So great has been the affliction that has befallen thee that yellow spots have developed within thy body, and truly thy life forces have become greatly weakened thereby; truly thou dost now suffer.

It is that, therefore, that in ancient times it thus came to pass that the Federal Chiefs, our grandsires, made a formal rule, saying, 'Let us unite our affairs; let us formulate regulations; let us ordain this among others that what we shall prepare we will designate by the name Water-of-pity or compassion which shall be the essential thing to be used where Death has caused this dreadful affliction, inducing bitter grief.'

Condolence Ritual, article 4

VIII.9 *Curing chants in the notebooks of two Cherokee doctors*

Heirs to the southern Mound Builders and highly organized politically, the Cherokee held their territory and towns in the southern Appalachians well into the nineteenth century. Their voluminous literature awaits foreign readers. Much of it is written in the syllabary invented by Sequoyah in 1819. With its 80 or so characters (which stem in part from old Iroquoian signs), the syllabary is better adapted than the Roman alphabet to Cherokee phonetics. Newspapers were printed in it well into this century and it has served the purposes of daily life. The fluid hands in these notebooks, kept by doctors named Ketigisti Thomson and W. W. Long, show the ease with which it could be written.

The English translation is of the first text, by Thomson, an eastern Cherokee born in North Carolina about 1870. It is the first of the four stanzas of a shamanistic chant. In each stanza a different

Ketigisti Thomson, Notebook

W. W. Long, Notebook

creature is invoked as an agent against the disease: after the kingfisher come fishing-hawk, mink and otter. All are white and rare. They are called upon to take away the effect of a bad spell cast on the patient which works through the saliva and produces worms and parasites. Once all four are gathered they are asked to step on the shaman's white cloth, on which the steeped medicine is ready. There is a characteristic shift of tenses within and between the stanzas which produces a hypnotic effect.

> *ʃ}ɾᶜ* rapidly you have come here, kingfisher, you white one
> *ᶜᵗ* you are magical
> *ᶜᵗ* you never fail
> *ᶜᵗ* high above, resting there
> *ᶜᵗ* rapidly you are descending
> *ᶜᵗ* the disease you have come to take away with you
> *ᶜᵗ* a second time you never appear.

Note:

ʃ}ɾᶜ = *s-ge* or '*ske*', the formal opening of the chant
ᶜᵗ = *ha*, a noise of stress and encouragement.

VIII.10 *The climax of the Cuna 'Serkan Ikala' chant*

Residents of the continental isthmus, the Cuna belong to the language family of the Chibcha, which extends from Maya territory in the north to the old Inca empire in the south. Like their Carib and Arawak neighbours, these modern Chibchas use ideographs, in boustrophedon, to record prayers, both Christian and native American. Such is the script used to preserve this healing ritual, the Serkan Ikala or 'Spirits of the Dead Way' which, though written with crayons on paper, has antecedents in the more traditional use of painted balsa-wood boards. During the ritual, the patient lies in a hammock, with shaman's dolls beneath him. This quotation is from the final section of the 572-line Serkan Ikala chant. The ideographs shown here form stanzas as follows: 1-4; 5-9; 10-13; 14-17; 18-21; 22-26.

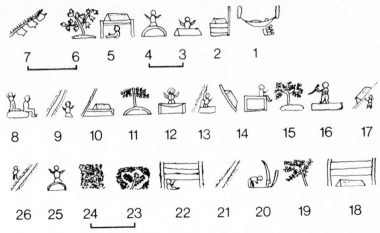

1. The Neles are the defence under the patient's hammock.
2. From the east the chiefs come, summoned
3. against the place of the Ancient Spirits they are the defence
4. making the whole place scarey.
5. From the west the chiefs come, summoned.
6. Nele Nettle with his men comes, summoned;
7. he comes with prickly leaf-cloths; comes stinging;
8. against the white-faced ancients they are the defence;
9. they are entangling the way, making the whole place scarey.
10. From the big sea the chiefs come, summoned.
11. Nele Small Peppers are the defence;
12. against the white-faced ancients they are the defence;
13. they are entangling the way, making the whole place scarey.
14. From opposite the big sea the chiefs come, summoned.
15. Nele Cabur Pepper with his men comes, summoned;
16. against the ancient spirits they come as the defence;
17. they are entangling the way, making the whole place scarey.
18. From above the chiefs come, summoned.
19. Nele Red Pepper with his men comes, summoned;
20. against the ancient spirits they are the defence;
21. they are entangling the way, making the whole place scarey.
22. From below the chiefs come, summoned.
23. Nele Mupakkaopinale Pepper with his men comes, summoned;
24. Muppakka Oparpalele the chiefs come, summoned;
25. against the place of the ancient spirits they are the defence;
26. they are entangling the way, making the whole place scarey.

Serkan Ikala

255

Each of the six stanzas with which the chant closes falls into two halves: the first concerns the residences from which the shaman's own forces or chiefs (*sailakan*) arrive, beginning with east; the second, the action they are to perform as Neles or herbs-in-person, barring the approach roads to the patient, against the spirits of the dead, the Serkana. The symbols are written out in boustrophedon, giving details of residence and plant, antagonist and defensive action. These sets of 'constant variables' recall those of Midewiwin scrolls or of the sandpaintings of Navajo 'Ways'. Cuna writing, however, varies somewhat from individual to individual; Guillermo Hayans, the author of this text, chose to employ different symbols from those used by his master, Nele Rubén Pérez Kantule. And in the work of both subtle syncopations in the oral chants are often noted at the expense of symmetry in the writing. In the second stanza here, for example, the pungent and prickly qualities of the nettle are specially brought out in an 'irregular' extra symbol (7), which shows three *molas*, the shaman's leaf-cloths, strung on a line. The six residences (*neka*) are the only absolutely regular item, at the start of each stanza. They recall the 'world-directions' of peoples on either side of the isthmian Cuna. East, 'sunrise' (2), takes priority and, faced by west (5), makes a binary continuum on which the other residences – 'big sea' (10), and its opposite (14); above (18) and below (22) – depend in both time and space; *neka* is 'moment' as well as house, like *pacha* in Quechua. Together, these six stanzas recapitulate the idea of the whole ritual (*ikala*), confirming the shaman's control over all imaginable ways (*ikala*).

VIII.11 *Initiation into Mide medicine*

Originally inscribed on birchbark, these symbols were used in the initiation ceremonies of the Midewiwin; the text was copied out at Mille Lacs, Minnesota, in the late nineteenth century by the Mide shaman Sikassige, an Ojibwa Algonkin who also dictated the oral text. As in the Walam Olum, the symbols come in fours, while each pair represents the dialogue between the initiator and the candidate, fresh from his steam bath. The initiator opens by stating his knowledge of magic herbs, roots and plants (1). A very wide range of such medicines is listed on Midewiwin 'prescription' sticks, usually in groups of four. This knowledge, first imparted by the Venus-like Great Rabbit (Manabozho), is integral to the Midewiwin and has as its aim the regeneration of ailing humanity;

it is intricately related to knowledge of the sky, especially the phases of the moon, and to the experience of the shaman's trance journey to the heart of the sky. It will be lost (2, 3) if the Midewiwin Society does not replace healers who have grown old or died. Once his application is accepted the candidate has his head 'put on' (4).

After the pause (two vertical lines), we see a pouch of otter skin, an animal sacred to Manito, filled with 'migi' shells (5). When opened within the Mide lodge its power is enormous; as a test the candidate is asked to place the energy-filled migi shells, at a maximum of twenty, at twenty agreed points on a patient's body – a procedure reminiscent of the medical placing of the Twenty Signs (cf. *VIII.6*) in Mesoamerica. Next (6) the candidate is shown on his journey into the sky, his feet towards the eastern half of the celestial arch. At his destination the thunderbird is invoked (7) as a token of enhanced vision (8). In the last stanza the candidate is confirmed as a fellow Mide, in touch with spirits who have previously walked into the sky; the communication between them is like that between celestial bodies or heads (11). As a whole, this ceremony may be adapted to each of the four stages of Midewiwin initiation, here shown as four dots inside the lodge (9).

My arm is almost pulled out with digging medicine.
It is full of medicine.
    Almost crying because the medicine is lost.
Yes, there is much medicine you may cry for.
    Yes, I see there is plenty of it.

When I come out the sky becomes clear.
    The spirit has given me power to see.
I brought the medicine to bring life.
    I too, see how much there is.

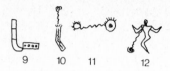

9 10 11   12

I am going to the medicine lodge.
 I take life from the sky.
Let us talk to one another.
 The spirit is in my body, my friend.

Sikassige, Midewiwin text

VIII.12 *The journey of the soul after death*

As a medicine man in the fullest sense, the shaman helps the soul through its most perilous journey, death. The text here was collected around 1910 among the Winnebago Sioux in Wisconsin, who used a syllabary borrowed from the Algonkin to record their medical literature. The words are typical of those confided to the deceased during his four-day wake, in which he passes through the Underworld before walking into the sky. The journey itself can be undertaken only after certain ritual tests and examinations, for which the deceased is also prepared. On the way he may be helped by the spirits of people killed by the shaman as a warrior in battle, though for this to work and not have adverse effects the shaman must not exaggerate his prowess. The actual course of the journey in time and space corresponds exactly with that described by Algonkin shamans from their trances; and, more dramatically, with the cosmological narratives of Mesoamerica. As if referring to a well-known doctrine, this Sioux text alludes briefly but firmly to the ritual stations of Venus and the sun: west – the setting sun; the Underworld – Herecgunina's lodge; east – the footprint of the day; and the zenith, the lodge of the Earthmaker at midday. Like the lords of the Maya and Nahua underworlds, Herecgunina had to be outwitted for the soul to pass; the four days of the journey to his abode correspond to the half-period of Venus's absence at inferior conjunction (cf. *V.2*). What is more, the instructions given by the grandmother regarding the footprints in the eastern sky enable us to understand the Maya account of the *uinal* as a rising into true life (cf. *V.14*). Like the *uinal*, the Sioux soul has to get the rhythm of the footsteps printed in the sky in order to join his relatives in the heart of heaven. Given the historical and geographical distance between the Sioux and the Maya, the correspondence of the detail here is little short of astonishing. The only way of explaining it is to see the movements of Venus – the only planet besides the much smaller and hastier Mercury to pass through the 'underworld', i.e. inferior conjunction – as a paradigm for the journey of both the shaman and epic heroes like Quetzalcoatl.

My grandchild, Earthmaker is waiting for you in great expectation. There is the door to the setting sun. On your way stands the lodge of Herecgunina, and his fire. Those who have come [the souls of brave men] from the land of the souls to take you back will touch you. There the road will branch off towards your right and you will see the footprints of the day on the blue sky before you. These footprints represent the footprints of those who have passed into life again. Step into the places where they have stepped and plant your feet into their footprints, but be careful you do not miss any. Before you have gone very far, you will come into a forest broken by open prairies here and there. Here, in this beautiful country, these souls whose duty it is to gather other souls will come to meet you. Walking on each side of you they will take you safely home. As you enter the lodge of the Earthmaker you must hand to him the sacrificial offerings. Here the inquiry that took place in the first lodge will be repeated and answered in the same manner. Then he will say to you, 'All that your grandmother has told you is true. Your relatives are waiting for you in great expectation. Your home is waiting for you. Its door will be facing the mid-day sun. Here you will find your relatives gathered.'
Sioux liturgy

IX Singer and scribe

THE preceding chapters in this book present texts which have, or have had, some demonstrable function, ritual or social. At the same time these texts have intrinsic qualities; the singers and scribes who composed them were normally aware of their own skill as professionals, of using specific conventions, styles and modes, and of having what in some cases amounts to theories of creativity.

Speech and script

At the most fundamental level, with the faculty of speech the artist imitates the god who speaks to create. In the properly ordered thread of his words he mimics and indeed records the divine utterance through which the world was created in oral cosmogony. Wholly dependent on memory, he composes chants and narratives with a strong and conscious emphasis on this same basic principle of coherence, which is sufficient to itself.

Insofar as this verbal discourse is modified by or relies on visual symbols and signs, these are recognized as a means of creative expression which is analogous to speech. Such is certainly the case throughout the area north of the Maya, with its common fund of iconography and even principles of writing (anticlockwise reading, inversion as negation, for example). In recounting the origins of their ritual, the Mide shamans, the sandpainters of the Southwest and the Toltecs alike refer to 'culture-bringers' whose identities are similar and who are distinguished by having provided song and writing as reciprocal arts. The Great Rabbit figure said to have founded the Midewiwin invented their four-line chants as the complement to the four-symbol stanzas of the script he gave them, just as songs and sandpaintings were brought as a twin gift to the Navajo.

In the Toltec tradition it is Quetzalcoatl who has this role, the singing master and the teacher of the screenfold scribe. In the Nahua language 'to utter a flower' and 'to paint a song' are phrases

which well illustrate the degree to which this reciprocity was felt
between the two media. Sustained comparison between them led
further to the idea of craftsmanship for its own sake, as it did among
the Parnassians of nineteenth-century Europe; there are passages in
Aztec poetry which catch exactly the correspondence between verse
and the visual and plastic arts, and their promise of enduring fame,
celebrated in Gautier's poem 'L'Art'. The Nahua word for artistry
in this sense was *toltecayotl*, 'Toltec-ness', in honour of Quetzalcoatl of Tula whose brush-pen was the foil for Tezcatlipoca's spear.

The Maya made an apt image of their own tradition in an incised
bone from Tikal, which shows a hand holding a brush-pen
emerging from a mouth like a tongue. Here, the voice and the
graphic image are not just reciprocal media: the tongue finds direct
expression in the pen, as indeed it did in hieroglyphic writing which
in this respect was as much at the service of speech as the Roman
alphabet into which it was later transcribed. In the calendar of their
Classic Era, the Maya wedded the rich iconography of north
America to arithmetical principles of place-value used by their
predecessors and, to the south, by the Chibcha and the Inca, with
their *quipus*. The result of this combination, Maya hieroglyphic
writing, is unique in the New World; and in reflecting upon their
literature Maya authors point to its origins in their calendar and
arithmetic. They write songs which contrive to recount the
beginning of time, and narratives which end but do not end. Maya
authors are also distinguished by their attention to the *idea* of the

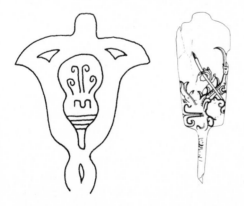

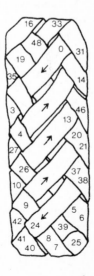

Figs. 18–20. (*Left*) Flower with inset guitar (after a
modern Cuna applique *mola*; cf. *VIII.10*); (*centre*)
incised bone, Tikal; (*right*) hieroglyphic text 'woven' in
stone, Stela J, Copan – cf. fig. 1(e).

book, *uooh* in Yucatec, *vuh* in Quiche. In valuing the power of the book, at its highest, to sustain and regulate, they see it less as God's actual scripture than as the work of authors who may become god-like in the exercise of their art. This in turn involves the idea of the text as literally textile or woven, the 'mat' (*pop*) of authority on which calendrical time units are seated during their rule, and the base of wisdom which gives the *Popol vuh* its title. A similar notion is found in the Toltec tradition, where the mat of authority is equated with the matted fibres of the screenfold book, and is evoked also in Inca textiles, e.g. in the figured belts of authority so carefully detailed by Guaman Poma.

Mode

Enquiry into the social origins of literature reveals how certain types of composition have developed from having an actual function in society into genres and modes cultivated for their own sake, regardless of context. The connections of Gilgamesh with shamanist therapy and of the pastoral mode with songs once actually sung by Dorian shepherds are well-known cases in point. We find the same development in America, especially in the complex societies of Mexico and Peru where urban poets cultivated their art in modes derived from the tasks of the countryside and from the ritual occasions of public life. Such poets formed a 'Brotherhood' at the Aztec imperial court and were known as *haravek* in Peru. In its immense wealth, Quechua poetry still bears the imprint of the Inca state, which designated songs for a wide range of tasks; in the Quechua play *Ollantay*, for example, the song-for-scaring-birds-from-the-crops is recited to great dramatic effect before Pachacuti at his court. Basic types or modes of song which deserve special attention are those originating in planting, warfare, and funeral liturgy.

Of itself planting implies creativity, a germination and flowering. Like the plant growing from its seed, the poem grows organically and unfolds. The poets of the Aztec Brotherhood referred to their works as perfect plants while the very word for poetry, *xochicuicatl* or flower-song, stems from the same idea. The element '*xo-*', to grow or flourish, is found also in the Nahua mode in which this idea is most highly developed: the *xopan-cuicatl* or burgeon song. In this mode not just the poem but the poet himself may be the flower or plant, erect and resplendent: through his art he acquires the essence of the perfect substance maize or embodies the plant which has

262

enhanced his sensation or expanded his consciousness, cocoa or peyote, for example. Like his creation he is shaped from within, genetically and organically. In the 'burgeon' mode of Nahua poetry, as in the American cosmogonical doctrines of man's vegetal essence which it implies, there is far less emphasis on inspiration, on the breath from outside filling the poet like an empty vessel, than on growth from within. It is just this aesthetic which fascinated the Surrealists, notably Antonin Artaud, in their dealings with Mexico when searching for alternatives to Western norms.

A second mode in the repertoire of the Aztec Brotherhood was the war- or eagle-song (*yao-* or *cuauhtli-cuicatl*). In part this mode recalls the warrior's origins as a hunter. Indeed, the very convention (widespread in northern America) of depicting capture by drawing a 'voice' line from the heart of the hunter's trophy corresponds to the conqueror's practice of demanding the war- and other songs of an enemy as tribute, these being used at will by the court poets of Peru as well as Mexico. Also the risk run by the hunter is celebrated in the bravery of the warrior who in his profession gains an enhanced understanding of existence. The words of the Pawnee warrior faced with death: 'Let us see, is this real, this life I'm living', are elaborated in many Nahua poems in the war mode. Also the excitement of the battle itself and the glory of conquest produce poetry which is best described as heroic.

A third major mode of Nahua poetry is the lament or 'orphan song', *icno-cuicatl*, which explores feelings of cosmic abandonment and the precariousness of mortal life before the unknown. In his *Key into the Language of America*, Roger Williams reports that, at the onset of their long winter night in New England, the Algonkin would cry, as a song, 'ntouag onnausinnummin' ('we are orphaned'). In this mode we find the suspicion that all attempts to guarantee the survival of the soul, and the shaman's journey to the heart of the sky and the 'transformation' effected there, may after all be self-delusion and that the only reality is here and now. The 'orphan song' doubtless originated in funeral liturgy, which posed the question: 'Where does this being really go from here?' – compare the lament from Tupac Amaru, for example, *I.11*. In examples of the orphan mode as it was cultivated at the Aztec court we find the remembrance of dead heroes who have left on the irreversible journey past death and whose characteristic bravery acts as encouragement to those left behind.

Insofar as it explores ideas of regeneration and survival through art, Nahua poetry draws particularly on the twin notions of planting and hunting, on the contrast between maize man rooted in earth and man able to walk into the sky, between agro- and astronomical existence. As we saw above (p. 180), reconciling these two ways of being was the principal object of such graphic texts as the Sky and Earth sandpainting; and in the *Popol vuh* the maize planted at the centre of Xmucane's house by her Twin grandsons, as what they call 'the sign of our word', thrives – or not – as they fare on their cosmic journey. In this chapter we find further variations on the same theme. The very definition of the Toltec poet is the traveller who becomes a plant; and the logic behind it is also found in the converse Chimu depiction of the beanseed sprouting legs to become the messenger.

Style

Still with the Aztec Brotherhood as a guide, we see that styles of poetry differ from modes in stemming not so much from activities and experiences common to most societies as from the peculiarities of a region, in speech, manners and dress. It is just this regional diversity in America which makes it impossible to give anything like an adequate account of its oral literatures (though certain anthologists have attempted the task). In the main 'foci' of the continent however, native poets themselves have modified the situation by explicitly recognizing the differences between their work and that of others, translating and commenting upon it. One of the main bonds and sources of encouragement between the different nations who took part in the Ghost Dance movement was the exchange of songs, a practice which may be traced back to the Midewiwin or more generally to the common links of the Algonkin and Sioux with the Mound Builder tradition. In this respect the practices of the Inca and the Aztecs were more systematic, since they saw themselves exercising the conqueror's right to their subjects' songs. Also, since the system was centralized in both cases we find 'styles' defined as something different from the metropolitan norm, with touches of the exotic. In Part I of his Chronicle, Guaman Poma defines the very geography of the Tahuantinsuyu through the songs and 'flowery music' typical of each of its four parts, all contributing to the wealth of Cuzco: large drums and quena flutes from the Collasuyu; deer-horns and tambourines from the Chinchasuyu; topless dancers and transvestites from the Antisuyu and Amazon with pan-pipes; and satirical singers with death-masks from the Condesuyu. Similarly, in the Aztec *Cantares mexicanos* manuscript and a companion manuscript called *Romances de los señores de la Nueva España* (Ballads of the Lords of New Spain) styles are designated after songs from the regions conquered by Tenochtitlan: to the west and north those of the 'wild' Otomi and Tepanec; to the east, beyond the Colhua towns and Tlaxcala, those of the Huaxtec Maya and Totonac of Cuextlan on the Gulf Coast, whose exquisite etching in shell was also much appreciated far beyond them again, in the townships along the Mississippi.

The silencing and the obliteration of the native Americans have been predicted as inevitable and imminent almost since Columbus. Yet, against all odds, that catastrophe has not happened; nearly half a millennium later, in more than one part of the continent, American speech and signs persist, and their coherence. During this time, in order to survive, native singers and scribes have however sometimes chosen to be overlooked, to dissemble before an invader whose incomprehension has been eclipsed only by greed. To this extent, the texts gathered in this book may be understood as fragments of a larger message, which has yet to be heard and read.

IX. 1 *Nainu-ema the world-maker and Rafu-ema the word-maker*

Like the Guarani, the Witoto near the Caqueta river on the upper Amazon form part of the 'Amazonian cosmos', as it has been called; also like the Guarani, they have oral literature, and their ritual chants concerning the origin of the world and that of man are so constructed that they build up cumulatively, phrase by phrase. The fragment of their oral cosmogony here does honour to their power of conceptual and associative thought-as-voice. With the utmost mental effort, at first lying down as if in a hammock, the father Nainu-ema struggles to win a firm place to stand on the antediluvian 'dream earth'; his persistence closely resembles that of the father Ñamandu as he probes the 'eldest darkness' in the opening chants of the Guarani 'Ayvu Rapyta' or 'Origin of Human Speech' (cf. *V.10*). Just as Nainu-ema thinks reality into existence, so Rafu-ema, the story-teller, threads words into a continuous narrative. Creation of god and the artist alike *is* human utterance, here pristine and devoid of written support.

a phantasma, *naino*, nothing else
the father touched the image of the phantasm
                touched a secret, nothing else
the father Nainu-ema, who-has-the-phantasm, held it by a dream
to himself
                thought hard about it
he held nothing substantial
he held the phantasma by the thread of a dream
                by the line of his breath
in the void he probed for the mass of the phantasma
the probe was nothing: 'I fasten on the void'
                he probed nothing
Then the father thought hard and probed for the mass of the word-
    thing
in the void he fastened on to the mass of the phantasma with the
    thread of a dream
in the void the father pressed his adhesive
                dreamed his adhesive on to it
    held it by the thinnest thread
he seized the mass of the phantasma
    pressed and pressed it
    seized, held and seized it again
then he set himself on the plain, this dream earth
    stepped on to the plain
he held the phantasma
he spat spittle from his mouth he spat again and again
he held the phantasma firm
then he set himself on this earthly part
he peeled off the sky, he seized the earth
    peeled off the blue sky and the white sky
        At the base of the sky, Rafu-ema, who-has-the-story,
                            thought hard about it
let these words be made
here above we relate them

Witoto Genesis

naino mikade inyede nainona
fore hetaide momade
hana hetaide dyiide mikade
moma Nainuema nikaido abi mosinyote
 abina
   henorite
mika amena inyede mosinyote
nainokoni nikai igaido mosinyote
   hafaikido
ninomo hinade naino ihiyake fakaode
fakademo dyiide hinade dyireike
    fakade dyiide
habi henode momade bikino hidyake fakade

hinade naino hidyake medyeridode
 nikai igaido dyirireidode
momade hinade arebaike nitanode
   arebaike nikariode
 iseikedo mosinyote
naino hidyake naino gaitanode
 nitade nitade
 gaitanode mosinyote gaitaikeda
iesa rainadate inikoni nikaranikoni
 inidyomoreidade
naino mosinyote
muitade imugi ie fue imugu imuguri muitade
naino mosinyokeda
iesa rainadate birunyukoni
ie biko hirenote birunyu gaiktaikeda
  hirenote biko mogoguito koreko
   ie henikekoni iesaai abina
    henohenorite
bikino komuitate
kai ari atidiekino Rafuema

1   2   3   4   ‖ 5   6   7   8

9   10   11   12   ‖ 13   14   15   16

Kweweziashish: Midewiwin scroll

Midewiwin song-board

IX.2 *Midewiwin song-symbols*

In its closeness to Sikassige's medical initiation text (cf. *VIII.11*), this scroll by a near-contemporary Kweweziashish ('Bad Boy') points up the importance of 'capturing' songs and symbols for use by the Mide shamans. The one who endowed the Midewiwin with this treasure, as well as with its medical knowledge, is the Great Rabbit, whose first identity is the hunter who walks into the sky as Venus. Here, instead of the arm of the medicine digger in Sikassige's text, we have hunting symbols (1 and 10), and the emphasis is less on personal healing power than on the celestial journey as such and on the winning of song (8 and 12). The introduction of music into the Midewiwin is celebrated in the additional final stanza, where we see a drummer (15) and the song-symbol of a bear (16; before the upright 'magic panther' at the end). The bear has the conventional 'heart-line' to show that its voice has been captured and that its song is known.

In the other text, a song-board, eight such song-symbols (that is two stanzas) are set out in pairs, male and female, showing the antiphonal nature of the chants they match. Applied to the bodies of patients in curing rituals, the board, with its superb line and balance, leaves no doubt about the sophistication of the Midewiwin inciser of symbols.

IX.3 *Quetzalcoatl teaches the arts of song and painting*

According to the Vienna screenfold, Quetzalcoatl was an artist and a 'culture-bearer' as well as an agent in Toltec cosmogony. Before emerging as Venus (cf. *V.4*), he appears in a series of eight paired figures as model and instructor in matters of dress, dance, warfare and other arts: in the two pairs of figures in the series shown here, both times he raises his index finger as a mark of authority (1 and 3), and then points it forward as the teacher, wearing his round hat (2 and 4). In the first pair he brings knowledge of Flower-song, the fine speech of poetry and rhetoric. The speech sign with the Flower entwined in it rises from his mouth, just as the feathers of his head-dress rise. In the second pair he is the scribe with his brush, the 'tlacuilolli' setting down thought with his hand, once again according to the movement of his feathered head-dress. Moreover, a highly ingenious counterpoint is made between the two arts. In design, the voice flames (3) in the scribe's heart (*yolteutl*) recall the

Flower-song of the singer (2), while the coloured stones set like palette paints in the body of the singer (2) echo the idea of the painted page (4). Quetzalcoatl the Toltec thus illustrates the idea of art which transcends its dual expression in word and sign. He is also shown to be the philosopher because the colours under his brush are red and black, the essential terms of knowledge.

Vienna screenfold, p. 48

IX.4 *Toltec definitions of the poet*

In this elaborate sequence, taken from the *Cantares mexicanos* manuscript, the Aztec Brotherhood of poets show a professional concern with the art they are engaged in. For they put together two of the modes of Nahua poetry, the 'orphan' and the 'burgeon' modes, in order to arrive at an idea of poetry itself. In the first mode, in the first part of the poem, we hear of the lost Toltec hero Nacxitl.

His successor at Tula, 10-Flower (reigned AD 895–930?), bemoans the loss in the phrases of funeral and installation liturgy (lines 13–14). Leaving his people orphaned, Nacxitl is said to have journeyed east. This corresponds to the actual journey of conquest he made, which is also noted in Maya sources (cf. *II.2* and *V.6*). Following the road past Cholula, the volcano Poyauhtecatitlan, Acallan and Xicalanco (lines 7–9, 22), he crossed to Yucatan, where he erected the columns of inverted snakes characteristic of Toltec architecture (line 2) at Chichen Itza and other cities in that area. However, Nacxitl's departure, remembered so long afterwards in poetry, is also symbolic, insofar as he is implicitly identified with the Venus-like Quetzalcoatl. Like Quetzalcoatl he endows Tula with script and other arts (lines 31–2, 36–7) and is said to be both the 'victim' and the 'lord who pierces' (line 12), to whom his people are devoted and who ascends into the sky.

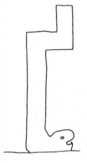

Fig. 21. Snake Column, one of the *coatlaquetzalli* (designed by Quetzalcoatl), found notably at Tula and Chichen Itza; the tail is arched forward to act as a beam bearer, while the jaw is pressed on the ground.

Fig. 22. Aztec musical instruments (after Florentine (Codex).

Having walked, like Venus, up to Tlalocan, the heart of heaven rich in both quetzal plumes and water, 'transformation is effected' (lines 41–5; see above p. 104): the hero is switched from astro- to agronomy, from traveller to plant. In this second part of the poem, and in the 'burgeon' mode, the poem like the poet is reborn, emerges like a resplendent maize plant. We now witness the artistry of the interplay between the twin crafts of the singer and the scribe. The counterpoint between the 'uttered flower' and the 'painted song' (lines 51–2) corresponds exactly with the pairs of Quetzalcoatl figures in the Vienna screenfold. The 'royal fibres' of the screenfold book (line 47) are the woven mat of authority, 'textile' text which yet is transcended in the finely expressed vision, the 'complete' heart (line 55). Awareness of his power gives the poet hope for survival and continuity through its being implanted in others (line

69). The Prince, Cocoa and Peyote flowers he invokes are fellow poets, with perceptions heightened like his own.

As a whole, the poem turns on the *idea* of Tula, the home base of the conqueror, the abundant paradise of the planter, and, now, a city of the mind. The details of its architecture are elaborately woven into the tense-structure of the poem. The sanctuary once 'stood' (line 1): the columns that bore its beams 'still remain', like the upright flowers (lines 2 and 81). Though the ceremonially laid sand has disappeared and the pyramid has cracked (lines 15–16), the houses sacred to Quetzalcoatl 'will always be there' (line 25), like the implanted word. The 'painted stone and wood' of Tula (lines 31 and 61) which Quetzalcoatl abandoned speak for themselves; and through memory the heart will come back (line 65).

> At Tula stood the beamed sanctuary,
> only the snake columns still stand,
> our prince Nacxitl has gone, has moved away.
> Our vanguard is wept for with conches;
> 5   he is going to his destruction in Tlapallan.
>
> He was there in Cholula,
> made an end at Mount Poyauhtecatitlan,
> crossed the water at Acallan.
> Our vanguard is wept for with conches;
> 10   he is going to his destruction in Tlapallan.
>
> I come to the frontier with winged finery,
> the lord who pierces and the victim.
> My fine-plumed lord has gone away
> has left me, 10-Flower, an orphan.
>
> 15   The pyramid burst apart hence my tears
> the sacred sand whirled up hence my desolation.
> My fine-plumed lord has gone away
> has left me, 10-Flower, an orphan.
>
> Tlapallan is where you are expected
> 20   is where you are destined to rest;
> you are moving on, my fine-plumed lord,
> destined for Xicalanco.
> Still yet, still yet . . . .
> Your house will always be there, your gates
> 25   your palace will always be there.
> You left them orphaned here at the Tula frontier.

You wept endlessly, great lord;
   your house will always be there, your gates
   your palace will always be there.
30   You left them orphaned here at the Tula frontier.

Stone and wood, you painted them
in the city of Tula.
   Where you ruled, our prince Nacxitl,
   your name will never be destroyed;
35   your people will always cry for you.

The turquoise house and the snake house, you built them
in the city of Tula.
   Where you ruled, our prince Nacxitl,
   your name will never be destroyed;
40   your people will always cry for you.

As white and yellow maize I am born,
The many-coloured flower of living flesh rises up
and opens its glistening seeds before the face of our mother.
In the moisture of Tlalocan, the quetzal water-plants open
    their corollas.
45 I am the work of the only god, his creation.

   Your heart lives in the painted page,
   you sing the royal fibres of the book,
   you make the princes dance,
   there you command by the water's discourse.
50 He created you,
he uttered you like a flower,
he painted you like a song:
a Toltec artist.
The book has come to the end:
55 your heart is now complete.

Here through art I shall live for ever.
Who will take me, who will go with me?
Here I stand, my friends.
A singer, from my heart I strew my songs,
60 my fragrant songs before the face of others.
I carve a great stone, I paint thick wood
my song is in them.

It will be spoken of when I have gone.
I shall leave my song-image on earth.
65 My heart shall live, it will come back,
my memory will live and my fame.
I cry as I speak and discourse with my heart.
Let me see the root of song,
let me implant it here on earth so it may be realized.
70 My heart shall live, it will come back,
my memory will live and my fame.
The Prince Flower gently breathes his aroma,
our flowers are uniting.
My song is heard and flourishes.
75 My implanted word is sprouting,
our flowers stand up in the rain.
The Cocoa flower gently opens his aroma,
the gentle Peyote falls like rain.
My song is heard and flourishes.
80 My implanted word is sprouting,
our flowers stand up in the rain.

Cantares mexicanos, ff. 26v.–27v.

IX.5 *The 'burgeon' mode of Aztec poetry*

Nahua poems in the 'burgeon' mode (see p. 263) offer sensations to
the mind through the sight, taste and smell of growing things which
strongly recall the iconography of Teotihuacan mural painting. Its
images of growth and splendour draw on the botanical expertise of
the Nahua and their cults of hallucinogens. In this example, such a
'flower' is both the agent of perception and the shape which
possesses the imagination. It is also what the poet himself becomes,
as he moves between the immediacy of here, the 'I-place' (*ni-can*),
and the oblivion of space, expressed as 'sometime'. His fellow poets
are similarly transformed, in the refined society or Brotherhood of
poets, as they dance round the upright drum (*huehuetl*) mentioned
here. As a guild, they took care of the correctness of the mode and
style, of the instruments used, and of rhythm and tone (for which an
exact notation exists in the *Cantares mexicanos* manuscript).
Consciousness of their art comes through in notions like the flower
'staining', that is, dyeing or painting the heart, which conjoin the
arts of song and painting in the way taught by Quetzalcoatl.

274

nichuana teihuinti xochitl
yehcoc ye nican poyoma
xahuallan timaliuhtihuitz
maxochitl oyehcoc ye nican
zan tlaahuixochitla moyahua
motzetzeloa ancazo yehuatl nepapan xochitl
        zan comoni huehuetl maya nehtotilo
in quetzalpoyomatl a ic icuilihuic noyol, nicuicanitl
in xochitl a ya tzetzelihuipancuel nicuiya, maxonahuiacan
zan noyolitic ontlapani in cuicaxochitl
nicyamoyahua in xochitlacuicatl
ninoquinilotehuaz in quenmanian
        xochineneliuhtiaz noyollo
        yehuan tepilhuan in tetecutin
zan ye ic nichoca in quenmanian
zan nicayaihtoa noxoichiteyo nocuicatoca
nictalitehuaz in quenmanian
        xochineneliuhtiaz noyollo
        yehuan tepilhuan in tetecutin

I am drinking the liquor of the flower
the narcosis is here
switch into it
the flowers are here in your hands
the flowers of pleasure spread
so shaken in themselves each is irisdescent
        the drum is a growing intrusion, dance
exquisite narcosis stains my heart, the singer's
I bear the irisdescent downpour, receive it
just inside my heart the song-flower snapped
I disperse the flower-song
I am going to be frozen in rapture sometime
      my heart will be mixed with the flowers
      and *Les fleurs nobles*, corolla of the Princes
I could cry over the 'sometime'
I tell my flower fame, my song name
I'll be somnambulant sometime
      my heart will be mixed with the flowers
      and *Les fleurs nobles*, corolla of the Princes

Cantares mexicanos, f. 29r.

IX.6 *The heroic mode*

Experience of battle much enriched the vocabulary of the Nahua, as poetry came to be cultivated for its own sake and the rhythm of the war-drum became prosody. Just as funeral and planting rites furnished the orphan and burgeon modes, so war did the heroic Eagle song. In this mode, exemplified here from the *Cantares mexicanos*, we read of the war storm, the clash of elemental opposites – boiling fire and blazing water (line 7) – as the wild excitement of the imagination; of the precious-Water of blood as 'streaming' energy; of 'shield-fame' (line 8, the exact equivalent of the Anglo-Saxon phrase) as glory; and, above all, of the supremacy of the Flower, that multiple concept, referred here to lordliness like the equivalent Sign – Ahau (XX) – of the Maya. This song is described in the manuscript as coming from the Colhua towns of Chalco and Amecameca, southeast of Tenochtitlan, and it doubtless entered the court repertoire as an item of tribute. Chimalpahin reports how warrior performers from Chalco and Amecameca were required to travel up to Axayacatzin's palace after a defeat in 1479, and that a high standard of entertainment was expected from them.

> Between the Eagles and the Jaguars
> let the embrace happen, oh princes.
> To the clash of shields
> the Capturers join company.
> 5 The battle blossom spreads over us and rains down
> in godly delight.
>
> There, the blaze seethes and streams along:
> ambition to fulfil and shield-fame to win
> dust rises over the bells.
> 10 The war-flower will never end.
> Jaguar-Flower and the shield Flower
> open their corollas,
> dust rises over the bells.
>
> With the Eagle bucklers the Jaguar banners entwine;
> 15 with the quetzal shields the gold-black banners mingle.
> There they seethe and turn.
> The Chalcan and the Amecamecan arise,
> the clash of war turns around
> The arrow shattered,

20   the obsidian splintered:
     the shield-dust covers us,
     the Chalcan and the Amecamecan arise.

Cantares mexicanos, f. 18r.

IX.7 *The Otomi lament of Nezahualcoyotl*

Nezahualcoyotl (1402–72), the 'poet-king' of Texcoco, has been made famous in English by Prescott's *Conquest of Mexico*. He was both dedicated to learning and language and the man who engineered the aqueduct brought to Tenochtitlan for his uncle Moctezuma I (above, p. 213). Several of the poems in the *Cantares mexicanos* collection refer to him and suggest that he was a highly respected composer of songs, who ranged easily among the various modes and styles of the Brotherhood. One of his styles was the 'Otomi', they being the western Tepanec people conquered by the Nahua. Tonal and rich in 'uncouth' consonants, the Otomi language was appreciated for its poignant broken effects by translators who strove to reproduce them in Nahua. On occasion, Nezahualcoyotl actually composed in Otomi, his mother tongue, although the only known text of his in that language, first printed in the eighteenth century and quoted here, is at least partly fraudulent. Nonetheless, the manner of these stanzas of his 'Flower Song' as it is entitled in both Otomi and Nahua, resembles that of songs which have survived in the folk tradition. Also the images of the lyric – willow, Rainstorm axe, Wind, the ephemeral count of life, Earth's belly – are readily recognizable in the pre-Columbian screenfolds.

the willow stands erect	gumbgue na tzitzo
so pride flourishes	tzu teranetzi
here in the world	nugua tzimajay
it may live long	matzi nadunthi danvuigui
but the fire-axe	tzagueto narantzivi natzi
	narancuay
splits it	dijequi dithiegmi
the Wind	narandohi
throws it down	di tzirajahy
ephemeral is the count	nestihi napehde
of Flower life	nadeni nuarabuiy
at sunrise	nubui tziudi
it burgeons	tiumbi nua rantzu

at sunset
  it weeps in death
the whole thing on earth
  must end
life is ephemeral
  and sinks into the pit
the whole earth belly
  is a grave
there is nothing
  it can sustain
it hides
  it buries
the water course, the river
  the stream, the spring:
none
  goes back

nubui istindee
  ytzoni nadu aranbuiy
gato nua namethi najay
  da huadi
nua na nestihi nanbuigui
  dibgetze na octzi
gato na tzandi najay
  nanigee
otho tevea
  da pay unime
ogui
  agui
ytzege ya dothte
  ya ne ya puethe
ajonto
  tambengui

Nezahualcoyotl, *Nadeni tzandu*

IX.8 *Modes of Quechua poetry*

Once an instrument of Inca collectivism, *runa simi*, the 'language of men' or Quechua, is unusual in the range of resources with which it may express nuances of individual feeling. Each of these three brief examples of Quechua verse bear marks of the society which produced them yet invoke the power of poetry itself. The first, taken from Guaman Poma, is a *yaravi*, that is, in the lyrical mode which derives from the Inca term for poet (*haravek*) and which not only survives in Quechua but has entered the repertoire of Spanish American poets. The poet compares his pain of love with the night and with the thought of being swept away, as if by a river in spate, to the *zancay*, the Inca state prison (above pp. 76, 77). Urgently appealing, the poet hints at the animal irrationality in his passion. Guaman Poma reports that love songs were carefully monitored by the state; when judged capable of driving the listener to suicide, echoing in an Andean chasm, they were actually prohibited. The second is a 'needling' piece, in the mode of the satirical *wawaki* songs once sung at the old Moon festival, and sung today to elicit *chicha* (maize beer) from bystanders during carnival in Cochabamba (Bolivia). It intimidates obliquely, with its suggestions of a hollow laugh, like that uttered by the satirists of Inca times through their skull masks. The last example, a *wanka* or field work-song, appears in José María Arguedas's novel *Todas las sangres* (1964) where it is sung by a modern Quechua community in the Andes to fend off attack by government agents. Beyond sustaining the rhythm of work it wins over these hostile outsiders – reminding them, with its sheer verbal power, that they too once sang in Quechua.

(a)
doesn't your heart hurt
don't you want to cry
you, my precious flower
you, my queen,
you, my princess
see how justice takes me off in
    spate
and imprisons me
when I glimpse your mantle
when I see your dress
the day does not exist for me
in this night I awake to know
it will never dawn;
I think that you,
my queen, my señora,
don't remember me
I'm eaten up
by the puma and the fox of the
    zancay
I'm alone,
disheartened and lost, my lady.

(a)
mana soncoyqui queuiccho
mana uacaycunyacuy
cicllallay caspa
coyallay caspa
ñustallay caspa
uniyuiquellan apariuan

yucuy parallan pusaiuan
chay llicllayquita ricuycuspa
chay acsoyquita camaycuspa
mananam pachapas chiciancho
tuta ricchariptipas
mana tacmi pacha
pacarincho
camca coya, camca senora
mananachi yuyariaunquicho
cay zancaypi poma atoc
micouaptin

cay pinaspi
uichicasca quicasca tiapti palla

(b)
The carnival was
a sad old man it was
under the bridge
sniffing around he was
I saw him with his
such'i fish moustache
in his bag
two eggs there were
I tried to grab them
but hollow they were

(b)
Carnavalmá kasqa,
uj machitu kasqa.
Chaka uramanta
wataqamusqasqa;
ñóqay rikurqoni,
such'i barbas kasqa;
alforjasninpipis
ískay runtus kasqa;
upirísaj nini,
meq'arájtaj kasqa.

(c)

The swallow moves its wings
not so fast as you
boy, man.

The silver fish moves through
    the waters
of river and lake
not so fast as you
boy, man.

(c)

Wayanaysi rapran
manaya k'an hinachu,
mak'ta, runa.

K'ollk'e chalwas *ahujan*

mapu k'ochapi,
manaya k'an hinachu
mak'ta, runa.

IX.9 *An express message in beans*

In the ascending spiral painted around the Chimu pot from
which this drawing is taken, we move from the seed bean to the
reception of the message. The message grows out of the bean itself;
as its roots and sprouts and eyes develop into the messenger's legs
and arms and eyes it itself also remains the medium, carried in the
messenger's pouch. In the inset (from another pot) intricately
patterned beans are being read by a feline creature with greatly

Chimu vase decoration

Detail of decoration from
a Chimu pot showing
bean reader

enlarged eyes and the tail of speed behind him. The Chimu messenger, then, resembles the Inca *chasqui*, a runner whose job it was to speed information to and from the capital, patterned beans being the equivalent of the knots on the *quipu* which in turn, in Guaman Poma's drawings (cf. *II.3*), become the equivalent of a letter written in the alphabet. This text plays on the familiar connection between the seed of growth and of ideas; among the Chibcha it is Mica (fig. 5), expert in agriculture, who 'reads' bean-seeds, to see if they are good genetically, with his wide-set eyes. Moreover, as in Mesoamerican and Southwestern texts, the seed bean becomes a plant man who moves. This Peruvian bearer of thought uses two legs, like the Maya *uinal*, bearer of the Twenty Signs (the runners proper, each with a different head-dress, total twenty; also, preceding them, it is the eighth bean which begins to walk, possibly a reference to the eight days spent by Venus in the dark underworld before walking up into the sky; cf. p. 151). This Chimu text deals not just with actual systems of communication in Peru but with the capacity to think creatively and express.

IX.10 *Wisdom lost and preserved in the* Popol vuh

In telling how the maize men of this world age were created, the *Popul vuh*, of the Quiche Maya, describes the god-like perception which they at first enjoyed. Born from the perfect substance 'white and yellow maize', like the poet celebrated in Nahua poetry (cf. *IX.4b*), they have enhanced vision and a universal understanding of the world's time and space. However, so that their creative power does not rival that of the gods who made them, and is turned rather to sexual reproduction of their kind, their eyes are chipped, like the eyes of figures on certain Maya stelae. Yet there is a paradox here. For in their relative blindness they lose their understanding of precisely the matters dealt with at such length in the *Popol vuh*: the 'four creations, the four destructions' of the world in American cosmogony (see p. 164). The authors of this account, descended through direct genealogy from the first maize men, thus imply that they are nonetheless 'quite like gods' in preserving that lost wisdom; as the *Popol vuh* says (alluding to the essence or saliva through which the Twins are engendered), 'there is no destruction for the image of a lord or of a sage'. And the means by which they preserve it is the written words of their book, whose name is synonymous with the 'mat' of authority (cf. 'Pop' in Table 4a and fig. 20).

They had breath
  And existed.
And they could see too;
  Immediately their sight began.
They came to see;
  They came to know
Everything under heaven
  If they could see it.
Suddenly they could look around
  And see around
In the sky,
  In the earth.
It was scarcely an instant
  Before everything could be seen.
They didn't have to walk at first
  So as to gaze at what was under heaven:
They were just there and looked.
  Their understanding became great.
Their gaze passed over trees,
  Rocks,
Lakes,
  Seas,
Mountains
  And valleys.
Truly then
  They were the most beloved of men,
Jaguar Quiche,
  Jaguar Night,
Nought
  And Wind Jaguar.

And so then they came to see everything under heaven,
  And so then they gave thanks
To Former,
  And Shaper,
'Truly then twice thanks,
  Thrice thanks that we are created already,
And that we are mouthed
  And faced.
We can speak;
  We can hear;
We ponder;
  We move;

Q'ok uxilab
X uxik.
X e muqun nay puch;
Hu zuq x opon ki muqubal.
X k'iz k ilo;
X k'iz k etamah
R onohel xe kah,
Ve k e muqunik.
Libah chi chi ki zol vachih,
Chi zol muquh puch
U pam kah,
U pam ulev.
Ma hu q'atahil na
Chi k ilix tah r onohel.
Ma k e bin ta na' on nabe
Kate ta chi k il ri 'u xe kah:
Xa vi chiri 'e q'o vi ta k e muqunik,
Tzatz k etamabal x uxik.
X iq'ov ki vachibal pa chee,
Pa 'abah,
Pa cho,
Pa palo,
Pa huyub,
Pa tak'ah.
Qitzih vi chi 'e
Loqolah vinaq
Ri Balam Kitze,
Balam Aqab,
Mahuq'utah,
Iq'i Balam.

Kate puch x l iz k il r onohel u xe kah,
Kate q'ut ki qamovanik ri
Chi r e Tzakol,
Bitol.
'Quitzih vi ka mul qamo,
Ox mul qamo mi x oh vinaqirik,
Mi pu x oh chiinik,
X oh vachinik.
K oh ch'avik;
K oh taonik;
K oh bizonik;
K oh zilabik;

We think very well;
   We understand
Far
   And near,
And we can see large
   And small,
What is in heaven,
   What is on earth.'

They came to understand everything;
   They saw it:
The four creations,
   The four destructions
The womb of heaven,
   The womb of earth.
And not very happily
   Did they listen to this,
The Former
   And Shaper.

'It is not good
   What they say.
Aren't their names just formed
   And shaped?
But quite like gods
   Will they become then
Unless they begin to multiply
   And begin to grow numerous
When it whitens,
   When it brightens:
Unless it increases.
   Then so be it!'

And their eyes were chipped
   By the Heart of Heaven.
They were blinded like the clouding of the surface of a mirror;
   Their eyes were all blinded.
They could only see nearby then,
   However clear things might be,
And thus they lost their understanding,
   And all the wisdom of the four men
At the start,
   At the beginning.

Utz ka qa nao.
X q etamah
Nah.
Naqah.
Mi pu x q ilo nim,
Ch'utin
U pa kah,
U pa 'ulev.'

X k'iz k etamah r onohel.
X ki muquh
Kah tzuq,
Kah xukut,
U pam kah,
U pam ulev.
Ma q'u 'utz
X ki tao
Ri 'Ah Tzak,
Ri 'Ah Bit.

Ma vi 'utz
Ri ka ki biih.
Ma pa xa tzak,
Xa bit ki bi?
Xa labe 'e kabavil
K e 'uxi chik,
Ve ma vi k e poq'otahik,
K e k'iritahik.
Ta chavax ok,
Ta zaqir ok!
Ve ma vi chi k'iyarik,
Ta ch ux ok!

Xa q'u x vabax u baq' ki vach
R umal u K'ux Kah.
X moyik kehe ri x uxilabix u vach lemo;
X moyomobik u baq' ki vach.
Xa naqah chik x e muqun vi,
Xere chi q'alah ri 'e q'o vi.
Kehe q'ut u zachik k etamabal
R uq r onohel ki naobal e kahib chi vinaq
U xe,
U tikaribal.   *Popol vuh*

285

IX.11 *Last words in the Book of Chumayel*

Chilam Balam or Priest Jaguar, the scholar-sage after whom the Yucatec community books are named, was one of many who anticipated the Spanish invasion of eastern Yucatan from the Caribbean islands. His statements epitomize the energy devoted by the Maya to finding ways of dealing with foreign economies and religions without being destroyed by them. Linking morality with the rhythms of the calendar, this text draws heavily on *katun* rhetoric (cf. *IV.9*). In addition to images familiar from earlier quotations, here we find an extraordinarily dense triad, towards the end, which invokes the process of pronouncement and utterance itself: to 'turn back the neck' also means to 'pervert the voice'; 'eye' is also face, like that of the *katun* (see p. 146); and 'drooling at the mouth' evokes the identification of saliva with semen in Maya (and Inca) creation concepts, and hence the balance between head and

10   This alone is the word
11   I, Chilam Balam, have interpreted the word
12   of the true god of all places in the world
13   in every part of the world it is heard, oh father
14   of sky and earth. Splendid indeed is his word in heaven
15   oh father, his rule over us, over our souls.
16   Yet as thrice the offspring of animals are the old men
17   of the younger brothers of the land. Snarled minds, hearts dead
18   in carnal sophistication, who too often turn back, who
19   propagate Nacxit Xuchit through the sophistication of his circle
20   the two-day rulers, lustful on their thrones
1   lustful in their sophistication. Two-day men, their words
2   two-day their seats, their bowls, their hats
3   the day crime, the night crime, hoods of the world.
4   They turn back their necks, they wink their eyes, they drool
                                                                at the mouth
5   before our own representatives, oh father. See,
6   when they come the foreigners bring no truth.
7   Yet great secrets are told by the sons of the men
8   and the women of seven ruined houses
                                                        Who is the prophet
9   who is the priest who shall read
10   the word of this book
                        Finis

belly as the exit of the heart. Compare the proper face (*uich*) and mouth (*chi*) of the first maize men in the *Popol vuh*. The 'sons of the ruins' are the Maya themselves, whose creative power is unperverted and who ask who has the sense to read their literature. The question is not simply sarcastic, and carries forward Maya faith in the universal intelligence of man, towards 'the end of the loss of vision and shame'. Moreover, the line numbering (which is in arabic numbers in the original text) of this 'final' passage leaves it open to continuity. Like the Twenty Signs of the *uinal*, and like the twenty tuns of the *katun*, these twenty lines fall into two decimal sets, which prepares them for the next step in time. Ending on 10 at the end of the first set, the text is poised, ready to move on into the second, wherever it is written. The 'Finis' then means not the end of the book (*uooh*) but the inadequacy of its reader, an image found in the *Popol vuh*, a book (*vuh*) whose reader in our times is said to be 'hiding his face from it'.

10	Yok tuba in than,
11	cen Chilam Balam, ca in tzolah u than
12	hahal Ku tuzinile yokol cabe; yubi
13	hunac tzuc ti cabe, yume, u than Dios, u Yumil
14	caan y luum. Hach utz ka u than ti caan,
15	yume, Cokol yahaulil, yokol ix ca pixan/
16	hahal Ku. Heuac heob ti ulez lae, yume, ox al a mukil
17	<i>x cuch lum idzinil. Dzaman yol, cimen ix u puc-
18	zikal tu nicteob xan, ah uaua tulupoob, ah ua
19	tan zinaob, Nacxit Xuchit tu nicte u lakob,
20	ca-ca-kin yahaulilob, coylac te tu dzamob,
1	coylac te tu nicteob. Ca-ca kin uinicil u than-
2	[n]ob. Ca-ca-kin u xecob, u luchob, u ppoocob,
3	u co kin[n]ob, u co akab, u maxilob yokol
4	cab. Kuy cu cal, mudz cu uich, pudz cu chi,
5	ti yahaulil cabob, yume. He, cu talel minan
6	hah tu thanob u dzulilob cah. Bin yalob
7	hach talanilob, u mehen Uuc-tocoy-naob,
8	yalob Uuc-tocoy-naobe, yume.

Mac to ah

9	bovat, mac to ah kin bin tohol cantic
10	u than uooh lae?

Finis.

8

16 hahal kin: keuac ჳ v les lae yume: Ox alam v kil =
17 x Cuch Luum y ꝛi nii: ꝛamen yol = Cimenix v puu
18 Ɛi kal tunii tecō xan = ah na ua tulupoob = ah va
19 tan Ɛinaob = Nac xit = xu chit tunü ta udaklob =
20 Cacakin yahaulilob Coylae te tu ꝛamoob =
1 Coylae tatu nuctaob Cacakin uini cil = v than
2 nob = Cacakin u xe cob = v lu chob = v pootob
3 v Cohin nob = v Co akab = v maxilob = yoktol
4 Cab = Huy cu Cal = mu꞉ cu uich = pu꞉ cuchi =
5 ti yahaulil Cabob = yume he cu ta lel Minan
u than nob, V ꝛuli lob Cah Bin yalob
6 tatani lob = V mehen uic to coy naob =
yalob Vuc to coy naobe yume = Mac to ah
9 Bouat = Mac to ah kin = bin to hol cantic
v than Vooh lae

Finis

Notes

Details of authors and titles alluded to in the text and notes are given in the Bibliography.

Introduction
The idea of the New World, and American Indian Texts

1 Two valuable recent accounts of the continent's early history are *The New World*, by Warwick Bray *et al.*, and G. H. S. Bushnell's *The First Americans.*

2 This term is used to refer to roughly the area now occupied by the United States and Canada. (Strictly speaking, *North* America includes Mexico.)

3 Indispensable guides are the seven volumes of the *Handbook of South American Indians*, and the fifteen volumes of the *Handbook of Middle American Indians*, of which the last two are entirely devoted to Mesoamerican texts. On northern America, the Annual Reports and Bulletins of the Bureau of American Ethnology (BAE) are a massive source of materials.

4 Anthologies of northern American texts include: M. Astrov, *The Winged Serpent*; J. Bierhorst, *In the Trail of the Wind*; and J. Rothenberg, *Shaking the Pumpkin*. G. Baudot's *Les Lettres précolumbiennes* deals with the Latin American area. A continental view is taken in J. Alcina Franch's *Floresta literaria de la América indígena* and

within J. Rothenberg's *Technicians of the Sacred*. Popular selections of pages from the Mesoamerican screenfolds are C. Burland's *Magic Books from Mexico* and H. Biedermann's *Altmexikos heilige Bücher*.

5 For example in items *I.16*; *II.1* and *VII.10*; *IV.8* and *9*; I.14, *V.11* and *VII.3.*

6 These arguments are rehearsed briefly in the introduction to Chapters VI and VIII; see also index entries under 'Shaman's journey' and 'zenith'. They are developed in more detail in my articles 'Mesoamerican description of space II: signs for direction', *Ibero-Amerikanisches Archiv*, 2 (1976), 39–62; 'Time and Script in Mesoamerica', *Indiana*, 3 (1976), 9–40; 'The literate Maya and their Golden Age', *The New Scholar*, V (1976), 275–98; 'Continuity in Maya writing: new readings of two passages in the Book of Chumayel', *comparison*, 5 (1977), 98–128, revised version in *Maya Archeology and Ethnohistory*, ed. G. Willey and N. Hammond, Austin, Tex., 1978; and 'The journey of the Mide Shaman: a paradigm of American cosmology', *Festschrift Gerdt Kutscher*, ed. J. Golte and A. Mönnich, Berlin 1978 (in press).

7 The break between Jung and Freud was perhaps in part stimulated by Jung's fascination with America via

(of all books!) Longfellow's *Hiawatha*; in *Symbole der Wandlung* Jung follows up Longfellow's sources in H. R. Schoolcraft's editions of Algonkin texts. American Indian texts have also, of course, long been ingeniously quoted to prove the existence of 'lost continents' such as Atlantis (Braghine, Le Plongeon, Brasseur de Bourbourg) and Mu (Churchward), as well as of cataclysms and extra-terrestrial visitations (Veleikovsky, Däniken).

CHAPTERS I–IX
The following notes refer to the individual texts quoted and to my introduction to each. Dates given in individual headings refer not to the texts but to events described in them.

I Invasion from the Old World
1 Codex Ríos, pp. 86v.–88r. Number 270 in the census of Mesoamerican texts in volumes 14 and 15 of the *Handbook of Middle American Indians* (=HMAI Census), which makes clear the complex bibliography of this and other texts from that area. In Kingsborough 1831–48, ii. Sections of both the Rios and the Telleriano Remensis (HMAI Census 308) codices, of the late sixteenth century, derive from the lost Huitzilopochtli screenfold and preserve its typical squarish format on their folio pages; the pages for the years 1519–28 survive only in the Ríos. On the iconography and style of Toltec historical writing see D. Robertson, *Mexican Manuscript Painting of the early Colonial Period. The Metropolitan Schools*. On the events in question, W. H. Prescott's *Conquest of Mexico* remains a standard work.

Year-Bearer: see Table 3.
Royal Funeral in 11 Flint: of Nezahualpilli, ruler of Texcoco

and son of Nezahualcoyotl; see *IX.7*.

2 Lienzo of Tlaxcala, scene 42; HMAI Census 350. In *Antigüedades mexicanas*, 1892. Early versions of this work existed as murals, and on native paper made from the maguey plant, the American papyrus. Compare this scene with *III.5* and *VII.2*.

3 From part 5 (§§ 103–394) of the *Annals of Tlatelolco*, or *Unos anales históricos de la nación mexicana*; HMAI Census 1073. This translation was made with the help of those by Menguin, Berlin and Barlow, and Garibay 1953–4, 2: 258. The *Annals of Tlatelolco* form an important part of M. León-Portilla's two excellent anthologies of responses to invasion, in Mexico (1959) and in America more widely (1964a).

Nahua lyric poetry: see Chapter IX.
Shafts: of arrows and spears – that is, reeds –, and human bones; cf. *V.4*.
Torn hair: snatching hair conventionally meant victory; see Chapter VII.
Zacatl: depicted in *I.4*.
Price... maize: cf. *VI.15*.

4 Huitzilopochco: Contrat de Commanderie; HMAI Census 145. Cf. Boban 1891, 1: 387–9. Charles Gibson's *Spain in America* gives a succinct summary of the *encomendero* system in both New Spain and Peru, and of the role of the Spanish Crown and the Church.

Huitzilopocho: listed in the Mendoza Codex, p. 20 (cf. *VII.10*). Turkey: one of the Thirteen Birds of Mesoamerican ritual; see Table 2.

5 Manuscrito del Aperramiento; HMAI Census 9. Cf. Wagner 1944. Coyoacan: compare the sign for this town in *I.2*.

Malinche: this name possibly derived not from Maria but from Malinalli (Grass/Tooth), the Nahua term for one of the Twenty Signs of Mesoamerica (XII); see Table 2c. She died in 1529. Deer, Snake, Dog: VIII, V and X, of the Twenty Signs.

6 Paxbolon-Maldonado Papers, pp. 160–61, HMAI Census 1164. In Scholes and Roys 1948 and Smailus 1975. This translation is based on Smailus's Spanish (1975: 56–61), with reference to the facsimile of the Chontal Maya text in Scholes and Roys. For further details of the invasion of Maya territory see R. S. Chamberlain, *The Conquest and Colonization of Yucatan, 1517–1550.*

Mapa de Tepechpan: HMAI Census 317.

Mactun: the Chontal Mayas' name for themselves; 'Chontal' is Nahua for 'foreigner'.

Capitán del Valle: Cortés was given the title Captain or Marquess of the Valley of Oaxaca in 1528.

Head was hung: compare the passage in the *Popol vuh* discussed on p. 218.

Ceiba: a giant spreading tree often found as the focal point of villages in tropical America.

Yaxdzan: a town near Itzamkanac, capital of Acallan.

7 Ah Nakuk Pech, *Chronicle of Chac-Xulub-Chen*; HMAI Census 1166. This translation by D. G. Brinton, 1882: 199, 206–7 and 214–5, slightly modified by comparison with J. Martínez Hernández's Spanish translation (1926) of the very similar *Chronicle of Yaxkukul*, by Ah Macan Pech.

Mastiffs: cf. *I.5*; they are also mentioned in the Maya *Chronicle of Calkiní* (HMAI Census 1143).

8 The Chilam Balam Book of Chum-ayel, pp. 14–15; HMAI Census 1145. Facsimile edition by Gordon 1913. In all our translations from this work (see *II.2*, *IV.9*, *V.14* and *IX.11*), Dorn and I gratefully acknowledge help from those by Médiz Bolio (1930) and above all Roys (1933).

9 *The Book of the Cakchiquel*, HMAI Census 1172, translated by A. Recinos and D. Goetz, 1953: 129. Written by Francisco Hernández Arana and Francisco Díaz, of the Xahil or Dancer clan of the Cakchiquel. See Edmonson, 'Historia de las tierras altas mayas', in Vogt and Ruz Llullier 1971: 273–302. In Cakchiquel, the calendar name 'Maize' is actually 'measure' or 'net' of maize cobs (like that gathered by the mother of the magic Twins in the *Popol vuh*).

10 Huarochiri Narrative, ff. 83r–83v, in H. Trimborn and A. Kelm, *Francisco de Ávila: Tratado de los errores . . .*, and J. M. Arguedas, *Dioses y hombres de Huarochiri*. This and succeeding translations (*V.8*, *VII.13*) are based mainly on Trimborn's German. Huarochiri was visited by Guaman Poma (see next item) on his information-gathering travels as a place rich in Quechua lore, despite the Christianizing efforts of Francisco de Ávila and other missionaries. W. H. Prescott's *Conquest of Peru* gives a stirring account of the Spanish advance to Cajamarca.

11 Felipe Guaman Poma de Ayala, *Nueva corónica [sic] y buen gobierno*, p. 451. Facsimile edition, with an essay, by R. Pietschmann 1936. Guaman Poma's pun on *corona* (crown) and *crónica* (chronicle) echoes native thought. Throughout, my commentaries on his work (see also items *II.3*, *V.8, 9*, and *VII.12*) are indebted to the edition of the *New Chronicle* by Luis Bustios

Gálvez (1956–66). Guaman Poma's work is a key source for John Hemming's new appraisal of Quechua resistance at Vilcabamba, *The Conquest of the Incas* (1970); and for Nathan Wachtel's recent *Vision of the Vanquished* (1977).

12 Abbreviated translation from the Spanish of Lucas Fernández Piedrahita, *Noticia historial de las conquistas del Nuevo Reino de Granada* [1688], Bogotá 1973: 400. Though pedestrian, this work has the unique merit of transcribing speeches, like this one, from the manuscript of the conquistador Jiménez de Quesada, which is now lost, a service the more appreciable in view of the paucity of Chibcha-language documents from the Conquest period. Besides, Piedrahita was the first to explain Colonial affairs in terms of native precedent; and he continuously relates the life of his day to the past he records. For further remarks about Bochica, see note to *II.2*. Millennial architecture and stone carving in the territory around Las Papas, at San Agustín and Tierradentro, offer hard evidence of the age of the Chibcha tradition and of its connections with Mesoamerica; cf. figs. 5, 13, and notes to *III.9* and *IX.9*.

13 Yves d'Evreux, *Voyage dans le nord du Brésil*, 1864: 51. See N. González, 'El diálogo de los caciques', *América indígena*, xvii: 221–31.

14 Walam Olum, ed. Brinton 1884: 210–17 (symbols 159–64 and 165–84). The only known text of the Walam Olum (or Red Score) was published in C. S. Rafinesque, *The American Nations*, Philadelphia, Pa., 1836, I: chapter 5, which also contains Rafinesque's alphabetic transcription of the accompanying Lenape-Algonkin oral text. Among subsequent editors (Squier, Black, *et al.*), Brinton has raised the ques-

tion of the work's authenticity. He concludes that the oral text is 'a genuine native production', but does not pronounce on the written text, beyond saying that it uses the Algonkin pictographic system (for a 'Synopsis' of which see H. R. Schoolcraft 1851–7, I: 408). Indeed it does and is related to the Midewiwin ritual of the Algonkin to a degree unsuspected by both Rafinesque and subsequent editors including Brinton. The Algonkin author Kah-gegagah-bowh (David Copway) vouched for its authenticity (Squier 1877: 17). Had Rafinesque simply written this text himself rather than copy it, as he said he did in his unpublished papers, from a wooden original given by the Lenape to his friend Dr Ward in gratitude for a cure, then he is hardly likely both to have understood the ritual intricacies of the Walam Olum and to have effaced all trace of such understanding, as he does in his commentaries and English translation. The translation of the oral text offered, and that in later chapters (*V.11* and *VI.3*), is basically Brinton's emended according to new readings of the symbols. Just as W. H. Prescott narrated the conquests of Mexico and Peru, so another New Englander and his near-contemporary, Francis Parkman, dealt with that of northern America, though from a very different point of view from that of the Walam Olum.

Scioto: a tributary of the Ohio and the site of the Mound Builder and Algonkin town of Chillicothe, the eastern twin of Piqua, not far from the Wabash, where the Walam Olum was obtained from the Lenape shortly before their removal west of the Mississippi in the 1820s.

Large ships: the first large ship

on the Great Lakes was La Salle's *Griffin* (45 tons), launched in 1679.

184 days: due to unevenness in the sun's course, the northern hemisphere summer is longer than the winter of about 181 days, a fact recognized in several American calendars.

15 Reproduced in G. Mallery, *Picture-Writing of the American Indians*, p. 230, a work unsurpassed as a source of northern American texts.

16 Lahontan, Baron de (Lom d'Arce), *Voyages* . . ., 1703: 62–4 (British Library call no. G 15867), who as a witness of the occasion also offers a plan, showing the wampum belts and the calumet laid by Grangula before M. de la Barre. The speech appears in Thatcher 1832, ii: 41, and in the excellent *Chronicles of American Indian Protest*, pp. 21–4. On the connection between the Iroquois League and the Constitution of the United States, see Benjamin Franklin's *Autobiography*, chapter 10, and Lewis Henry Morgan, *League of the Ho-de-no-sau-nee, or Iroquois*, 1851. Strengthened by the addition of the Tuscarora as a Sixth Nation in 1721, the League was not displaced from its 'Castles' until the early 19th century.

Akonessan: 'partridge' in Iroquois, the nickname of the interpreter, M. le Moine.

castles: the stockaded towns of the Five (later Six) Nations. Miami, Illinois, Ottawa, Shawnee: all Algonkin tribes.

17 Reproduced in Mallery 1893, plate xliii; one of 41 drawings, in part in colour, on manila paper, by Red Horse, along with his description of the battle, translated and discussed by Mallery, *ibid.*, pp. 563–6. Cf. Petersen 1971 and Dee Brown 1971.

18 Photograph by A. P. Niblack, reproduced in *The Coast Indians of Southern Alaska*, Washington, D.C. 1890; Barbeau 1950: 406. Like other Northwest chiefs, Skowl was a slaver and adept at potlatch, the material exchange system peculiar to the area. He was later converted to Western Christianity and his daughter married an Austrian, Baronovich, from Trieste. One of the earliest British visitors to the Haida in 1797 remarked upon their 'Huge Images intended to represent Human Figures' (Charles Bishop, *The Journal and Letters*, ed. M. Roe, Cambridge, 1967: 64). After the Alaska purchase (1867) Abraham Lincoln became a favourite subject for pole carvers.

II Defence of traditional values and forms

1 Nahua original in the Secret Archive of the Vatican, edited and translated by W. Lehmann 1949; often referred to by the Spanish title 'Coloquios de los Doce Primeros Misioneros de Mexico'. This translation is based on Lehmann's German, corrected against binary and other norms of Toltec writing as exemplified in both the Mendoza Codex and the Borgia screenfold. Good introductions to the Aztec tradition in English are: G. C. Vaillant, *Aztecs of Mexico*; J. Soustelle, *The Daily Life of the Aztecs*; M. León-Portilla, *Aztec Thought and Culture*; and E. R. Wolf, *Sons of the Shaking Earth*.

Purslane: amaranth or pig-weed, cultivated from New Mexico to Peru for its small seeds, which the Aztecs ground into a flour, as they did sage.

Aromatic leaf: chiefly tobacco.

2 The Book of Chumayel, pp. 19–21. For accounts of the Maya, see Roys's introduction and notes to his translation of the Chumayel (1933) and his *The Indian Background of Colonial Yucatan*; also J. E. S.

293

Thompson, *The Rise and Fall of Maya Civilization*, and M. Coe, *The Maya*. Nelson Reed's *The Caste War of Yucatan* is one of the few works devoted to Maya military resistance.

hab: the 360-day period more commonly known as '*tun*' (see Table 5). 1900 *hab* (about 1874 years) puts the founding of Maya society in the 4th century BC, 7.0.0.0.0 of the Maya Era when counted back from 11.15.0.0.0 (1519), two *katuns* prior to the Katun 11 Ahau discussed above, p. 42, and below, p. 146.

three emblems: found on Monument 13 at La Venta – stone, jaguar roar, and bird (fig. 2). The footprint behind the walking figure recalls petroglyphs found in northern South America which the Chibcha explicitly associate with the culture hero Bochica, who is said to have arrived in Sogamoso at about the same period (5×400 years ago). Moreover, Bochica's epithets – Nemqueteba (Jaguar), and Sue (Bird) – recall the Maya emblems (also '-hica' is stone); cf. Krickeberg 1928: 177–8, 199.

Nacxit: compare the 'Nacxitl' discussed in *IX.4*.

Mayapan: 'walled town' in Nahua; called Tancah in Maya in this text.

3 The upper set of illustrations shows pp. 250, 350, 360 and 302 of Guaman Poma's work; the lower set shows pp. 1153, 811, 814 and 694. On the Inca and their predecessors, see P. A. Means, *Ancient Civilizations of the Andes*, and J. Alden Mason, *The Ancient Civilizations of Peru*. J. H. Rowe's concise 'Aspects of Inca Socio-Political Organization and Religion at the Spanish Conquest' is reprinted from the *Handbook of South American Indians* in

R. Wauchope, *The Indian Background of Latin American History*.

In Guaman Poma as in the Chilam Balam books we find ironic surprise at the sheer extent of Spanish greed, which made fair targets of old people and the poor who were least able to meet their demands, and the same ridicule of such figures as the vigilante choirmasters. In particular, Guaman Poma records a series of 'typical threats' made to the Quechua, in their language, by the animal figures in picture 2b, revealing the rivalry between them. On one side the priest says: 'I'm your father and owner' and the *encomendero* claims on the other: 'I count more than the priest or the corregidor; I inherited you from my conquistador father'. In their Quechua sermons to the Indians the priests went much further, saying: 'If an Indian makes you pregnant you'll give birth to a bear. If a Mulatto makes you pregnant it'll be a monkey. If a white man makes you pregnant you'll have a lovely child. If a mestizo [half-breed] makes you pregnant you'll have a slave. You should not go to bed or sleep with an adult Indian, who is potent, because you may later find yourself ashamed: my beautiful women, don't anger God in this way. My daughters, hear me.'

Inca socialism stimulated Tupac Amaru II's rising in 1780 (cf. Regis Debray, *Revolution in the Revolution?*, Harmondsworth, 1968, p. 28). It is emblemized in the figure of the headless Inkarri ('Inca king') waiting to be rejoined to the body of the state which, as in the Quechua lament quoted above (*I.10*), remains incomplete without it; cf. J. M. Arguedas and J. R. Pineda, 'Tres versiones del mito de Inkarrí', in J. M. Ossío 1973.

4 For the French version of this speech, see Robert Navarre [?], *Journal ou Dictation d'une conspiration*, ed. R. Clyde Ford, 1913: 22–4 (Navarre, a French-Algonkin interpreter, witnessed the speech). English versions are in B. B. Thatcher, *Indian Biography*, ii: 85–120; H. R. Schoolcraft, *Algic Researches*, 1839; and in *Chronicles of American Indian Protest*, pp. 39–40; see also Witt and Steiner, *The Way*, p. 8.

By October 1763, fearing defeat at Pontiac's hands, the British government proposed the famous Proclamation line along the Appalachians as a permanent westward limit on white settlement. Eventually accepted by Pontiac, the line was hugely resented by speculators like George Washington, who had illegally taken options on large tracts of land to the west in the Ohio valley. The will to make good this speculation became a main motive for creating the independent United States of America, consisting of thirteen states, which soon came to pose a more immediate and, above all, populous, threat to Indian interests.

The Algonkin have stood as an important term of political reference since the times of Cromwell's New England friend Roger Williams, author of the highly suggestive *Key into the Language of America*. In the 19th century, Lewis Henry Morgan turned his attention to them and as a result deeply influenced Engels and Marx. At the same time, though from a very different angle, the Algonkin were studied by H. R. Schoolcraft who provided the source material for *Hiawatha* (see Janet Lewis's novel *The Invasion*).

sky and earth: this phrase echoes the Walam Olum; see *V.11*.

all you see . . . all you have seen: compare the Mide songs in *VIII.11*.

III Ritual

1 Drawn and interpreted by Naumoff (an Aleut Eskimo from Kadiak) in San Francisco 1882; in Mallery 1893: 507.

2 Taken from the Ojibwa chief Jim Greenhill in Minnesota in 1915; Denver Art Museum, Cat. No. Coj-36. Reproduced in N. Feder, *American Indian Art*, item 169. There is an important commentary on the Midewiwin standardization of shamanistic practices in Mircea Eliade, *Shamanism* (1964: 314ff.).

3 Black Elk, *Black Elk Speaks: Being the Life Story of a Holy Man of the Oglala Sioux*, as told through John G. Neihardt, New York 1932, pp. 25–7. See also his *The Sacred Pipe. Black Elk's Account of the Seven Rites of the Oglala Sioux*, recorded and edited by J. E. Brown, Norman, Okla. 1953.

Tipi: a Sioux word; often painted on the 'south' side; the larger 'tipi lodge' was used for ceremonial purposes.

Name: the importance of names among the Sioux is shown by their several pictographic censuses and rosters, discussed by Mallery, 1893.

Neighed to cheer: these singing animals show their 'voice lines' from the heart in Standing Bear's drawings; see also *IX.2*.

4 Made by Mr. Fred Stevens [Klah], a Navajo, in 1966 and preserved in the Horniman Museum, London. Stevens's native name, Klah ('Left-handed'), is also that of a celebrated painter of the previous generation. Because it is sacrilegious to create a painting outside Navajo ritual, this one was made on the understanding that it is imperfect. A basic study of these rituals is Gladys A. Reichard's

invaluable *Navaho Religion. A Study of Symbolism.* During the Taos rising of 1680–92, sandpaintings played an important part in the general cleansing of the population from the effects of Christianity.

5 Borgia screenfold, p. 30; HMAI Census 33. My notes on this screenfold, as well on the Vienna and the Laud, are heavily indebted to Karl Nowotny's *Tlacuilolli. Die mexikanischen Bilderhandschriften: Stil und Inhalt*, the fundamental study of these works. The numbers in the explanatory diagrams given here and subsequently refer to the ritual sets in Table 2: q.v. The Borgia and all other ritual screenfolds in Toltec writing discussed in this book, except the Borbonicus, are parchment.

6 Laud screenfold, p. 2; HMAI Census 185.

7 These hymns appear in the Manuscript of Tepepulco 1559–61 (HMAI Census 1098), the earliest research material for the project which two decades later culminated in Sahagún's monumental *General History of the Things of New Spain.* Though he included the Hymns in the appendix to Book 2 of the Florentine Codex (HMAI Census 1104), the bi-lingual Nahua-Spanish draft of his History, Sahagún left them untranslated, out of religious scruple, fearing their demonic power. This translation draws on those by Seler 1904 and Garibay 1958, listed under Twenty Sacred Hymns; see also Brinton 1890. Anticipating the comparative studies made by J. G. Frazer in *The Golden Bough*, K. T. Preuss related these Hymns to analogous Old World texts in Greek and Sanskrit ('Dialoglieder des Rigveda im Lichte der religiösen Gesänge mexikanischer Indianer', *Globus*, xcv, 1909, no. 3). An important part of

early Christian missionary work in Mesoamerica and elsewhere was the substitution of pagan with Christian ritual dramas, some of which survive in Nahua, Quechua and Tupi-Guarani (Ricard 1933; Brinckmann 1970).

8 Laud screenfold, p. 1. The alignment follows that suggested by Burland in his edition (1966).

9 Borgia screenfold, p. 17; lower two-thirds of the page. Compare Burland 1953:22–4. The banner held by Tezcatlipoca designates both the ritual victim and the number 20; this specific definition of man's vigesimal digits also exists in Chibcha ritual and calendrics, in the sign *gueta* (fig. 5). The posture and head-dress of this Chibcha victim recall both the paintings at Tierradentro (fig. 13) and *timehri* found throughout northern South America. Humboldt (1810) was the first to discuss vigesimal arithmetic in America. For other Chibcha number signs see *III.6* and *IX.9*.

11 Laud screenfold, pp. 26–25. For the Navajo Turkey, see G. Reichard, *Navaho Religion*, p. 488. Though it quite misrepresents the 'poor Indian's' knowledge of the solar walk, Pope's *An Essay on Man* has a remarkable insight into Indian burial, saying that the Indian 'thinks, admitted to that equal sky,/His faithful dog shall bear him company'.

12 Vienna screenfold, pp. 18–17; HMAI Census 395. Facsimile editions by Lehmann and Smital 1929, and Adelhofer 1963.

13 Nuttall screenfold, p. 15; HMAI Census 240. Dates given according to Alfonso Caso's correlation, 1968. On sacred sand see my article: 'Sacred Sand in Mexican Picture-Writing and later literature', *Estudios de cultura náhuatl*, ix (1974), 303–9. Coloured sand is found

overlying burials at Olmec sites. The underground ball-court resembles that owned by the Lords of Xibalba whom the magic Twins (Quetzalcoatl's counterparts in the *Popol vuh*) overcome on their underground passage from west to east.

14 After Maudlsay 1889–1902, 4: 62. Cf. Kelley 1976: 261–8.

15 First prayer in Garcilaso el Inca, *Comentarios reales*, book 2, chapter 27, where it is taken from Blas Valera who transcribed it from a *quipu*. Second prayer in J. H. Rowe, 'Eleven Inca prayers from the Zithuwa ritual', Kroeber Anthropological Society Papers, Berkeley, Cal., 1953, who re-edits and translates Quechua liturgy gathered by Father Molina and others and published by Markham (1873). My article 'Inca hymns and the epic-makers', *Indiana*, i (1973), 199–212, deals with these and similar prayers in relation to the French novelist Marmontel and the poets of Spanish-American Independence.

IV Calendar

1 Mallery 1893: 266–87. Each winter includes the end of our calendar year and the beginning of the next: here I have given only one year date, 1800 for the winter of 1800–01, etc.

2 Borbonicus screenfold, pp. 21–22; HMAI Census 32. See A. Caso 1968: 103–29.

3 Annals of Texcoco screenfold, p. 3; HMAI Census 84. It is interesting to note that the emergence of major Nahua texts, e.g. the Legend of the Suns and the Twenty Sacred Hymns, coincides with the end of the Calendar Round in 1558.

4 Selden screenfold, p. 7; HMAI Census 283 (not to be confused with the Selden Roll, HMAI Census 284, also Mixtec, but written on native paper and not a screenfold). See Spinden 1935 and facsimile

edition by Caso 1964, for commentaries on this screenfold and on this page from it.

5 Fejérváry screenfold, p. 1; HMAI Census 119. See: Seler 1901; C. Burland, *The Four Directions of Time*; V. Castillo, 'El bisiesto nahuatl', *Estudios de cultura náhuatl*, ix (1971); 75–99; and my article 'Mesoamerican description of space II: Signs for direction', *Ibero-Amerikanisches Archiv*, ii (1976), 39–62.

6 Stela C, Tres Zapotes, in M. Coe, 'The Olmec style and its distribution', HMAI 3: 739–75. On the connection between Olmec and Maya, see Benson 1968, Joralemon 1971 and Coe 1966: 52–73; also note to *II.2* above.

7 In J. E. S. Thompson, *Maya Hieroglyphic Writing*, fig. 56 (Tila); Maudslay 1889–1902, 2: pl. 47 (Copan). The most accessible accounts of the complexities of the Maya calendar are this work of Thompson's and S. G. Morley's *An Introduction to the Study of Maya Hieroglyphs*. For the late date at which celestial and terrestrial time were correlated in the Old World see S. Toulmin and J. Goodfield, *The Discovery of Time*. It is not at all impossible that the Classic Maya were aware of the precession of the equinoxes and the differences between the solar and the sidereal year.

8 Paris screenfold, p. 5; HMAI Census 247. All three Maya screenfolds are of native paper. The quotation of Avedaño is from Roys 1933: 184. Note how the Sacred Round number 260 reappears as the total of the *tuns* in the Katun Round.

9 Text of the Katun 13 Ahau of the first of the two series of Katun Rounds extant, based on Roys 1954; Barrera Vásquez 1948: 65–6; Chumayel 73–4; Códice Pérez 1949: 172–3 (Chilam Balam Book of

Mani) and 308–9 (Chilam Balam Book of Oxkutzcab); Chilam Balam Book of Kaua, f. 86; Chilam Balam Book of Tizimin, trans. Makemson 1951. Other passages in the Chilam Balam books show that the Maya worked effortlessly in *three* calendars: their own (as here), the Toltec, and the Christian.

V Cosmos and man

1 The original is in the Museonacional de antropología, Mexico City. On American world-ages in general, see Spence 1923; Krickeberg 1968; Imbelloni 1956; Lahourcade 1970. It is interesting to speculate how far the unstable seismic zone of Mesoamerica and Peru encouraged a view of geology which was accepted in Europe only with the triumph of the Vulcanists over the Sedimentarians as late as the late eighteenth century (H. Butterfield, *The Origins of Modern Science*, London 1957). The Nahua term 'olin', XVIII in the Twenty Signs in Toltec, exactly matches the Quechua 'pachacutec', one of the set of Inca imperial names, meaning both earthquake and movement. 'Olin' also means rubber (hence the 'Olmec' of the coastal lowlands), the material essential for the Ball Court game (cf. note to *III.13*), in which the ball is seen as a celestial body.

2 The History of the Kingdoms (*c.* 1570) is also known by the title *Anales de Cuauhtitlan*; HMAI Census 1033. This translation after Lehmann's German edition 1938, §§ 141–54. Other endings to the Quetzalcoatl 'story' are in the Florentine Codex, Book 3, chapters 12–14, and the *Cantares mexicanos*: see *IX.4*. The one quoted here inspired one of the brighter moments in D. H. Lawrence's *The Plumed Serpent* (chapter xv).

Atecpan . . . Amochco: these are places where Quetzalcoatl bathed 'even at midnight', near his four palaces in Tula, where he withdrew completely, to escape Tezcatlipoca's sorcery.

1 Reed: the date of Quetzalcoatl's birth and death in these Annals, 52 years apart.

roseate spoonbill, cotinga . . .: for the names of these birds I rely gratefully on the erudition of J. Bierhorst 1974: 77. Note the implicit numerical value of macaw (11) and parrot (13) in the set of Thirteen Birds, and of the quetzal bird itself (12). In the *Popol vuh* there is an opposition between the raucous parrot and the shy quetzal as bringers, respectively, of the third and fourth world ages; the quetzal also features in the creation of this world age in the Book of Chumayel. For similar roles of the Thirteen Birds as harbingers and auguries, good and bad, see *III.11*, *V.3*, *VI.5*, *VI.6*, *VIII.1* and note to *IX.11*.

6 *Popol vuh* HMAI Census 1179, translation by Edmonson 1971: 145–8. Through comparison with Quechua and Nahua texts I have dared to revise the textual divisions made in this magisterial version, making Edmonson's 'First Creation' into the first and second and putting his Third and Fourth together as the fourth. In the Xibalba sequence the very length of the Quiche text corresponds to the journeys made respectively by the father and his Twin sons. The story of the father is said to go only to 'the middle' (*niq'ah*); that of his sons is literally twice as long. The story of man's creation from American corn is still told by the Maya (see Tibertius Kaal) and is a theme taken up by several Latin American writers,

notably the Guatemalan novelist Miguel Angel Asturias.

7 Dresden screenfold, pp. 24 and 46 (the discontinuous pagination is due to the fact that the screenfold once fell apart); HMAI Census 113. Thompson 1972: 62–70, offers translations of the glyphic passages. Otto Neugebauer's recently published *History of Ancient Mathematical Astronomy*, Berlin and New York 1976, while not dealing at all with the Maya, none the less reveals how like their astronomy was to that of Mesopotamia, contrary to established opinion. Neugebauer says: 'From the cuneiform texts we learned the ephemerides had been computed exclusively by means of intricate difference sequences which, often by the superposition of several numerical columns, gave step by step the desired coordinates of the celestial bodies – all this with no attempt of a geometrical representation, which seems to us so necessary for the development of any theory of natural phenomena. It is a historical insight of great significance that the earliest existing mathematical astronomy was governed by numerical techniques, not by geometrical considerations, and, on the other hand, that the development of geometrical explanations is by no means such a "natural" step as it might seem to us who grew up in the tradition founded by the Greek astronomers of the Hellenistic and Roman period.'

10 Ayvu Rapyta, recited by Pablo Vera, mayor Francisco of Tava'i and others, edited and translated into Spanish by León Cadogan 1959: 18–25. See also López Austin 1965, and Metraux 1928. Guarani theology (noted in Europe as early as 1514 in the Fuggers' *Nieue Zeitung*) has been an important source for the Paraguayan novelist Augusto Roa Bastos.

11 Walam Olum, ed. Brinton, pp. 170–7 (symbols 1–24). Note how the 'discord' sign in 22 opposes three to one, above and below the four-square house.

12 David Cusick, *Sketches of Ancient History of the Six Nations*, Tuscarora Village, 1825; also in W. M. Beauchamp, *The Iroquois*, New York 1892. On the Tuscarora, see *I.16*. Other cosmogonical accounts of the Foundation of the League include the bi-lingual text (Iroquois and English) written in 1885 by the Mohawk Seth Newhouse (in the American Philosophical Society Library, Philadelphia).

13 In: Newcomb and Reichard 1937: 37.

14 Book of Chumayel, pp. 60–2. Previous translations are by D. Sodi, 'Como nació el uinal', *Estudios de cultura maya*, i (1961), 211–19, and M. Edmonson, in 'Metáfora maya en literatura y en arte', *Verhandlungen des XXXVIII. Internationalen Amerikanistenkongress*, Stuttgart-Munich, 1968, ii: 37–50.

1 Ape: through his skill man becomes god-like, just as the ape can mimic man. Degrading their elder brothers into apes, by making their loin-cloths look like tails, is one of the deeds of the magic Twins in the *Popol vuh*; cf. also the *timehri* in fig. 15 (*a* and *c*).

2 Eb: 'Eb' means (amongst other things) 'stairway', and as such it gives the vertical dimension to the 'heart of heaven'. Steps were thought of as teeth; cf. the equivalent Toltec sign 'malinali'.

6 Cib: in this conceit the candle (of beeswax; *cib*), abhorred in Revelation (18:23 and 22:5) as the source of intellectual enlightenment in Babylon, is made to antedate even sun and moon.

Candle is the same as the number one in Indian sign language.

11 Imix: this event could be read as 'rocks and trees were created on this day'. However, the verb 'patic', meaning 'to mould' or 'to invent', is one of no less than seven distinct Maya verbs in this passage meaning 'to create'. The materials involved, stone and wood, may conventionally evoke the art of painting and carving and hence of writing. 'Within the day' has the inherent meaning of 'in the face of one day' and could thus refer to the formula on which hieroglyphic writing was based (1 day = 1 unit). Thus, what looks like a dull echo of God's creation day by day could again be a subtle allusion to Maya cosmology.

12 Wind: winds and draughts have a dangerous power in shamanism; cf. chapter VIII.

13 Night: this event refers both to the 'sloppy' race of men made in the *Popol vuh* (cf. *V.7*), and to the biblical man of clay.

2 Snake: 'covered' like the Snake in the Walam Olum; cf. *V.11*.

VI Hunting and Planting

1 Mallery 1893:582, where it is accompanied by a text in Innuit (Eskimo); from the same source as *III.1*.

2 Buffalo robe, Museum für Völkerkunde, Berlin, Cat. no. IV B 205. Collected from the Mandan Sioux by Prince Maximilian von Wied in 1833. Ghost Dance song in Mooney 1896: 216. In some of the songs collected by Mooney (e.g. p. 269), Algonkin tribes like the Cheyenne recall their lost home to the east.

3 Walam Olum, ed. Brinton, pp. 180–5 (symbols 41–52), that is the first three stanzas of the opening chapter (five stanzas in all) of Part 2. The four- and five-stanza structure

of this historical part of the text is recorded by the small horizontal lines in the symbol for sachem Walamolumin – see fig. 6, p. 96.

rich in mind: the triple-cross sign here is the same as the sachem Much-Honoured's sign in *I.13*.

canoes: see the remarks on the Maya canoe hieroglyph in the commentary to *VI.9*.

4 Newcomb and Reichard 1937: pl. xxxv.

6 Boturini screenfold, pp. 1–4. HMAI Census 34. Kingsborough 1831–48, 1. Cf. Robertson 1959: 83–6.

7 Cristobal de Castillo, *Historia*, ed. Paso y Troncoso 1908: chapter 2. HMAI Census 1021.

8 Told (to me) by the Arawak Indian Cuthbert Simon at his village on the upper Mahaica River, Guyana, 5 August 1978. This and other stories, told to Simon by his grandmother, were copied down by him in notebooks in Arawak, in the alphabet or in a syllabary devised by him. For the Carib version of the story, collected in northwest Colombia *c.* 1920, see the *Handbook of South American Indians*, 4: 326; cf. also the snake design, taken from a totuma, in C. D. Dance, *Chapters from a Guianese Log-Book*, Georgetown 1881: 305.

9 S. W. A. Gunn, *The Totem Poles in Stanley Park*, Vancouver, 1965: 10.

10 D. Kelley 1976: 231.

12 Fejérváry screenfold, pp. 34–33 (top third of those pages). The connection between the planting stick and the snake-penis is made very clear in the Borgia, pp. 18–21. For modern Maya planting practices see Cardoza y Aragón 1955, chapter 2.

13 Borgia screenfold, p. 27. Compare the central disk, divided between night and sun, with that in *III.8*, and with the 'first fruits' symbol in

the Walam Olum (*V.11*). In some Mesoamerican languages there are separate words for day-rain and night-rain.

15 Chimalpahin (for full name see bibliography), *Relaciones*, f. 168v (7th Relación); HMAI Census 1027. This translation was made with help from Siméon 1889. See *VII.8* for another example taken from this work. Writing *c*. 1600, Chimalpahin was literate in several languages and in his Mexican histories he drew on screenfold Year-Bearer annals, on transcriptions of these in Nahua, and on previous historians like Castillo (see *VI.7*). Integrating all this information with European histories gleaned from Spanish *reportorios* (almanacs), he was one of the first scholars to tackle the problem of correlating the Christian and the Toltec calendars and of reconciling biblical with native American world history: see Zimmermann 1960.

Nezahualcoyotl: cf. *I.1* and *IX.7*.

VII Conquest

1 Museum of Mankind, London, item 917. See Petersen 1971 for later Cheyenne records of conquest and notes on their Dog Soldiers and other military orders. On his travels through Creek and Cherokee territory, De Soto found the houses of chiefs covered with skins recording their conquests. A Creek account of migration and conquest, 'curiously written in red and black characters' on buffalo skin, was presented to James Oglethorpe in 1735 and was once preserved in the Georgia Office, Westminster; see A. S. Gatschet 1884 and 1892.

2 Aubin Manuscript no. 20; HMAI Census 14. In the Bibliothèque Nationale, Paris, where an accompanying copy gives details of the faded central area.

3 Nuttall screenfold, p. 75. The conquered town 'Loin-cloth' is shown by the hill or pyramid sign ('tepetl' in Nahua), used for place names in Toltec writing, along with House (cf. *I.2*), Wood, Ford and other conventional signs (an inverted star indicates Valley or lowland, for example). When he conquered the Mixtecs Cortés was presented with copies of their historical screenfolds so that he might continue the story. On Mixtec political history, see J. C. Clark, *The Story of 8-Deer*, and P. Dark, *Mixtec Ethnohistory*.

4 See Alfonso Caso, 'El Mapa de Teozacoalco', *Cuadernos Americanos* VIII (1949), 5: 145–81. The dimensions of the map are 138 × 176 cm. ($54\frac{1}{2}$ × $69\frac{1}{2}$ in.). Similar MSS. including columns of married pairs were prepared to support land claims – The Geneaology of Tlazultepec, for example, was produced as evidence in a lawsuit in 1597.

5 *Annals of Cuauhtinchan* (also known as the *Historia Tolteca-Chichimeca*), pl. 24–5, HMAI Census 1129. The 52 leaves of visual and alphabetic (Nahua) text cover the period AD 1116–1544. This commentary draws on Berlin and Rendón 1947.

6 Slab 14, Monte Albán, in A. Caso, 'Zapotec writing and calendar', HMAI 3: 937.

7 Lintel 8, Yaxchilan, in Museum of Mankind, London. Cf. Coe 1966: 172–3. The struggle between the two 'legitimate' older brothers and their junior rivals, the Twins, is a main theme in the Underworld chapter of the *Popol vuh*, lines 2203–4659.

8 Chimalpahin, *Relaciones*, ed. Siméon 1889: 116–7.

Tlacaelel: this figure is discussed by León-Portilla 1956.

9 See note to *III.7*; also my article, 'Huitzilopochtli and what was made of him', *Mesoamerican Archeology*,

ed. N. Hammond 1974: 155–66.

10 Mendoza Codex, p. 39; HMAI Census 196. Prepared for the viceroy Antonio de Mendoza *c.* 1542, this document forms part of the valuable collection of American materials published in Part 2 of Samuel Purchas, *Hakluytus Posthumus or Purchas his Pilgrimes*; see Robertson 1959 and J. C. Clark's magnificent edition of 1938.

The tribute lists form part 2 of the Codex (pp. 17–55) and are modelled on the Tribute Roll of Moctezuma (HMAI Census 368), in which however the reading order begins at bottom left. For details of song as tribute, see chapter IX.

11 G. Kutscher 1954: item 21. Here, I have followed the convention of calling the civilization which preceded the Chimu in this area early Chimu rather than 'Mochica'; cf. E. P. Benson, *The Mochica*, 1972. Larco Hoyle 1965: 95–6 has a fine copy of a pre-Inca weaving which celebrates a conquest by showing rows of naked prisoners, male and female, with ropes around their necks.

VIII Healer

1 Dresden screenfold, pp. 16c–17c (cf. *IV.9*). On shamanism in general and in America, see Eliade 1964: 288–336. The sixth interval of this table, no. 47 in Thompson's edition of 1972, should read '10', not '12'. At a shrine at Izamal the macaw is also revered as a *curer*, of yellow fever: Kinich Kakmo, Sun-eye Fire-macaw (Roys 1933: 141).

2 Chilam Balam Book of Kaua, p. 4. HMAI Census 179 and 1148. This photograph is printed direct from T. Maler's nineteenth-century negatives, The zodiac date, Cancer on 12 June, is prior to the Gregorian Reform of 1582. The Chilam Balam Books of Tekax, Nah, Ixil and Chancah also contain medical literature.

3 Ritual of the Bacabs; HMAI Census 1142. This translation based on Roys 1965: 114–5, who also comments on the text of *VIII.2*.

4 Martín de la Cruz, *Libellus de Medicinalibus Indorum Herbis*; HMAI Census 85. Translation from Gates's edition 1939: 98.

5 Hernando Ruiz de Alarcón, *Tratado de las supersticiones . . .* (1629), a collection of Aztec cures from the area southwest of Tenochtitlan. This translation and commentary based on Hinz 1970, a fundamental study of these texts. Some of this lore survives in the rituals of the Native American Church.

7 Osuna Codex, p. 38; HMAI Census 243.

8 Original Iroquois versions of the Book of Rites were written out in the nineteenth century by the Onondaga chief John Arthur Gibson and the Mohawk Smoke Johnson and others; this translation is by John Bierhorst 1974: 145, an excellent edition of this and other basic texts of American Indian literature.

The religion founded in 1799 by the Seneca preacher Handsome Lake draws on traditional Iroquois notions of medicine and of the opposition between hunter and planter, and guards against the anarchy caused by alcoholism and by grief in the face of death. Learning about the ancient Condolence ritual of the Iroquois from an Indian who returned with Cartier to France, Rabelais lustily satirizes it, in his fashion, in *Pantagruel*, IV, 26.

9 Notebooks by Thomson and Long in the Speck collection in the library of the American Philosophical Society, Washington, D.C., items 669 and 688. Cf. Mooney 1896, and Kilpatrick 1965. ‹

10 Holmer and Wassen, *Dos cantos*

shamanísticos de los indios Cuna, Göteborg 1963: 52. The numbers placed above the symbols here correspond to numbers 546–72 in that source (14 = 559 and 560). See also Holmer and Wassen 1953, a discussion of the Mu Iglala ritual. For the relationship of Cuna script to ritual and myth see Kramer 1970. Rubén Pérez Kantule's work is discussed by Nordenskjöld, 1928–30 and 1938, and his political role in the Cuna rising of 1925 is celebrated in a poem in Ernesto Cardenal's *Homage to the American Indians*. On the Cuna use of painted balsa boards see the *Handbook of South American Indians*, 4: 262–3.

11 Quoted by Mallery 1893: 236–8 and pl. xviii; pp. 255–6 give a cosmological drawing and verbal text by Sikassige. A Mide text referring explicitly to the phases of the moon is in the same work, 241–3. Cf. also Catlin 1841: pl. 309 for lunar signs by a Pawnee shaman. The fifth line of the present text was taken by A. G. Day as the title for his study of American Indian poetry (1951), *The Sky Clears*. The first published examples of Mide texts are in Tanner 1830. Copies of prescription sticks may be found in R. T. Coe, *Sacred Circles* 1976: item 162.

12 Paul Radin, *The Winnebago Tribe*, 1923: 104–5.

IX Singer and Scribe

1 K. T. Preuss 1921: 166–7. This translation based on both Preuss's German and his transcription of the Witoto original. On the history of this region, see G. Reichel-Dolmatoff, *Amazonian Cosmos*; and D. Lathrap, *The Upper Amazon*. It was only in 1886 with the development of rubber tapping by foreign companies, that Witoto territory was first seriously invaded.

2 Museum of Mankind, items 2252 and uncatalogued. On Mide music see F. Densmore, *Chippewa Music*, Washington 1910–13, whose work is very well reviewed by Kenneth Rexroth, 'American Indian Songs', *Assays*, New York 1960. Rexroth also singles out Yvor Winters as the only major U.S. critic to appreciate native American literature: cf. Winters 1967: 352–8, and his pupil Day 1951. For more recent studies see Zolla 1973 and Rothenberg 1968. For Sikassige's initiation text see *VIII.11*, above. Modern Algonkin songs using Mide symbols are published by H. A. Norman in *Alcheringa*, 3 (1971): 64–7.

3 Vienna screenfold, p. 48. On Toltec artistry see León-Portilla 1956; Séjourné 1957 (an important source for Nicholson 1959 and for W. C. Williams and other U.S. poets.

4 *Cantares mexicanos*, ff. 26v–27v; HMAI Census 1019. This and the following translations of this text are indebted to Schultze Jena 1957, and Garibay 1965–8, 3. An exhaustive historical study of the first part of this poem was made by Lehmann, 'Ein Tolteken Klagegesang', *Festschrift E. Seler*, Stuttgart 1922, who compares it with similar Toltec 'orphan' songs in the *Popul vuh* (lines 6058–80) and the Book of the Cakchiquel, ed. Recinos and Goetz, pp. 50–4. Bierhorst 1974: 17–97 well vindicates the unity of the piece as a whole.

Nacxitl: cf. *II.2*.

Conches: these and other musical instruments are played in farewell ceremonies depicted in the *Annals of Cuauhtinchan* and other Toltec sources.

10-Flower: reigned in Tula AD 895–930.

Sacred sand: cf. note to *III.13*.

Where you are expected: this is a shamanistic formula.

6 *Cantares mexicanos*, f. 18r. The Pawnee war song is quoted by Brinton 1890: ch. 3; see also Brinton 1887.

Bells: these were worn round the ankles of the performers.

7 Otomi text in J. Granados y Galvez 1778: 77. On its origins and authenticity see my article 'An Indian Farewell in Prescott's *Conquest of Mexico*', *American Literature*, xiv (1973), 348–56. The Otomi version of the Twenty Signs is noted in Caso 1968. León-Portilla 1967 has discussed the question of authorship in Mexican poetry; on Nezahualcoyotl in particular see Gilmor 1949 and V. Castillo 1972.

8 (a) Guaman Poma, op. cit., p. 237; translated by W. S. Merwin under the title 'My ragged sea-lettuce' (Rothenberg 1968: 238); (b) Jesús Lara, *Poesía popular quechua*, p. 69 (modern orthography); (c) J. M. Arguedas, *Todas las sangres*, 1964: 292. J. G. Herder included Quechua poems, taken from Garcilaso el Inca, in his own *Stimmen der Völker in Liedern*, the first large-scale anthology of poetry outside the classical European tradition. See also the remarkable local collection of Quechua literature, *Tarmap Pacha Huaray / Azucenas quechuas*, Lima 1905; and R. and M. d'Harcourt's *La Musique des Incas et ses survivances*, 1925.

9 Kutscher 1954: item 29; inset from *Handbook of South American Indians* 5, fig. 187 (after Larco Hoyle). Other Chimu and Moche runners include foxes and centipedes with legs like plant leaves. The tail 'of speed' behind the bean-reader exactly resembles the Algonkin sign of the same meaning – cf. *I.13*. On ideography, see C. Wiener, 1880: 650–2, 772 and 774, and Ibarra Grasso 1953. As for the Chibcha seed reader Mica, the ritual

number three (see fig. 5), he recalls the bicephalous statues found from San Agustín, Colombia, to Nicaragua.

10 *Popol vuh*, lines 4865–94, 4909–28, 4939–48, 4963–74 and 4997–5006, ed. and trans. by Edmonson 1971.

11 Book of Chumayel, pp. 106–7. The one well-known collection of modern Maya verse, as such, edited by A. Barrera Vásquez, is entitled *El libro de los cantares de Dzitbalche*, HMAI Census 1159. The deep connection between ritual calendrics and forms of literacy and literature may be held characteristic of America (and appear to defy in principle Structuralist approaches to the 'mythologies' of the continent). Equivalent in this respect to the Maya text here, with its vigesimal lines, are: the Walam Olum, with its 184 'equinoctial' symbols (see p. 51); the Vienna screenfold and the *Annals of Cuauhtinchan*, with their 52 'year'-pages; the *Popol vuh*, where journeys through the underworld are closely measured in the numbers of lines and the words which respectively record them (see note to *V.6*); and the Quechua drama *Ollantay*, with its 30 'day of the month' dialogues.

Seven ruined houses: cf. note to *VI.5*.

Note the identity, between Yucatec and Quiche Maya, of the words *balam* (Jaguar), *utz* (good), *ox* (three), *chi* (mouth), and the similarity of the terms for night (*akab*, *aqab*), sky (*caan*, *kah*), earth (*luum, ileu*) and eye, face or image (*uich, uach*).

night crime: *co akab*, also the name of the Screech owl (Roys 1933: 169), sixth of the Thirteen Birds; employed by the Lords of Xibalba (in the *Popol vuh*) as a night patrol in the flower gardens of their hell.

Bibliography

The following list is meant for general reference and by no means aspires to be exhaustive – an impossibility given the vastness of the subject. It does not include all the works cited in the notes above and is confined to books and main publications. Details of different editions are given chiefly for the sources of native texts, though in several cases the quotations in this book are taken directly from originals.

Abbreviations:

BAE Bureau of American Ethnology, Washington, D.C.

LAAL Library of Aboriginal American Literature, ed. D. G. Brinton, Philadelphia, Pa., 1882–90.

Alcina Franch. J.:
1957 *Floresta literaria de la América indígena. Antología de los pueblos indígenas de América*, Madrid.

Alvarado Tezozomoc, Hernando:
1949 *Crónica Mexicayotl* (*c.* 1600); Spanish trans. from the Nahuatl by Adrian León, Mexico.

Álvarez, María Cristina:
1974 *Textos coloniales del Libro de Chilam Balam de Chumayel y textos glíficos del Códice de Dresde*, Mexico.

Annals of Cuauhtinchan:
1942 *Historia Tolteca-Chichimeca*; facsimile in *Corpus Codicum Americanorum Medii Aevi* by Ernst Menguin, Copenhagen.
1947 *Historia Tolteca-Chichimeca: Anales de Cuauhtinchan*, Spanish trans. by H. Berlin, Mexico.

Annals of Cuauhtitlan – see History of the Kingdoms.

Annals of Texcoco (Códice en cruz) – in Boban (q.v.) 1891: vol. 1.

Annals of Tlatelolco:
1948 *Unos annales* [*sic*] *históricos de la nación mexicana* (1528), ed. and trans. into Spanish by H. Berlin and T. Barlow, Mexico.

Antigüedades de Mexico:
1974 *Antigüedades de Mexico*, basadas en la recopilación de Lord Kingsborough (q.v.), Mexico (4 vols.).

Antigüedades mexicanas:
1892 *Antigüedades mexicanas*, publicadas por la Junta Colombina de Mexico, Mexico.

Arguedas, José María:
1938 *Canto Kechwa*, Lima; English translation by R. W. Stephen, *The Singing Mountaineers. Songs and Tales of the Quechua*, Austin, Tex. 1957.
1964 *Todas las sangres*, Buenos Aires.
1966 *Poesía quechua*, Buenos Aires.

Arias-Larreta, A.:
1968 *Literaturas aborígenes de América*, Buenos Aires.

Artaud, Antonin:
1971 *Lettres du Mexique. Les Tarahumaras*, in *Oeuvres complètes*, nos. 8–9. Paris.

Astrov, Margot:
1946 *The Winged Serpent*, New York; republished as *American Indian Prose and Poetry*, 1962.

Asturias, Miguel Angel:
1930 *Leyendas de Guatemala*, Madrid.

1949 *Hombres de maíz*, Buenos Aires.
1960 *Poesía precolombina*, Buenos Aires.
1971 *Trois des quatre soleils*, Geneva.

Austin, Mary:
1923 *The American Rhythm*, New York.

Aveni, A. F.:
1975 *Archeoastronomy in Pre-Columbian America*, Austin, Tex.

Ayvu Rapyta:
1959 *Ayvu Rapyta. Textos míticos de los Mbya-Guarani del Guaira*, ed. León Cadogan, São Paulo.

Bagrow, Leo:
1964 *History of Cartography*, London.

Bancroft, H. H.:
1874–5 *The native races of the Pacific states of North America*, San Francisco, Cal.

Barbeau, M.:
1950 *Totem Poles, according to crests and topics*, Toronto.

Barrera Vásquez, A., and S. Rendón:
1948 *El libro de los libros de Chilam Balam*, Mexico.

Basadre, J.:
1938 *Literatura Inca*, Paris.

Baudin, L.:
1964 *Les Incas*, Paris.

Baudot, G.:
1976 *Les Lettres précolumbiennes*, Paris.

Benson, Elizabeth P.:
1968 *Dumbarton Oaks Conference on the Olmec 1967*, Washington, D.C.
1973 *Mesoamerican Writing Systems*, Washington, D.C.
1972 *The Mochica. A Culture of Peru*, London and New York.

Biedermann, H.:
1971 *Altmexikos Heilige Bücher*, Graz.

Bierhorst, J.:
1971 *In the Trail of the Wind. American Indian poems and ritual orations*, New York.
1974 *Four Masterworks of American Indian Literature. Quetzalcoatl | The Ritual of Condolence | Cuceb | The Night Chant*, New York.

1976 *The Red Swan. Myths and Tales of the American Indians*, New York.

Black Elk (Hehaka Sapa):
1932 *Black Elk Speaks. Being the Life Story of a Holy Man of the Ogalala Sioux as told to John Neihardt*, New York; revised edition, Lincoln, Neb., 1961.
1953 *The Sacred Pipe. Black Elk's Account of the Seven Rites of the Oglala Sioux recorded and edited by J. E. Brown*, Norman, Okla.; Penguin edition Harmondsworth, 1971.

Boas, F.:
1927 *Primitive Art*, Oslo; new edition 1955, Toronto, New York and London.

Boban, E.:
1891 *Documents pour servir à l'histoire du Mexique*, Paris (2 vols. and atlas).

Bodley screenfold:
1831–48 In Kingsborough (q.v.), vol. 1.
1960 *Interpretation of the Codex Bodley 2858*, by A. Caso, Mexico.

Book of Chumayel – see Chumayel, Book of.

Book of the Cakchiquel:
1953 *Annals of Cakchiquels*, translated from the Cakchiquel Maya by Adrian Recinos and Delia Goetz, Norman, Okla.

Borbonicus screenfold:
1899 *Codex Borbonicus*, ed. E. T. M. Hamy, Paris.

Borgia screenfold:
1898 *Codex Borgia*, ed. F. Ehrle, Rome.

Borsari, F.:
1888 *La letteratura degl' indigeni americani*, Naples.

Borunda, I.:
1898 *Clave general de jeroglíficos americanos*, Rome.

Boturini screenfold:
1831–48 In Kingsborough (q.v.), vol. 1.

Boturini Benaducci, L.:
1746 *Idea de una nueva historia general de la América septentrional*, Madrid.

Bowra, C. M.:
1963 *Primitive Song*, New York.

Braghine, A.:
1938 *The Shadow of Atlantis*, London.
Brasseur de Bourbourg, C. E.:
1868 *Quatre Lettres sur le Mexique*, Paris.
1871 *Bibliothèque Mexico-Guatemalienne*, Paris.
Bray, W., *et al.*:
1975 *The New World*, London.
Brinckmann. B.:
1970 *Quellenkritische Untersuchungen zum mexikanischen Missionsschauspiel 1533–1733*, Hamburg.
Brinton, D. G.:
1882 *The Maya Chronicles*, Philadelphia, Pa.; Library of Aboriginal American Literature (=LAAL), vol. I.
1883 *Aboriginal American Authors*, Philadelphia, Pa.
1887 See Cantares mexicanos.
1890 *Essays of an Americanist*, Philadelphia, Pa.
Brown, Dee:
1971 *Bury my Heart at Wounded Knee. A History of the Sioux uprising of 1870*, New York and London.
Burga Freitas, A.:
1939 *Ayahuasca. Mitos y leyendas del Amazonas*, Buenos Aires.
Burkitt, R.:
1920 *The Hills and the Corn. A legend of the Kekchi Indians of Guatemala, put in writing by the late Tiburtius Kaal*, Philadelphia, Pa.
Burland, C.:
1950 *The Four Directions of Time*, Santa Fe, N.M.
1953 *Magic books from Mexico*, Harmondsworth.
1965 *North American Indian Mythology*, London.
1967 *The Gods of Mexico*, London.
Bushnell, G. H. S.:
1968 *The First Americans*, London and New York; reprinted 1978.
Campos, R. M.:
1936 *La producción literaria de los aztecas*, Mexico.

Cantares mexicanos:
1887 *Ancient Nahuatl Poetry*, ed. D. G. Brinton, Philadelphia, Pa. (LAAL vol. 7).
1957 *Alt-aztekische Gesänge*, ed. L. Schulze Jena, Stuttgart.
1965–8 *Poesía náhuatl*, ed. A. M. Garibay, Mexico (vols. 2 and 3).
Cardenal, Ernesto:
1969 *Homenaje a los indios americanos*, León, Nicaragua; English trans., *Homage to the American Indians*, Baltimore, Md, 1973.
Cardoza y Aragón, L.:
1955 *Guatemala. Las líneas de su mano*, Mexico.
Carrasco Pizana, P.:
1950 *Los Otomies*, Mexico.
Casas, J. Broda de:
1969 *The Mexican Calendar as compared to other Mesoamerican systems*, Vienna.
Caso, Alfonso:
1954 *El pueblo del sol*, Mexico; English trans. *The Aztecs. People of the Sun*, Norman, Okla., 1958.
1968 *Los calendarios prehispánicos*, Mexico.
Castaneda, Carlos:
1968 *The Teachings of Don Juan*, New York.
Castillo, Cristobal de:
1908 *Fragmentos de la obra general sobre historia de los mexicanos ... escrita en langua nahuatl (c. 1600)*, ed. F. del Paso y Troncoso, Florence.
Castillo, Victor:
1972 *Nezahualcoyotl. Crónica y pinturas de su tiempo*, Texcoco.
Catlin, George:
1841 *Letters and Notes*, London (2 vols.).
Chamberlain, R. S.:
1955 *The Conquest and Colonization of Yucatan 1517–1550*, Washington, D.C.
Chilam Balam, Books of – see Chumayel, Mani (Códice Pérez), Tizimin, Books of.

Chimalpahin Cuauhtlehaunitzin, Domingo Francisco de San Antón Muñón:
1889 *Annales de . . . 6e et 7e Relations*, ed. R. Siméon, Paris.
1958 *Das Memorial breve*, ed. W. Lehmann and G. Kutscher, Stuttgart.
1963 *Die Relationen C.'s zur Geschichte Mexikos*, ed. G. Zimmermann, Hamburg (2 vols.).
1965 *Relaciones originales de Chalco Amaquemecan*, ed. S. Rendón. Mexico.
Chronicle of Calkini:
1957 *Códice de Calkini*, ed. A. Barrera Vásquez, Campeche.
Chronicles of American Indian Protest:
1971 *Chronicles of American Indian Protest*, New York.
Chumayel, Book of:
1913 *The Book of Chilam Balam of Chumayel*, ed. G. B. Gordon, Philadelphia, Pa.
1930 *Libro de Chilam Balam de Chumayel*, ed. A. Médiz Bolio, San José, Costa Rica.
1933 *The Book of Chilam Balam of Chumayel*, ed. R. L. Roys, Washington, D.C.
1956 *Livre de Chilam Balam de Chumayel*, ed. Benjamin Péret, Paris.
Churchward, J.:
1931 *The lost continent of Mu*, New York.
Cid Pérez, J.:
1964 *Teatro indio precolumbino*, Madrid.
Clark, J. Cooper:
1912 *The Story of Eight Deer*, London.
Códice en cruz – see Annals of Texcoco.
Coe, M. D.:
1966 *The Maya*, London and New York.
1973 *The Maya Scribe and his World*, New York.
Coe, R. T.:
1977 *Sacred Circles. Two thousand years of North American Indian Art*, London.
Copway, George (Kah-gegagah-bowh):
1847 *The Life, History and Travels of Kah-gegagah-bowh*, Albany, N.Y.
Cornyn, J. H.:
1930 *The Song of Quetzalcoatl*, Yellow Springs, Ohio.
Cortés, Hernán:
1961 *Cartas de relación de la conquista de Mexico*, Mexico.
Courlander, H.:
1971 *The Fourth World of the Hopis*, New York.
Cranfill, T. M.:
1959 *The Muse in Mexico. A Mid-Century Miscellany*, Austin, Tex.
Cronyn, G. W.:
1918 *The Path on the Rainbow. An anthology of songs and chants from the Indians of North America*, New York.
Cruz, Martín de la:
1939 *The de la Cruz-Badiano Aztec herbal of 1552*, ed. W. Gates, Baltimore, Md. (2 vols.).
1964 *Libellus de medicinalibus indorum herbis (1552)*, Mexico.
Cumming, W. P., *et al.*:
1974 *The Exploration of North America 1630–1776*, London.
Curtis, Natalie:
1923 *The Indians' Book*, New York.
Cusick, David:
1825 *Sketches of Ancient History of the Six Nations*, Tuscarora Village, N.Y.
Däniken, E. von:
1968 *Erinnerung an die Zukunft*, Düsseldorf.
Dark, P.:
1958 *Mixtec ethnohistory: a method of analysis of the codical art*, Oxford.
Day, A. G.:
1951 *The Sky Clears. Poetry of the American Indians*, New York.
Díaz, Bernal:
1963 *The Conquest of New Spain*, trans. J. M. Cohen, London.

Dibble, C. E.:
1963 *Historia de la nación mexicana. Reproducción a todo color del Códice de 1576 (Códice Aubin)*, Madrid.

Densmore, Frances:
1926 *The American Indians and their Music*, New York.

Diringer, D.:
1968 *The Alphabet*, London (2 vols.).

Dorn, Edward:
1966 *The Shoshoneans*, New York.
1974 *Recollections of Gran Apachería*, San Francisco, Cal.

Dresden screenfold:
1892 *Die Maya Handschrift der Königlichen öffentlichen Bibliothek zu Dresden*, ed. E. Förstemann, Dresden.
1972 – see Thompson, J. E. S.

Driver, H. E.:
1961 *Indians of North America*, Chicago, Ill.

Dundes, N.:
1964 *Morphology of the North American Indian Folk-Tales*, Helsinki.

Dunn, Dorothy:
1968 *American Indian Painting of the Southwest and Plains Areas*, Albuquerque, N.M.

Durán, Diego:
1971 *History of New Spain*, Norman, Okla.

Edmonson, Munro:
1971 *Lore*, New Orleans, La.
1971a – see *Popul vuh* 1971.

Edwards, Emily:
1966 *The Painted Walls of Mexico from prehistoric times until today*, Austin, Tex., and London.

Eliade, Mircea:
1964 *Shamanism. Archaic techniques of Ecstasy*, Princeton, N.J. (trans. from the French, *Le Chamanisme*, Paris 1951).

Feder, N.:
1971 *American Indian Art*, New York.

Fejérváry screenfold – see Seler, E. 1901.

Fernández, Justino:
1954 *Coatlicue, estética del arte indígena antiguo*, Mexico.

Fernández de Piedrahita, Lucas:
1973 *Noticia historial de las conquistas del Nuevo Reino de Granada* [1688], Bogotá.

Fiedler, Leslie A.:
1968 *The Return of the Vanishing American*, New York and London.

Fletcher, Alice C.:
1900 *Indian Story and Song from North America*, Boston, Mass.

Flor y canto:
1964 *Flor y canto del arte prehispánico de México*, Mexico.

Florentine Codex:
1950–69 *Florentine Codex: General History of the things of New Spain* (Bernardino de Sahagún), trans. (from the Aztec) C. Dibble and A. J. O. Anderson. Santa Fe, New Mexico, and Salt Lake City, Utah (11 vols.).

Fouchard, Jean:
1972 *Langue et littérature des aborigènes d'Ayti*, Paris.

Franco, Alfonso Arinos de Melo:
1937 *O indio brasileiro e a revoluçao francesa, as origens brasileiras da theoria da bondade natural*, Rio de Janeiro.

Fuentes y Guzmán, F. A. de:
1932–3 *Recordación Florida ... del Reyno de Guatemala*, Guatemala (3 vols).

Gamio, Manuel:
1972 *Arqueología e indigenismo*, Mexico.

Garcilaso de la Vega, 'El Inca':
1966 *The Royal Commentaries of the Incas*, trans. H. V. Livermore, Austin, Tex., and London.

Garibay, K. A. M.:
1940 *Llave del Nahuatl*, Otumba; 2nd enlarged ed., Mexico, 1961.
1940a *Poesía indígena*, Mexico.
1953–4 *Historia de la literatura náhuatl*, Mexico (2 vols.).
1965–8 – see *Cantares mexicanos*.

Garza, Mercedes de la:
1975 *La conciencia histórica de los antiguos mayas*, Mexico.

309

Gatschet, A. S.:
1876 *Zwölf Sprachen aus dem Südwesten Nordamerikas*, Weimar.
1884 *A Migration Legend of the Creek Indians*, Philadelphia, Pa. (LAAL vol. 4).
1892 *A Migration Legend of the Creek Indians*, part 2, St Louis, Mo. (vol. 5 of the Transactions of the Academy of Sciences).

Gelb, I. J.:
1963 *A Study of Writing*, Chicago, Ill.

Genet, Jean, and P. Chelbatz:
1927 *Histoire des peuples Mayas-Quiches (Mexique, Guatemala, Honduras)*, Paris.

Gibson, Charles:
1966 *Spain in America*, New York and London.

Gilmor, Frances:
1949 *Flute of the Smoking Mirror (A Portrait of Nezahualcoyotl)*, Albuquerque, N.M.
1964 *The King danced in the marketplace*, Tucson, Ariz.

Gonçalves Dias, A.:
1858 *Dicionario da lingua tupi*, Leipzig.

González, Nicolás:
1958 *Ideología guarani*, Mexico.

Granados y Gálvez, J. de:
1778 *Tardes americanas*, Mexico.

Grant, Campbell:
1967 *Rock Art of the American Indian*, New York.

Gross, Donald:
1976 *Native Cultures of South America*, New York.

Guaman Poma de Ayala, Felipe:
1936 *Nueva corónica y buen gobierno*, facsimile edition, Paris.
1956–66 *La nueva corónica y buen gobierno*, ed. L. Bustios Gálvez, Lima (3 vols.).

Guardia Mayorga, C.:
1961 *Diccionario Kechwa-castellano*, Lima.

Guiteras-Holmes, Calixta:
1961 *Perils of the Soul. The world-view of a Tzotzil [Maya] Indian*, New York.

Gunn, S. W. A.:
1965 *Totem Poles of British Columbia*, Vancouver.

Hagen, Victor Wolfgang von:
1944 *The Aztec and Maya papermakers*, New York.

Haile, B.:
1938 *Origin Legend of the Navaho Enemy Way*, New Haven, Conn.

Hale, Horatio:
1883 *The Iroquois Book of Rites*. Philadelphia, Pa. (LAAL, vol. 2); 2nd enlarged edition, Toronto 1963.

Hammond, Norman:
1974 *Mesoamerican Archeology: New Approaches*, Austin, Tex., and London.
1978 *Maya Archeology and Ethnohistory* (ed. with Gordon Willey), Austin, Tex.

Handbook of the American Indians North of Mexico:
1907 *Handbook of the American Indians North of Mexico*, ed. F. W. Hodge, Washington, D.C. (2 vols.; BAE Bulletin 30).

Handbook of Middle American Indians:
1964–75 *Handbook of Middle American Indians* (general editor, R. Wauchope), Austin, Tex., and London (15 vols.). HMAI Census numbers are quoted in this book; the Census, compiled by J. B. Glass and C. Gibson, appears in vols. 14 and 15.

Handbook of South American Indians:
1963 *Handbook of South American Indians* (general editor, Julian Steward), New York (7 vols).

Harcourt, Raoul and Marie d':
1925 *La Musique des Incas et ses survivances*, Paris.

Hariot, T.:
1590 *A Briefe and True Report of the New Found Land of Virginia*, Frankfurt.

Hemming, John:
1970 *The Conquest of the Incas*, London.

Hinz, Eike:
1970 *Die magischen Texte im Tratado Ruiz de Alarcóns 1629* (Antropologische Analyse altaztekischer Texte), Hamburg.

History of the Kingdoms:
1938 *Die Geschichte der Königreiche von Colhuacan und Mexiko* (Codex Chimalpopoca: Anales de Cuauhtitlan and Leyenda de los Soles), ed. Walter Lehmann, Stuttgart and Berlin.

Hoffman, W. J.:
1894 *The Beginnings of Writing*, New York.

Holmer, Nils M., and S. H. Wassen:
1953 *The complete Mu-Igala in Picturewriting, A native record of a Cuna Indian Medicine Song*, Göteborg.

Hopi, Book of the – see Waters, F.

Huarochiri Narrative:
1939–41 *Dämonen und Zauber in Inkareich. Fr. de Ávila, Tratado . . . de los errores*, ed. H. Trimborn, Berlin; new edition by Trimborn and A. Kelm, Berlin 1967.
1966 *Dioses y hombres de Huarochirí. Narración quechua recogida por Fr. de Ávila* [1598?], ed. J. M. Arguedas, Lima.

Humboldt, Alexander von:
1810 *Vues des cordillères et monumens des peuples indigènes de l'Amérique*, Paris.

Hyde, George E.:
1951 *The Pawnee Indians*, Denver, Col.; new edition, Norman, Okla., 1974.
1956 *A Sioux Chronicle*, Norman, Okla.
1962 *Indians of the Woodlands from Prehistoric Times to 1725*, Norman, Okla.

Hymes, Dell H.:
1967 *Studies in Southwestern Ethnolinguistics*, ed. D. H. Hymes, Paris–The Hague.

Ibarra Grasso, Dick Edgar:
1953 *La escritura indígena andina*, La Paz.

Imbelloni, J.:
1956 *La segunda esfinge indiana. Antiguos y nuevos aspectos del problema de los orígenes americanos*, Buenos Aires.

Ixtlilxochitl, Fernando de Alva:
1891–2 *Obras históricas*, ed. A. Chavero, Mexico (2 vols.).

Jones, Peter (Kahkewaquonaby):
1861 *History of the Ojebway Indians*, London.

Joralemon, P. D.:
1971 *A Study of Olmec Iconography*, Washington, D.C.

Josephy, Alvin M., Jr., and William Brandon:
1961 *The American Heritage Book of Indians*, New York.
1968 *The Indian Heritage of America*, New York; London 1972.

Jung, Carl G.:
1916 *Psychology of the Unconscious . . .*, trans. Beatrice M. Hinkle, New York and London; reissued 1951.

Kaal, Tibertius – see R. Burkitt.

Katz, Friedrich:
1969 *Vorkolumbianische Kulturen. Die grossen Reiche des alten Amerikas*, Berlin.

Keen, Benjamin:
1971 *The Aztec image in Western thought*, New Brunswick, N.J.

Keiser, Albert:
1933 *The Indian in American Literature*, New York.

Kelley, David H.:
1976 *Deciphering the Maya Script*, Austin, Tex., and London.

Kidd, K. E., and S. Dewdney:
1967 *Indian Rock Painting of the Great Lakes*, Toronto.

Kilpatrick, J. F., and Anna Gritts:
1965 *The Shadow of Sequoyah. Social documents of the Cherokees, 1862–1964*, Norman, Okla.

Kingsborough, Lord (Edward King):
1831–48 *Antiquities of Mexico, comprising facsimiles of ancient Mexican paintings and hieroglyphs*, London (9 vols.).

Klah, Hasteen:
1942 *Navajo Creation Myth: the Story of the Emergence*, Santa Fe, N.M.
Knorozov, Yuri V.:
1967 *Selected chapters from The Writing of the Maya Indians*, Cambridge, Mass.
Koch-Grünberg, Theodor:
1907 *Südamerikanische Felszeichnungen*, Berlin.
Kramer, Fritz W.:
1970 *Literature among the Cuna Indians*, Göteborg.
Krickeberg, Walter:
1928 *Märchen der Azteken und Inkaperuaner, Maya und Muisca*, Düsseldorf-Cologne.
1968 *Pre-Columbian Mexican Religions*, London.
Kubler, George:
1962 *The art and architecture of ancient America: the Mexican, Maya and Andean peoples*, Baltimore, Md.
Kutscher, Gerdt:
1954 *Nordperuanische Keramik / Cerámica del Perú septentrional*, Berlin.
La Barre, Weston:
1964 *The Peyote Cult*, Hamden, Conn.
Lafitau, J. F.:
1724 *Moeurs des sauvages américains comparées aux moeurs des Premiers Temps*, Paris.
Lahourcade, Alicia N.:
1970 *La creación del hombre en las grandes religiones de América precolombina*, Madrid.
Lambert, Jean-Clarence:
1961 *Les Poésies mexicaines. Anthologie des origines à nos jours*, Paris.
Lanczkowski, Günter:
1962 *Quetzalcoatl. Mythos und Geschichte*, Leyden (Numen IX).
Landa, Diego de:
1937 *Yucatan before and after the conquest, by Friar Diego de Landa* (his Relación de las cosas de Yucatan), ed. and trans. William Gates, Baltimore, Md.
Landes, Ruth:
1968 *Ojibwa Religion and the Midewiwin*, University of Wisconsin, Madison.
Lara, Jesús:
1947 *La poesía quechua*, Mexico.
1947a *Poesía popular quechua*, La Paz.
1967 *La cultura de los Incas*, Cochabamba.
Larco Hoyle, Rafael:
1965 *Checan. Essay on erotic elements in Peruvian art*, Geneva – Paris – Munich.
Las Casas, Bartolomé de:
1552 *Brevísima relación de la destrucción de las Indias*, Madrid; in S. Purchas, 1905, vol. 18.
Lathrap, Donald:
1970 *The Upper Amazon*, London and New York.
Laud screenfold:
1966 *Codex Laud*, ed. C. Burland, Graz.
Lawrence, D. H.:
1926 *The Plumed Serpent*, London.
Legend of the Suns – see History of the Kingdoms.
Lehmann Walter:
1938 – see History of the Kingdoms.
1949 *Sterbende Götter und christliche Heilsbotschaft*, Stuttgart.
Lenz, Hans:
1961 *Mexican Indian paper: its history and survival*, Mexico.
León-Portilla, Miguel:
1956 *La filosofía náhuatl estudiada en sus fuentes*, Mexico; English trans., *Aztec thought and culture*, Norman, Okla., 1963.
1959 *Visión de los vencidos. Relaciones indígenas de la conquista*, Mexico; English trans., *The Broken Spears*, Boston, Mass., 1962.
1964 *Las literaturas precolombinas de México*, Mexico; English trans., *Pre-Columbian Literatures of Mexico*, Norman, Okla., 1969.
1964a *El reverso de la conquista. Relaciones aztecas, mayas e incas*, Mexico.
1967 *Trece poetas del mundo azteca*, Mexico.

1968 *Tiempo y realidad en el pensamiento maya*, Mexico; English trans. *The Maya concept of time and reality*, Norman, Okla.

1968a *Quetzalcoatl*, Mexico.

Le Page du Pratz:

1758 *Louisiane*, Paris (3 vols.).

Le Plongeon, Augustus:

1886 *Sacred mysteries among the Mayas and the Quiches*, New York.

Léry, Jean de:

1580 *Journal de bord. Le Brésil en 1557*, Geneva, 2nd edition.

Levine, Stuart, and Nancy O. Lurie:

1968 *The American Indian Today*, Baltimore, Md.

Lévi-Strauss, Claude:

1964–71 *Mythologiques*, Paris (4 vols.).

Lewis, Janet:

1932 *The Invasion*, Denver, Col.

Lienzo of Tlaxcala:

1892 In *Antigüedades mexicanas* (q.v.).

Lom d'Arce (Baron de Lahontan):

1703 *Voyages du baron de Lahontan dans l'Amérique septentrional*, Amsterdam.

Longfellow, Henry Wadsworth:

1855 *The Song of Hiawatha*, Boston, Mass., and London.

López Austín, A.:

1965 *La literatura de los guaraníes*, Mexico.

Luxton, R., and Pablo Canché:

1977 'The Hidden Continent of the Maya and the Quechua' (unpublished manuscript).

Maclagan, David:

1977 *Creation Myths. Man's introduction to the world*, London and New York.

Madrid screenfold:

1967 *Codex Tro-Cortesianus (Codex Madrid)*, facsimile edition by F. Anders, Graz.

Mallery, Garrick:

1893 *Picture-Writing of the American Indians*, Washington, D.C. (BAE, 10th Annual Report); paperback edition, New York 1972.

Mani, Book of – see Pérez, Códice.

Markham, Clements Robert:

1856 *Cuzco: A journey to the Ancient Capital of Peru, with an account of the history, language, literature and antiquities of the Incas*, London.

1873 *Narratives of the Rites and Law of the Incas*, London.

Martínez Hernández, J.:

1930 *Diccionario de Motul, Maya-Español*, Merida, Yucatan.

Mason, J. Alden:

1964 *The Ancient Civilizations of Peru*, Harmondsworth and Baltimore, Md; revised edition.

Maudslay, A. P.:

1889–1902 *Archeology. Biologia centrali-americana*, London (5 vols).

McAfee, B., and Robert Barlow:

1949 *Diccionario de elementos fonéticos en escritura jeroglífica*, Mexico.

Means, Philip Ainsworth:

1931 *Ancient Civilizations of the Andes*, New York and London.

Mendoza Codex:

1938 *Codex Mendoza*, facsimile, ed. and trans. J. Cooper Clark, London (3 vols.).

Mera, Juan León:

1868 *Ojeada histórico-crítica sobre la poesía ecuatoriana desde su época más remota hasta nuestros días*, Quito.

Metraux, Alfred:

1928 *La Religion des Tupinamba et ses rapports avec celle des autres tribus tupi-guarani*, Paris.

1962 *Les Incas*, Paris.

Meyer, William (Yonv'ut'sisla):

1971 *Native Americans: The New Indian Resistance*, New York.

Miller, Arthur G.:

1973 *The Mural Painting of Teotihuacan*, Washington, D.C.

Molina, Alonso de:

1571 *Vocabulario en lengua castellana y mexicana*, Mexico; modern edition, Madrid 1944.

Montoya Toro, J., and Ernesto Cardenal:

1966 *Literatura indígena americana*, Antioquia.

313

Mooney, James:
1896 *The Ghost-Dance Religion and the Sioux Outbreak of 1890*, Washington, D.C. (Part 2 of the BAE 14th Annual Report); abridged paperback edition, Chicago, Ill., 1965.
1932 *The Swimmer Manuscript: Cherokee Sacred Formulas and Medicinal Prescriptions*, Washington, D.C. (BAE Bulletin 99).

Morgan, Lewis Henry:
1851 *League of the Ho-de-no-sau-nee, or Iroquois*, New York; paperback edition, New York 1962.
1909 *Ancient Society*, Chicago, Ill., 2nd edition.
1959 *The Indian Journals 1859–62*, University of Michigan Press, Ann Arbor.

Morley, S. G.:
1915 *An Introduction to the Study of the Maya Hieroglyphs*, Washington, D.C. (BAE Bulletin 57); paperback edition, New York 1975.
1956 *The Ancient Maya*, Stanford, Cal.; revised edition.

Navarre, Robert:
1913 *Journal ou dictation d'une conspiration* (French text with English trans. by R. Clyde Ford, *Journal of Pontiac's Conspiracy*), Detroit.

Needham, Joseph:
1956, 1959 *Science and Civilization in China*, London, vols. 2, 3.

Newcomb, Franc J., and Gladys Reichard:
1937 *Sandpaintings of the Navajo Shooting Chant*, New York; paperback edition, New York, Toronto and London 1975.

Nicholson, Irene:
1959 *Firefly in the Night. A study of ancient Mexican poetry and symbolism*, London.

Nicolau d'Olwer, Luis:
1963 *Cronistas de las culturas precolumbinas*, Mexico.

Nordenskiöld, Erland:
1925 *The Secret of the Peruvian Quipus*, Göteborg (2 vols.).

1938 *An historical and ethnographical survey of the Cuna Indians* (in collaboration with Rubén Pérez Kantule), Göteborg.

Noriega, R., *et al.* (ed.):
1959 *Esplandor del Mexico antiguo*, Mexico (2 vols.).

Nowotny, Karl:
1961 *Tlacuilolli. Die mexikanischen Bilderhandschriften. Stil und Inhalt . . .*, Berlin.
1969 *Beiträge zur geschichte des Weltbildes. . . .*, Vienna.

Nuttall screenfold:
1902 *Codex Nuttall*, facsimile edition by Zelia Nuttall, Cambridge, Mass.

Ollantay:
1853 German trans. in J. J. von Tschudi, *Die Kechua Sprache*, Vienna.
1868 Spanish trans. by J. S. Sebastian, *Ollanta*, Lima.
1871 English trans. by C. R. Markham, *Ollantay: An ancient Inca Drama*, London.

Olson, Charles:
1953 *Mayan Letters*, Mallorca; new edition, London 1968.

Ossío, J. M.:
1973 *Ideología mesiánica del mundo andino*, Lima.

Osuna Codex:
1973 *Pintura del Gobernador, Alcaldes y Regidores de Mexico (1565)*, Madrid; first edition, Madrid 1878.

Oxcutzcab, Book of – see Pérez, Códice.

Pachacuti, Salcamayhua: in Markham (q.v.) 1873.

Paddock, John:
1966 *Ancient Oaxaca*, Stanford, Cal.

Pagden, A. R.:
1972 *Mexican Pictorial Manuscripts*, Oxford.

Paris screenfold:
1887 *Codex Peresianus*, facsimile edition by Léon de Rosny, Paris; new edition by F. Anders, Graz 1968.

Parkman, Francis:
1851–92 *France and England in North*

America (series), Boston, Mass., Toronto, London etc.

Parsons, Elsie Clews:
1922 *American Indian Life*, New York; paperback edition, Lincoln, Neb. 1967.
1936 *Mitla. Town of the Souls and other Zapoteco-speaking pueblos of Oaxaca*, Chicago, Ill.
1939 *Pueblo Indian Religion*, Chicago, Ill. (2 vols.).

Paxbalon-Maldonado Papers – see Scholes and Roys; and Smailus.

Pech, Ah Macan:
1926 *Crónica de Yaxkukul*, ed. J. Martínez Hernández, Merida.

Pech, Ah Nakuk:
1882 *Crónica de Chac-Xulub-Chen (U belil u kahlil Chac-Xulub Chen)*; in Brinton 1882, also in Yáñez 1939 (qq.v.).

Péret, Benjamin:
1956 – see Chumayel, Book of.
1960 *Anthologie des mythes, légendes et contes populaires d'Amérique*, Paris.

Pérez, Códice:
1949 *Códice Pérez*; Maya text with free Spanish translation by E. Solis Alcalá, Merida, Yucatan (contains Chilam Balam Books of Mani and Oxcutzcab).

Pérez, José Cid, and Dolores Martí de Cid:
1963 *Teatro indio precolombino*, Madrid.

Petersen, Karen Daniels:
1971 *Plains Indian Art from Fort Marion. With a Pictographic Dictionary*, Norman, Okla.

Pferdekamp, Wilhelm:
1963 *Die Indianer-Story*, Munich.

Pontiac – see Navarre, Robert.

Popol vuh:
1950 *Popol vuh. The sacred book of the ancient Quiche Maya*, English version by Delia Goetz and Sylvanus G. Morley from A. Recinos's Spanish, Norman, Okla.; and London 1951; 1954 edition entitled *The Book of the People*, Norman.

1962 *Das Buch des Rates*, German trans. by Wolfgang Cordan, Düsseldorf-Cologne.
1971 *The Book of Counsel: the Popol vuh of the Quiche Maya of Guatemala*, English trans. Munro Edmonson, New Orleans, La.

Porras Barrenechea, Raul:
1951 *Mito, tradición e historia del Peru*, Lima.

Praus, Alexis:
1962 *The Sioux 1798–1922. A Dakota Winter Count*, Bloomfields, Mich.

Prescott, William Hickling:
1843 *History of the Conquest of Mexico, with a preliminary view of the ancient Mexican civilization . . .*, London (3 vols.); revised edition, Philadelphia, Pa, 1874.
1854 *History of the Conquest of Peru*, London (2 vols.).

Preuss, Konrad Theodor:
1912 *Die Nayarit Expedition*, Leipzig.
1921 *Die Religion und Mythologie der Uitoto*, Göttingen-Leipzig.
1968 *Nahua-Texte aus San Pedro Jicora in Durango*, Berlin.

Propp, V.:
1968 *Morphology of the Folktale*, Austin, Tex., 2nd edition.

Purchas, Samuel:
1625–6 *Purchas His Pilgrims. In five books*, London; new edition, Glasgow 1905 (20 vols.).

Radin, Paul:
1923 *The Winnebago Tribe*, Washington, D.C. (37th Annual Report of the BAE); paperback edition, Lincoln, Neb., 1970.
1928 *The Story of the American Indian*, London.
1954–6 *The Evolution of an American Indian Prose Epic. A Study in Comparative Literature*, Basel.

Rafinesque, C. S.:
1836 *The American Nations*, Philadelphia, Pa. (2 vols.).

Recinos, Adrian:
1957 *Crónicas indígenas de Guatemala*, Guatemala.

Redfield, Robert:
1941 *The Folk Culture of Yucatan*, Chicago, Ill.
Reed, Nelson:
1964 *The Caste War of Yucatan*, Stanford, Cal.
Reichard, Gladys A.:
1963 *Navaho Religion. A Study of Symbolism*, New York, 2nd ed.
Reichel-Dolmatoff, Gerardo:
1971 *Amazonian Cosmos. The Sexual and Religious Symbolism of the Tukano Indians*, Chicago, Ill., and London.
Reyes, Alfonso:
1915 *Visión de Anahuac*, Madrid.
1948 *Letras de la Nueva España*, Mexico, revised edition.
Reyniers, François:
1945 *Onze poèmes incaiques*, Lima.
Ricard, Robert:
1933 *La 'conquête spirituelle' du Mexique. Essai sur l'apostolat et les méthodes missionaires des Ordres Mendiants en Nouvelle Espagne de 1523-4 à 1572*, Paris.
Ríos Codex: in Kingsborough (q.v.) 1831–48, vol 2.
Rivet, Paul:
1958 *Miscelanea Paul Rivet: Octogenario Dicata*, Mexico (2 vols.).
Robertson, Donald:
1959 *Mexican Manuscript Painting of the early Colonial Period. The Metropolitan Schools*, New Haven, Conn.
Romances de los señores:
1964 *Poesía Nahuatl, I. Romances de los señores de la Nueva España*, ed. A. M. Garibay, Mexico.
Rothenberg, Jerome:
1968 *Technicians of the Sacred*, New York.
1972 *Shaking the Pumpkin: Traditional poetry of the Indian North Americas*, New York.
Roys, Ralph L.:
1933 – see Chumayel, Book of.
1943 *The Indian Background of Colonial Yucatan*, Washington, D.C.,

2nd ed., Norman, Okla., 1972.
1954 *The Maya katun prophecies of the Books of Chilam, series I*, Washington (Contributions to American Anthropology and History, no. 57).
1965 *Ritual of the Bacabs*, Norman, Okla.
Ruiz de Alarcón, Hernando:
1953 *Tratado de las supersticiones de los naturales de esta Nueva España*, Mexico; previous edition in the *Anales del Museo Nacional de Antropología e Historia*, 1892.
Sahagún, Bernardino de:
1956 *Historia general de las cosas de Nueva España*, Mexico (4 vols).
St. Denis, Ferdinand:
1850 *Une Fête brésilienne célébrée à Rouen en 1550*, Paris.
Satterthwaite, Linton:
1947 *Concepts and structures of Maya calendrical arithmetic*, Philadelphia.
Sánchez de Aguilar, Pedro:
1937 *Informe contra idolorum cultores* (1639), Merida.
Sauer, Carl Ortwin:
1966 *The Early Spanish Main*, Berkeley, Cal., and London.
1971 *Sixteenth Century North America*, Berkeley, Cal., and London.
Schaafsma, Polly:
1963 *Rock art in the Navajo Reservoir District*, Santa Fe, N.M.
Schlenther, Ursula:
1965 *Die geistige Welt der Maya. Einführung in die Schriftzeugnisse einer indianischen Priesterkultur*, Berlin.
Scholes, France V., and Ralph L. Roys:
1948 *The Maya Chontal Indians of Acalan-Tixchel: A contribution to the history and ethnography of the Yucatan peninsula*, Washington, D.C.
Schoolcraft, Henry Rowe:
1839 *Algic Researches*, New York (2 vols.).
1851–7 *Historical and statistical information respecting the history, condition and prospects of the Indian*

tribes of the United States, Philadelphia, Pa. (6 vols.).

Sejourné, Laurette:
1957 *Burning Water. Thought and Religion in Ancient Mexico*, trans. from the Spanish by I. Nicholson, London and New York; new edition 1978.

Selden screenfold:
1831–48 In Kingsborough (q.v.), vol. 1.
1964 *Interpretación del Códice Selden 3135*, facsimile edition by A. Caso, Mexico.

Seler, Eduard:
1901 *Codex Fejérváry-Mayer. Eine altmexikanische Bilderhandschrift*, Berlin; English edition by A. H. Keane, Berlin-London, 1901.
1902–23 *Gesammelte Abhandlungen zur amerikanischen Sprach- und Alterthumskunde*, Berlin (5 vols.); reprinted Graz 1960–61.
1927 *Einige Kapitel aus dem Geschichtswerke des Fray Bernardino de Sahagún aus dem Aztekischen übersetzt*, Stuttgart.

Smailus, Ortwin:
1975 *El Maya Chontal de Acalan. Análisis lingüístico de un documento de los años 1610–12* [The Paxbolon-Maldonado Papers], Mexico.

Smith, Mary Elizabeth:
1973 *Picture Writing from Ancient Southern Mexico. Mixtec Place Signs and Maps*, Norman, Okla.

Sodi Morales, Demetrio:
1964 *La literatura de los mayas*, Mexico.

Soustelle, Jacques:
1937 *La Famille Otomi-Pame*, Paris.
1940 *La Pensée cosmologique des anciens Mexicains*, Paris.
1955 *La Vie quotidienne des Aztèques à la veille de la conquête espagnole*, Paris; English trans., *The Daily Life of the Aztecs*, London 1961 and New York 1962.

Spence, Lewis:
1914 *The Myths of the North American Indians*, London.

1923 *The Gods of Mexico*, New York.

Spinden, Herbert Joseph:
1928 *Ancient civilizations of Mexico and Central America*, New York.
1933 *Songs of the Tewa. Preceded by an essay on American Indian Poetry*, New York.
1935 *Indian manuscripts of Southern Mexico*, Washington, D.C. (in Annual Report of the Smithsonian Institution for 1933).

Squier, Ephraim George:
1877 – see Walam Olum.

Sten, María:
1972 *Las extraordinarias historias de los códices mexicanos*, Mexico.

Stephens, John L.:
1841 *Incidents of Travel in Central America, Chiapas and Yucatan*, New York and London (2 vols.); paperback edition, London and New York 1969.
1843 *Incidents of Travel in Yucatan*, New York (2 vols.); paperback ed., London and New York 1963.

Steward, J. H., and L. C. Faron:
1959 *Native Peoples of South America*, New York.

Tanner, John:
1830 *Narrative of the Captivity and Adventures of John Tanner*, New York.

Tarmap pacha huaray:
1905 *Tarmap pacha huaray. Azucenas quechuas. Por unos parias*. Tarma.

Tavera Acosta, B.:
1956 *Los petroglifos de Venezuela*, Caracas.

Tax, Sol:
1967 *The Civilizations of Ancient America*, New York.

Tedlock, Dennis:
1972 *Finding the Centre. Narrative Poetry of the Zuni Indians*, New York.

Thatcher, B. B.:
1832 *Indian Biography*, New York (2 vols.).

Thompson, J. Eric S.:
1950 *Maya Hieroglyphic Writing*,

Washington, D.C.; 2nd edition, Norman, Okla., 1960.

1962 *A Catalog of Maya Hieroglyphs*, Norman, Okla.

1967 *The Rise and Fall of Maya Civilization*, Norman, Okla. (2nd enlarged edition).

1972 *A Commentary on the Dresden Codex*, Philadelphia, Pa.

Thompson, Stith:

1929 *Tales of the North American Indians*. Cambridge, Mass.; 2nd edition, Bloomington, Ind., and London 1966.

Tizimin, Book of:

1951 *The Book of the Jaguar Priest*, trans. Maud W. Makemson, New York.

1978 *The Book of Chilam Balam of Tizimin*, trans. Munro Edmonson, New Orleans, La.

Tomkins, W.:

1969 *Indian Sign Language*, New York.

Tozzer, Alfred Marston:

1921 *A Maya Grammar*, Cambridge, Mass.

Trimborn, Hermann:

1963 *Die indianischen Hochkulturen*, Berlin.

Twenty Sacred Hymns of the Aztecs:

1890 *Rig Veda Americanus: Sacred songs of the ancient Mexicans*, ed. D. G. Brinton, Philadelphia, Pa. (LAAL vol. 8).

1904 *Die religiösen Gesänge der alten Mexikaner* (in Seler 1902–23: vol. 2).

1958 *Veinte himnos sacros de los Nahuas*, ed. K. A. M. Garibay, Mexico.

Tylor, E. B.:

1861 *Anahuac; or Mexico and the Mexicans, ancient and modern*, London.

Vaillant, George C.:

1962 *Aztecs of Mexico: origin, rise, and fall of the Aztec Nation*, New York; revised edition, Harmondsworth 1965.

Valcárcel, Daniel:

1965 *La rebelión de Tupac Amaru*, Mexico (paperback edition).

Vienna screenfold:

1963 *Codex Vindobonensis Mexicanus I*, facsimile edition by Otto Adelhofer, Graz; reprint of 1929 edition by W. Lehmann and Ottokar Smital, Vienna.

Villa Rojas, Alfonso:

1945 *The Maya of East Central Quintana Roo*, Washington, D.C.

Villaseñor, David:

1965 *Tapestries in sand. The spirit of Indian sandpainting*, Healdsburg, Cal.

Villoro, Luis:

1950 *Los grandes momentos del indigenismo en Mexico*, Mexico.

Viscarra, J.:

1901 *Copacabana de los Incas. Documentos auto-linguísticos e isografiados del Aymaru-Aymara. Protogonos de los pre-Americanos*, La Paz.

Vogt, Evon Z.:

1969 *Zinacantan: A Maya Community in the Highlands of Chiapas*, Cambridge, Mass.

Vogt, Evon Z., and A. Ruz Lluillier:

1971 *Desarrollo cultural de los mayas*, Mexico (2nd edition).

Wachtel, Nathan:

1977 *The Vision of the Vanquished: The Spanish Conquest of Peru through Indian eyes, 1530–1570*, London.

Wagner, Henry R.:

1944 *The Rise of Fernando Cortes*, Berkeley, Cal.

Wallace, Anthony F. C.:

1970 *The Death and Rebirth of the Seneca*, New York and Toronto; paperback edition 1972.

Walam Olum:

1877 In E. G. Squier, 'Historical and Mythological Traditions of the Algonquins, with a translation of the Walam Olum, or bark record of the Lenni Lenape', in *The Indian Mis-*

cellany (ed. W. W. Beach), Albany, N.Y.

1884 *The Lenape and their Legends with the complete text and symbols of the Walam Olum*, a new translation, and an inquiry into its authenticity by D. G. Brinton. Philadelphia, Pa. (LAAL vol. 5); reprinted New York 1969.

1954 *Walam Olum or Red Score. The Migration Legend of the Lenni Lenape or Delaware Indians. A new translation* . . . by Glenn A. Black *et al.*, Indianapolis, Ind.

Waters, Frank:

1963 *The Book of the Hopi. The first revelations of the Hopis' historical and religious world-view of life*, New York.

Wauchope, Robert:

1962 *Lost tribes and sunken continents. Myth and method in the study of American Indians*, Chicago, Ill.

1970 *The Indian background of Latin American history; the Maya, Aztec, Inca and their predecessors*, New York.

Whorf, Benjamin Lee:

1956 *Language, Thought and Reality*, Cambridge, Mass.; paperback edition 1964.

Wiener, Charles:

1880 *Peru et Bolivie*, Paris.

Witt, S. H., and S. Steiner:

1972 *The Way. An Anthology of American Indian Literature*, New York.

Willey, Gordon:

1974 *Das alte Amerika*, Berlin.

Williams, Roger:

1963 *A Key into the Language of America* [1643], in *The complete writings*, New York, vol. 1.

Wilson, Edmund:

1959 *Apologies to the Iroquois*, New York.

Winters, Yvor:

1967 *Forms of discovery*, Chicago, Ill.

Wolf, Eric R.:

1959 *Sons of the Shaking Earth*, Chicago, Ill.

Yáñez, Agustin:

1939 *Crónicas de la conquista de Mexico*, Mexico.

1942 *Mitos indígenas*, Mexico.

Yves d'Evreux:

1864 *Voyage dans le nord de Brésil fait durant les années 1613–14*, Leipzig and Paris.

Zantwijk, Rudolf A. M. van:

1960 *Los indígenas de Milpa Alta, herederos de los aztecas*, Amsterdam.

Zimmermann, Günter:

1956 *Die Hieroglyphen der Maya-Handschriften*, Hamburg.

1960 *Das Geschichtswerk des Domingo de Muñon Chimalpahin Quauhtlehuantzin*, Hamburg.

1963–5 *Die Relationen Chimalpahins zur Geschichte Mexikos*, Hamburg (2 vols.).

Zithuwa Ritual:

1873 In Markham (q.v.) 1873.

Zolla, Elemire:

1973 *The Writer and the Shaman. A morphology of the American Indian*, New York.

Index

Bold type indicates the first page of discussion of a documentary item; italic, illustrations in the text. Abbreviations: NF = Nine Figures, TN = Thirteen Numbers, TS = Twenty Signs (cf. Table 2); l. = left, r. = right (referring to columns in the Notes). In Table 1 works and authors are grouped according to categories not included in the index because they occur too often: Algonkin, Aztec, Inca, Maya and Toltec. For individual screenfolds and codices, see under these two main entries.

Venus (as Lamat = TS VIII) 19, 64, 79, 86–8, 95–6, 104, 106, 116, 149–51, 155–69, 172, 180, 182–3, 187–8, 190–1, 194, 211–3, 218, 258–9, 269, 271, 281; see also rabbit, Sky
Viracocha 44, 119, 213–14, 218, 237, 240–1
Virgil 211, 243
voice-line 97, 263
vulture (TS XVI) 109, 207, 213, 243

Walam Olum 18–19, 50, 79, 95, 96, 150, 152, 162, 176, 189, 191, 193, 211, 256, 300r., 304r.
wampum, see under shell
Wapokenota 81
water (TS IX) 34, 67, 94, 97, 99, 109, 111–2, 155–6, 183, 187, 195, 213, 249
weaving 78, 88, 102, 170; belts 46, 173, loin-cloths 108, 208, 222, 235; mantles 35, 41, 64, 114, 131, 139, 201, 234–5; mats 29, 65, 71, 147, 261; 'woven' texts 131, 261, 262, 271, 281
willow 200, 277

wind, breath (TS II) 64, 102, 108, 134, 150, 155, 177, 242, 245, 277
Winnebago 258
Witoto 265
world ages 18, 19, 44–5, 148–86; see also eclipse, flood
'woven' texts, see under weaving

Xibalba, see Dead Land
Xicalanco 39, 155, 271
Xipe 106, 187
Xmucane, see Oxomoco
Xochimilco 32–3, 197–200, 231, 247

Yaxchilan 230
Yucatec 24, 39–42, 144, 218; — Community Books, see Chilam Balam

zancay 75, 278
Zapotec 24, 85, 90, 93, 102, 228–9
zenith 19, 64, 80, 85, 90, 104, 124, 140, 153, 159, 168, 195, 257, 271
Zithuwa Ritual 121, 214
Zuni 86

324